PATTERNS OF
DIPLOMATIC THINKING:

PATTERNS OF
DIPLOMATIC THINKING:

A Cross-National Study of Structural and
Social-Psychological Determinants

Luc Reychler

FOREWORD by Karl W. Deutsch

PRAEGER PUBLISHERS
Praeger Special Studies

New York   •   London   •   Sydney   •   Toronto

Library of Congress Cataloging in Publication Data

Reychler, Luc.
    Patterns of diplomatic thinking.

    Bibliography: p.
    Includes index.
    1. International relations--Research. 2. Diplomacy
--Research. I. Title.
JX1291.R53   327'.07'2   78-19774
ISBN 0-03-046636-9

PRAEGER PUBLISHERS
PRAEGER SPECIAL STUDIES
383 Madison Avenue, New York, N.Y. 10017, U.S.A.

Published in the United States of America in 1979
by Praeger Publishers,
A Division of Holt, Rinehart and Winston, CBS, Inc.

9   038   987654321

FOREWORD
by Karl W. Deutsch

HOW DIPLOMATS THINK AND WHAT
CAN BE FOUND OUT ABOUT IT

Professor Reychler has chosen a fascinating topic, and he has written an important book on it. How do diplomats think? How can one find out about it? And what does it matter, anyway?

To answer the last question first: it matters a great deal. Diplomats are more than mere messengers. They are the eyes and ears of their governments. What they do not report is not likely to get much attention from national decision makers. But what they do think will influence what they perceive and report to their home governments as facts. Their reports will include the perceived intentions and capabilities of other governments, as well as the perceived imminence of various economic, technological, or political crisis situations. In part, at least, the decisions of national governments will be influenced by these reports, and these decisions may then aggravate or mitigate international conflicts or crises, or sometimes tend to replace an adversary, conflict, or crisis by another.

But how can one find out about these matters? Most simply put, by asking a large and carefully chosen sample of diplomats a series of knowledgeable questions, encouraging them to talk freely and informally, listening patiently and carefully to the answers, and then, after the interviews are finished, analyzing the results by means of a battery of statistical techniques.

All these things Mr. Reychler has done. He has interviewed 266 diplomats from 116 countries, so chosen as to represent fairly the different categories of states in the international system. The average length of each interview was three quarters of an hour. The details of the interview methods used and the statistical techniques employed are set forth in this book, and for the expert they make very interesting reading. For the general reader, it may suffice to say that they fully establish the serious professional quality of the research. The results presented here constitute information that should not be lightly regarded.

Granted that Professor Reychler has demonstrated a method to find out about the thought patterns of diplomats, and that these thoughts matter, what has been found? How do diplomats think? They often think surprisingly differently. They differ both in their values and in their perceptions of reality. In some important

v

respects, diplomats from highly industrialized countries see themselves as living in one kind of world, and diplomats from the developing countries see themselves in quite another. Even the word "peace" means something different to the first group than it does to the second. Similar differences occur in what each group considers the best ways of promoting peace, and in what each sees as major obstacles to peace.

There are many other differences, in matters of substance as well as in style of analysis, that could have fateful consequences. They cannot be listed here, but they fill a good part of Professor Reychler's book.

In some other respects, however, diplomats think remarkably alike, regardless of the wealth or poverty of their nations. Above all, they want to be realistic. Some of their views of reality remain compatible and the areas of compatibility may grow. Here and now, they do not tend to moralize and most of them are wary of ideologies.

They do agree on some specific points. Professor Reychler found striking agreement among them about the need to improve detente between West and East, to improve communication across national boundaries, and to promote cooperation within regions and among "states that naturally belong together." All these goals and strategies are not only highly preferred, they are also considered to be realistic and attainable, and hence on the whole to be trusted.

Some other goals are also almost universally shared as aspirations, such as abolishing hunger and poverty, and general and complete disarmament. These goals, however, are seen as unrealistic in the present situation. Only the more moderate strategies of detente and economic aid to poorer nations are seen as having a realistic chance to help the world to move cautiously in these directions.

In sum, diplomats reflect the deep disparities and disagreements among the nations of the present international system. But they have enough in common to be able to communicate, to negotiate, and to arrive at significant agreements.

The important information, of course, is in the specific details. Only a hint of some of these could be suggested here. A great many of them, however, are in Professor Reychler's book. They make it very much worth reading; and they will repay deeper study.

Other groupings of countries might be used to reanalyze some of Professor Reychler's data. What significant differences, if any, would they show between the thought patterns of diplomats from Communist-ruled countries and from non-Communist ones, respectively? What are the differences between countries that possessed nuclear weapons at the time the interviews took place, and those countries which did not? And what differences, if any, were there among age groups or generations of diplomats? From what social backgrounds did these diplomats come and what education had they received? What cross-classifications among some of these various categories might still prove meaningful?

A special note must be added here to recommend this book to the attention of students and scholars in the field of diplomatic history. They cannot easily conduct surveys among hundreds of diplomats, nor can they interview the dead. But they could profit a great deal from many of Professor Reychler's questions. What image of the international system did statesman X carry in his head? What style of analysis did Ambassador Y employ? If political leader Z was seeking to promote peace, just what was his concept of peace, and what strategies did he see as realistic and desirable to bring it nearer? Broad questions of this kind have been asked before. But rarely, if ever, until now have they been broken down into so many specific details and dimensions within a framework of comparability as Professor Reychler has done here. This aspect of his methods may help historians, and their work might add historic depth to his present findings.

In writing this book, Professor Reychler has fulfilled the heavy but limited task he had set for himself. But at the same time he has opened new pathways for inquiry. It is to be hoped that the work he has begun here will be continued by him and many others.

Karl W. Deutsch
Harvard University

PREFACE

How does the international arena look from the vantage point of professional diplomats? What meaning do they attach to the international value of peace? What is their preferred world order? How do they analyze information about international relations? What is their strategic approach? How is their thinking about international relations formed and altered? How do we account for differences in diplomatic thinking?

These questions have not been adequately discussed by specialists of international relations. This study attempts to fill that gap. Patterns of diplomatic thinking stress the importance of the diplomat, not only as a missing link in the study of international relations, but also as a missing source of information for the student of international behavior. This book systematically probes four components of diplomatic thinking: the perception of the international environment, the operationalization of the international value of peace and preferred world order, the style of analysis, and the strategic approach. The variations in diplomatic thinking can be traced to the position the diplomat's country enjoys (or doesn't enjoy) in the international system, and to the international climate. It also sets out a methodology, tools, and techniques for tracing diplomatic thinking, and illustrates how elite interview material can be sensitively analyzed in ways that meet the standards of quantitative social science. Finally, the consequences of diverse conceptual approaches of international relations are evaluated in the light of international behavior.

Although the title does not indicate so, this book is a collaborative effort. For in a real sense I served for seven months as a scribe for the 266 diplomats from 116 countries who participated in this study. All of them deserve warm thanks.

In grappling with the perils of cross-national research, I was fortunate to have the guidance and assistance of two outstanding scholars: Herbert Kelman I thank for his tangible support, his sensitive advice, and his patient guidance of an impatient young European toward "a time to speak"; I am grateful to Karl Deutsch for his trusting support and manifold enlightening comments.

For special encouragement and thoughtful counsel, I also am grateful to Klaus Allerbeck, Robert Bower, Paul Braem, Pierce Barker, Paul Ghysbrecht, Helge Hveem, Harold Isaacs, Charles Judd, A. N. Oppenheim, John Steinbruner, Philip Stone, Paul Van de Meerssche, Sidney Verba, and Donald Wyman.

At various stages of this research I have had the skilled and indefatigable assistance of Elaine Exum: she did the reliability coding, provided sensitive editorial advice, and helped me deliver the study on time. My debt to her is profound.

Logistic support at various stages of this project was provided by the Behavioral Studies Program at Harvard University, Center for International Affairs, Grant MH-17669-05 to Herbert Kelman from the National Institute of Mental Health/U.S. Public Health Service, and by the Bureau of Social Science Research in Washington, D.C. The help of all these institutions was indispensable. For assistance of many kinds, a special mention is due to Marie-Paul.

The responsibility for what I have produced is mine.

CONTENTS

LIST OF TABLES

LIST OF FIGURES

1

Missing:
The Diplomatic Vantage Point

Diplomats always have been in the limelight of the international arena, but, paradoxically, few systematic studies of their behavior and thinking have been undertaken. In 1893 the president of the American Historical Association, James B. Angell, stated in his inaugural address that no class of public servants is so inadequately appreciated in the study of international relations as diplomats. This fact is still very much with us. The available resources on diplomats and diplomacy can be classified into six categories: personal memoirs of diplomats; handbooks on procedures and protocol; books on the art of diplomacy written by famous diplomats such as Machiavelli, Richelieu, François de Callières, Harold Nicolson, Jules Cambon, and Philippe de Commynes; specific diplomatic histories; a plethora of popular books on diplomacy which are very superficial, have an anecdotal base, and merely paraphrase statements made by diplomats such as those mentioned in the third category; and behavioral studies of substantive aspects of diplomacy. The last category is virtually empty. Iklé's (1967) work on negotiation, Modelski's (1970) study of foreign ministers, Russett and Lamb's (1969) analysis of global patterns of diplomatic exchange, Jacobson's (1967) study of delegates to international assemblies, and Alger's (1965) study of the impact of personal contact in intergovernmental organizations are a sample of the small number of studies about diplomats and diplomacy that can be fitted within the last category. All of these studies are serious steps in the right direction, although most are still based on anecdotal accounts or unrepresentative samples of diplomats. No sound comprehensive theory on the subject can emerge from such limited empirical data.

Recently the need for some organization in the study of diplomacy and diplomats was recognized by the American Academy of

Political and Social Science (1972): "We are concerned with an examination of the benefits to international studies which could emerge from a new and serious effort . . . to explore, to research, and to study and teach the field known as diplomacy." Diplomacy was officially recognized as the missing link in the study of international relations.

Although the failure of students of international relations to treat with sufficient fullness the work of diplomats cannot be justified, several causes of that neglect can be perceived. Angell (1893: 17) suggests as one of the causes the fact that diplomacy does not appeal to the imagination nor excite the passions of men as do the warrior's battles. A far more serious cause, however, appears to be the secrecy accompanying diplomatic interactions, where even open covenants are secretly arrived at. The processes by which agreements or disagreements ensue are often, perhaps generally, guarded by governments with varying degrees of secrecy. Another cause of inertia in the study of diplomacy is the vagueness of the term, which has been used with many meanings, ranging from the total foreign-affairs effort of a country to the highly specialized subject of negotiation. Clearly, before any research effort can be systematically organized, the term "diplomacy" must first be defined in a manageable manner. This task was facilitated by the work of a group of scholars and diplomatic practitioners which met in Philadelphia in September 1970 under the auspices of the American Academy of Political and Social Science. A methodological exploration of the possible definitions of diplomacy resulted in identifying "diplomacy" as the conduct of foreign relations. In this definition, diplomacy is treated as the operational function of international relations. This does not mean, however, that diplomacy has nothing to do with foreign-policy formulation. It does mean that the impact of diplomacy on policy formulation is tangential and incidental to its principal function, which is to carry the policy, once it has been formulated, across international frontiers and cultures in order to give effect to the aims and goals, explicit and implicit, of such policy (Poullada 1974: 194).

To appreciate the importance of the study of diplomacy in the understanding of international politics, we must make some important distinctions. First, it is important to distinguish between the roles of the professional and the nonprofessional diplomat (Poullada 1974). Both groups can be characterized in terms of their locus of operation and specific skills. The principal career of the professional diplomat is centered around a set of skills designed to enhance his effectiveness in the conduct of foreign affairs, and his skills are exercised in the international and transnational milieu. The professional diplomat may perform other functions, such as testifying to the Foreign Relations Committee. In this capacity, he may draw on his knowledge of diplomacy but does not function specifically as a diplomat. The reverse situation applies to the nonprofessional diplomat, whose principal career may be that of a politician, academician, industrialist, economist, or civil servant. For a given time, and during a given assignment, his position may involve him in the active conduct of foreign relations. A minister of foreign affairs, normally a member of the government, whose principal function centers on policy making, may assume the role of a nonprofessional diplomat when he heads his country's delegation to the Council of Ministers of the European Economic Community where he engages in an attempt to secure his country's interests. As a consequence of their different experiences and training, the nonprofessional diplomat is generally better skilled in assessing the effects of decisions taken on the domestic scene, whereas the professional diplomat is more sensitive to the international and transnational effects of the statements and actions of his own government. In this area the professional diplomat is an expert and can be a great asset for decision makers at home. Poullada (1974: 195) suggests that the frequent failure of governments to rely on their diplomats for guidance in these matters is a source of many unnecessary frictions in international relations generated by domestic events.

In this study we will limit our attention to the professional diplomat and will inquire into the specific functions the diplomat performs in the conduct of foreign policy. There are both substantive and procedural aspects to this process which must be distinguished (Poullada 1974). Substantive diplomacy can be described in terms of the rules the diplomat is expected to enact. In order to perform these roles, which we will examine later, the diplomat uses certain procedural arts and crafts, such as refinements of protocol, diplomatic drafting, press releases, and even enduring the treadmill of cocktail parties. These procedural and social activities are examined extensively in the literature and in the newspapers and are not of concern here. Instead we will focus our attention on the substantive functions or roles that diplomats perform.

Various authors classify the functions of diplomats differently. Most government classifications distinguish several areas of interaction between countries. The Plowden Report (1964: 43-82), for example, distinguishes policy planning, economic and commercial activities, information, consular work, aid and technical assistance, legal advice, research and library work, and registry and archives work. During their careers, most diplomats perform in several of these areas. For example, one diplomat interviewed for this study remarked that in his career he had to deal with subjects ranging from disarmament to artificial insemination of animals. This diversity allows diplomats a wide scope of experience in the diplomatic field.

Another classification system, which cuts across the above-mentioned areas of interaction, distinguishes the roles of diplomats in terms of the nature of their substantive functions. Poullada (1974: 195-99) categorizes diplomacy under five principal functional areas: conflict management, problem solving, cross-cultural interaction, negotiation and bargaining, and program management. The capacity to act as conflict manager is especially required when there is a high frequency of intersecting international interests. Adeptness at reconciliation, compromise, persuasion, bargaining, and accommodation is critical for adequate role performance.

> Although he is primarily the representative of the interests of his country, he knows that in international politics seldom does any party have a totally "right" case. More often there must be an accommodation of interests which depend on a range of options each with pluses and minuses. The diplomat attempts to harmonize these vectors of interest in such a way that there will be some net gain for all concerned (Poullada 1974: 196).

Problem solving is a second function required in diplomacy. The conduct of diplomacy presents itself to professionals as an infinite flow of problems, dilemmas, and choices. Even reporting can be considered an essential problem-solving exercise: "The diplomat must first of all choose between various interpretations, he must sort out the cultural bias inherent in the information, he must select the most creative way to utilize the information so as to influence both policy formulation and execution" (Poullada 1974: 196). A third area of substantive diplomatic activity centers on the transcultural functions of the diplomatic profession. This is an aspect which gives diplomatic work its unique character. Rossow (1962: 564), in an article in World Politics, depicts this function as follows:

> The diplomat finds himself operating between cultures, and sometimes in the midst of several simultaneously. . . . The principal contribution of the diplomat . . . comes from his skill in two directions. He interprets and appraises for his client situations and developments in foreign cultural contexts, and also acts as the advocate of his client in pursuing the latter's policy goals abroad. . . . Cross-cultural interpretation is therefore the basic professional function of the diplomat. . . .

A fourth role of the diplomat is negotiation and bargaining. A very substantial portion of the diplomat's time, whether as a junior or senior officer, consists of bargaining and persuasion designed to convince foreigners and fellow nationals alike to take some action, cooperate in some venture, or see a problem in a certain way.

A fifth area of substantive diplomatic function is program management, which refers to the implementation and management of such programs as intelligence gathering, technical assistance, or economic development. These five principal functional areas are, of course, not exhaustive. We could easily add another function such as communication management, which was considered by most diplomats interviewed to be of prime importance. This function refers basically to the preparation and efficient organization of contacts between nationals of his own country and of the host country-- for example, contacts between businessmen of the two countries designed to promote his country's commercial interests.

No serious studies have been undertaken of the above-described activities and their impact on international relations. I basically agree with Poullada that diplomacy is a missing link in the study of international politics and, more specifically, that a better knowledge of the substantive functions of diplomats could improve studies of power and influence, strategic interaction, bargaining and negotiation, and decision making. The inclusion of such variables as diplomatic persuasion, verbal strategy, perception, and interpretation could certainly refine the analysis of international behavior and show clearly that models based entirely on economic and coercive power are often off the mark because they do not take into account the empirical realities of diplomacy. In other words, the inclusion of diplomatic variables could give us a more sophisticated variety of realism in the study of international politics, for it would consider both material factors, such as geostrategic position or economic power of a country, and less-tangible factors, such as the climate of international action, international images, or verbal strategy in the assessment of the international situation.

Not only is diplomacy a missing link in the study of international politics, but diplomats are also an overlooked source of information for the students of international behavior. Diplomats are uniquely situated informants about the nature of international relations because of their vantage point and experience in the field. Close cooperation between management schools and business accounted to a great extent for the rapid improvement of management science. In the organization of international studies such a link is generally missing. A better information exchange between diplomats and scholars would be mutually beneficial.

What factors make the diplomat a unique source of information for the student of international politics? Before answering this question, we should make one further distinction, namely, that between the diplomat and other international actors, such as civil servants attached to the United Nations or the European Commission. The most important role of the diplomat is basically that of trustee of national interests. When I asked diplomats to describe their roles, they usually referred to themselves as representatives of their countries, as promoters of national interests (including their countries' economic and commercial interests), as the eyes of their countries, as advisors to their governments, and as protectors or beautifiers of their national images. The diplomat is expected to be completely loyal to his country and to have the national interests in mind in all his undertakings. Being a good diplomat and a successful promoter of national interests is one and the same thing. On the other hand, a civil servant seconded to the United Nations or European Commission is expected to be committed to this international organization or to have international loyalty.

With this distinction in mind, let us now look at the factors that make the diplomat an indispensable informant about the nature of international behavior. The first two factors are related to his influence on the outcome of the foreign-policy behavior of his own country and the country to which he is accredited. Diplomats have an input into the foreign-policy formulation of their own countries, by communicating their interpretations and appraisals of situations and developments in foreign areas, and by forecasting the international and transnational effects of the statements and the acts of their governments. Though the real impact of diplomats on the formulation of foreign policy is considered by some students of international relations to be tangential (Rosecrance 1973: 227-28), their "conduct" of foreign policy forms an important link between the formulation of policy and the success of its execution. Foreign-policy outcomes can be affected by the way the diplomat presents his government's goals; by his influence on the other actor's definition of the situation; and by his ability to create a favorable atmosphere and environment abroad based upon relationships with colleagues, officials, leading citizens, and other groups in the host country, so that negotiations can proceed with a minimum of friction and a maximum of communication. Information about the diplomat's definition of particular situations, his style of analyzing policy issues, and his strategic approach can add greatly to the understanding and predictability of international behavior; or in other words, academic models which ignore the profoundly transformational character of these intervening variables will tend to bear less relation to the empirical reality.

A third reason why the diplomat is a unique informant is related to his role as trustee of national interests. As national representatives, diplomats can be considered to be relatively good mirrors of their government's thinking about foreign policy. Thus it is reasonable to assume that information concerning the thinking of diplomats can be used to assess the foreign-policy thinking of the policy makers whom they represent. Therefore, the tapping of diplomatic thinking seems a very reliable substitute for the direct interviewing of foreign-policy makers. The fourth reason for selecting diplomats as prime informants about the nature of the international environment is the fact that they exercise their skills in several international and transnational milieux. As participant observers, they are trained to be accurate and sensitive analysts of the international environment. A fifth factor, which reinforces the choice of the diplomat as a reliable source of information, is the scope of his experience. In general this scope can be considered wide, for most diplomatic practitioners perform in several fields of international activity over the course of their careers.

In this study I asked a representative sample of the world's diplomats how they perceive the international environment; how they operationalize international values, such as peace or preferred world order; what style of analysis they use for interpreting international behavior; and what strategic approach they prefer for realizing the respective foreign policies of their countries. The term "diplomatic thinking" will be used to refer to all of these variables and each of them separately will be referred to as a component of diplomatic thinking. Chapter 2 will analyze the concept of diplomatic thinking and examine how a better knowledge of it could improve the fit between the reality of international behavior and our understanding of it.

2

Diplomatic Thinking

What do diplomats think diplomacy is all about? How do they perceive the international environment in which they operate? How do they analyze international issues? What do they consider to be a more preferred world order? How do they operationalize such values as peace or morality? What is their strategic approach? The answers to these questions are, I believe, fundamentally important for understanding the functioning of international systems. We can call this set of diplomatically relevant perceptions, values, analytic styles, and strategic approaches "diplomatic thinking," which is an aspect of diplomatic culture. Other aspects of diplomatic culture, which are not discussed in this volume, include diplomatic language and nonverbal components of diplomatic interaction, protocol, and communication patterns.

The present study, then, is a worldwide, cross-national study of diplomatic thinking. It lies at the juncture of five important approaches to the study of international behavior. First, there is decision-making theory (see Snyder et al. 1963), based on the notion that political action is undertaken by concrete human actors and that comprehension of the dynamics of this action requires viewing the world from the perspective of these identifiable actors. Second, elite theorists (see Bottomore 1965) and others have pointed to the crucial importance of elites in any political system. Diplomats can clearly be described as elites in the field of international relations. They are a small stratum of people who are much more highly involved in diplomatic thought, discussion, and action than most other groups in the nation they represent. Third, students of belief systems (see Kelman 1965; Deutsch and Merritt 1965; Putnam 1973; Burgess 1968) and the logic of images (see Jervis 1970) have directed our attention to the significance of images and beliefs of international actors. Fourth, to explain differences in diplomatic thinking, one can draw on the theory of international climate (Sprout 1965; Tagiuri and Litwin (1968). The international climate could be defined as the relatively enduring quality of the work environment that is experienced by diplomats, influences their thinking and behavior, and can be described in terms of values of a particular set of attributes of this environment. Finally, social-structure theory (see Singer and Small 1966; Schwartzmann and Arauja 1966; Galtung 1964; Gleditsch 1970; Lagos 1963; Hveem 1972) views international relations in terms of the structural positions of the actors in the international stratification system. One of the exponents of the theory, Helge Hveem (1972), hypothesizes that the world images and foreign-policy attitudes of the leading foreign-policy and opinion-making strata of a given national actor are a function of the position that actor occupies in the international system. In this chapter I shall say a word about the first two approaches; then most of the attention will be focused on image theory and its relation to diplomatic thinking. The social-structural and international-climate approaches will be discussed, respectively, in Chapters 3 and 5.

The decision-making approach to international relations does not focus on countries as reified abstractions or on governments, but instead it seeks to highlight the behavior of human actors involved in shaping decisions. By narrowing the subject of investigation from a larger, abstract collectivity to a much smaller group of persons who have a central position in the decision-making process, decision-making theorists make the locus of analysis more concrete and precise, and thus more amenable to the methods of social science.

The second approach to the study of international behavior, based on elite theories, starts with the proposition that in any political system some actors are more important than others and deserve closer scrutiny from students of politics. The significant core of the theory is the notion that some people are much more interested, much more involved, and much more influential in international politics than their fellows. In respect to these criteria, diplomats certainly qualify as one of the elite groups in international relations. They rank high as professionals on the dimension of interest and involvement. In relation to the conduct of foreign policy their influence is high, whereas in the formulation of foreign policy their influence is relatively low and basically indirect in nature.

The third approach to international behavior that is relevant to our study of diplomatic thinking focuses on the role of "images" in international relations. The major premise of this approach is that the character and development of international politics is conditioned by perceptions, beliefs, values, and habits of thought which define the situation in which political action takes place. In less-

formal words, images matter. The understanding of images and
their manipulation have always been required parts of the art of diplomacy. Machiavelli, a renowned mentor of diplomats and politicians,
never for a moment loses sight of the fact that a political circum-
stance is not an unequivocal happening in the world: Its meaning depends upon its reflection in the mind of the participant. "Fantasia,"
the term Machiavelli uses for image and imagination, functions as
his almost implicit alternative to reason in traditional political thinking. "To recognize it as such has the great advantage of allowing us
to understand politics a good deal more purely, less encumbered with
local pieties, than would otherwise be the case" (Minogue 1972: 162).
The concept "image" is now a notion central in the social psychology
of international relations. Kelman (1965: 24) defines it as "the organized representation of an object in an individual's cognitive system . . . the individual's conception of what the object is like." In
this study we will look at the diplomat's organized representation of
international relations. We should, however, be aware that the diplomat's image is very much a function of his role as national trustee
and therefore different from that of a neutral observer. We can
assume that his image will be biased so that it may serve the purpose of maximizing his country's interests. To indicate this strategic
quality, we could also refer to the diplomat's thinking or image as
his strategic image, a term coined by Burgess (1968).

As used in this study, the diplomat's strategic image is assumed to have four analytically distinguishable components: perceptual, analytical, evaluative, and action. The perceptual component
of a strategic image refers to the diplomat's view and definition of
the central features of the international environment. These characteristics of the international environment constitute "objective reality" from the point of view of the diplomat and are independent of his
response to it. The analytical component refers to the style of analysis or to the cognitive structuring of a situation. A full explanation
must await the clarifying examples given in Chapter 7 but, roughly
speaking, "analytic style" is used here to refer to the "how" of diplomatic thinking and analysis. People manifestly differ in the way
they cope with problems. Two persons who share identical beliefs
and values about a specific task can nonetheless handle it differently.
This is no less true of diplomats facing public problems than of other
individuals grappling with private concerns. Several styles of analysis can be distinguished: historical, structural, ideological, pragmatic, and so on. This study will focus on only a few styles of
analysis which we find intriguing. The reason for looking at some
styles, and not at all possible styles, is that this investigation is
meant to be illustrative rather than comprehensive. The third component of the strategic image refers to the evaluative orientation of

the diplomat's image. We must distinguish between different sorts
of evaluative orientations. Robin Williams (1968) emphasizes the
distinction between the specific evaluation of an object (for example,
"the use of nuclear weapons is immoral") and the criteria or standards in terms of which evaluations are made (for example, "international law is unacceptable because it reflects disproportionately
the interests of the center countries"). The emphasis in this study
will be on values as criteria, though inevitably specific evaluations
will be considered as well.

A large number of values guide and regulate a country's foreign policy. For example, much of the texture of international politics in any age is provided by the interplay among conflicting operative values such as peace, justice, morality, or conflicting visions
of a preferred world order. In this study we have elected to examine
at some length differing conceptions of peace and preferred world
order. The action component of diplomatic thinking consists of conceptions about the implementation of any given goals. It will be referred to as the strategic approach, which can be measured along
several distinct dimensions, such as gradualism versus absolutism,
compromise versus sticking to your guns, hawk versus dove, integration versus isolationism, or defense versus offense. Here again
I want to stress that I will glimpse only at some dimensions and not
at all possible ones. The distinction that I have implicitly drawn between perception, style of analysis, evaluation, and strategic approach must be interpreted with care. There are obvious connec-
tions between these four aspects of diplomatic thinking and generally
a single diplomatic statement can be discussed in terms of more
than one category. For example, this statement made by one of the
diplomats I interviewed in Washington, "There is no difference in the
nature of war and peace; there is always the fight for a better position in the world," has clearly perceptual, stylistic, evaluative, and
action components all at once.

The first priority of our research is to establish the measurable existence of the components of diplomatic thinking. This done,
we will place them into a causal context, looking at their effects and
origins. What difference does it make that a diplomat has a particular strategic image? And how did he come to have that image in the
first place? The following diagram captures the logical structure of
our inquiry.

I	II	III
Factors determining diplomatic thinking	Diplomatic thinking	International behavior

This inquiry will focus mainly on element II, but it also will look backward along the causal chain toward the sources of variation in diplomatic thinking and forward toward the consequences.

Let us first look at the relation between strategic images and action in the international environment. The term "strategic image" of the diplomat is used to summarize the way in which he or she perceives, analyzes, evaluates, and relates strategically to the international environment. In political science it is now well recognized that the practice of international politics is greatly influenced by the images the actors entertain (see Kelman 1965; Deutsch et al 1965; Waltz 1959; Aron 1966). The intermediary role of diplomatic thinking or strategic images in international interactions can best be illuminated by looking at some of the functions of those images for the decision maker. Burgess (1968: 6-7) distinguishes three functions. The first, which he calls the selecting function, involves filtering the great amount of information that is continually emitted by the environment. "Images serve as screens for the selective reception of new messages, and they often control the perception and the interpretation of those messages that are not completely ignored, rejected, or repressed" (Deutsch et al 1965: 134). The second function of a strategic image is the integrating function: images permit the diplomat to make sense out of the daily information he receives through organizing and integrating it. The image also has an orienting function, illuminating expectations about the future of the decision maker and thereby linking the different components with action. This permits the decision maker "to plan for contingencies and to select courses of action designed to modify, deter, accommodate, or accelerate subjectively probable trends or perceived conditions" (Burgess 1968: 7). For the purpose of analyzing international behavior, the orienting function of images has the greatest significance. Because international policy making is future-oriented, courses of action depend to a large extent on the decision makers' subjective calculations of future situations and their relation to their goals.

How can information on strategic images be of value to the student of international relations? Analytically, information about elite images can add greatly to our understanding and forecasts of the international behavior of particular states or groups of states. The utility of image analysis for forecasting is demonstrated by a considerable amount of research. Drawing on the theoretical work of Kenneth Boulding, several scholars have studied the extent to which images of decision makers correspond to the foreign-policy outputs of their countries. In a comparative study of Sweden and Norway between 1940 and 1949, Burgess (1968: 160) concludes that images and outcomes correspond very closely, and that potential mediating factors were not sufficiently powerful to alter the outcome.

The conclusion is based on his finding that the differences in the images of alliances led directly to the failure of negotiations between Sweden and Norway to establish a Scandinavian Defense Commission and to the decision of Norway to join NATO. Choucri (1969: 15) confirms the link between images and foreign-policy outputs for non-aligned nations. In a content analysis of the speeches of Nehru, Nasser, and Sukarno at the conferences of Bogor, Bandung, and Belgrade, she finds a congruent relationship between the images of the environment of these leaders and the acts of their respective nations. Her research also shows more congruence between images and concrete acts than between images and officially stated policies, suggesting that the latter are not a good indication of the intentions of foreign policy makers. Another interesting point is that she finds no congruency between the affective attitudes toward other actors in the environment and foreign-policy output. She is supported by a diachronic analysis of Indonesia between 1962 and 1970. The shift in Indonesia's general foreign-policy stance from emphasis on independence to emphasis on development cannot be explained in terms of a change in attitudes that saw hostility in the outside world, because these remained substantially the same during the period of the shift in policy (Weinstein 1973: 376-77).

In addition to their value for forecasting, strategic images may also have considerable explanatory power (Jervis 1970; Gamson and Modigliani 1971). For example, they may show us that what is perceived by actor A as irrational is quite rational when viewed through the strategic image of actor B. Finally, strategic images are susceptive of cross-national research, as will be demonstrated in this study.

Before leaving the discussion of the relationship of images to action, it should be noted that the images of elites represent only one of several types of independent variables that determine official behavior. Furthermore, images can be seen as mediating the effects of these other variables on behavior; that is, the conceptions of elites are intervening variables and necessary links between the sources of foreign policy and behavior itself.

Keeping in mind the artificiality of viewing image as either an independent or dependent variable, we will now treat the strategic image as a dependent variable and look at some sources of variation in diplomatic thinking. Among the determinants of diplomatic thinking are power, economic interests, historical experiences, membership in international organizations, culture, position in the international stratification, international climate, and geography of a given diplomat's country. This study tests the validity of two theories of international relations in explaining the sources of diplomatic thinking: the social-structural and international climate theories.

FIGURE 2.1

Schematic Overview of the Principal Variables
and Their Relations

Diplomatic Thinking Components

Chapter 5

Chapter 6

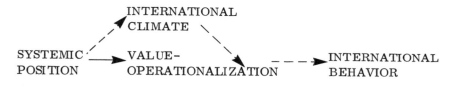

Chapter 7

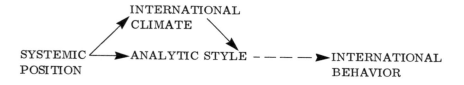

Chapter 8

Note: A dotted line links relevant, but not studied, relationships.
Source: Compiled by the author from his own research.

The main proposition of the first theory is that the strategic images of leading foreign-policy strata of a given national actor are a function of the position which that actor enjoys in the international system. To explain the interaction between individual and systemic variables the theory introduces another variable that can be labeled "positional awareness." A greater awareness is expected to enhance the impact of a country's position on the thinking of its representatives. In other words, "the international position of the actor is consequential or influential insofar as it is cognitively present to the persons constituting the milieu through their own perception or as it is perceived and taught them by others [other milieux]" (Hveem 1972: 70). The theory further proposes ways of classifying nations according to their positions in the international structure along several dimensions. Chapter 3 will discuss some of the relevant dimensions and procedures for positioning different countries along these dimensions.

The selection of the international climate theory is based on the finding that information about both the operational milieu (the environment as operationally defined, independent of the beliefs of those whose behavior is studied--in this case the structural position of a country) and the psycho-milieu (the environment as it is perceived) is important to predict an actor's style of analysis, value operationalization, and strategic approach (see Sprout 1965). In fact, this book will study the relation between the first component of diplomatic thinking (perception of the international environment) and the other three components (style of analysis, value operationalization, and strategic approach). This last theory will be treated in more depth in Chapter 5. In sum, this study is concerned with diplomatic thinking and its determinants. The term "diplomatic thinking" connotes the diplomat's perception of the international environment, his style of analysis, his operationalization of internationally relevant values, and his strategic approach. Chapter 3 will discuss the social-structural approach to international relations and the impact of the systemic position of a country on the thinking of its representatives. Chapter 4 sets out the tools and techniques that we will use to trace diplomatic thinking and its sources. Chapters 5, 6, 7, and 8 focus in turn on each of the components of diplomatic thinking and analyze how and to what extent they are affected by our systemic and perceptual independent variables. A schematic overview of the principal variables and their relations studied in Chapters 5 to 8 is presented in Figure 2.1. Chapter 9 provides a brief overview of the findings, summarizing a few of the broader implications for the study of international relations.

3

Diplomatic Thinking as a
Function of International Position

RELEVANCE OF THE SOCIAL-
STRUCTURAL APPROACH

The essence of international relations is a perpetual struggle between national actors for preferred positions. Looking back in history we find this competition symbolically expressed in the concern over precedence. Until the Congress of Vienna decided, in 1815, that ambassadors should rank according to their date of arrival in the host country, precedence depended on the seniority of their respective royal masters. However, "unfortunately, every monarch had his own ideas about his place in the royal scheme of things, and since no two crowned heads could ever agree, a diplomatic reception was rather like the last minute rush for drinks in a public house when the landlord calls out, 'Time, please,' with every one pushing, jostling and elbowing for position" (Roetter 1963: 29).

Countries think now more than ever in terms of comparison and improvement of their relative positions. To illustrate this fact, I will quote some statements made by diplomats whom I interviewed in Washington in 1975 in connection with this study:

> There is no difference in the nature of peace and war.
> There is always the fight for a better position in the
> world.
>
> Asian diplomat

> My country is one of the poorest among the richest. . . .
> We were once a source of raw materials and labor and
> know what it is to be at the other end.
>
> West European diplomat

The main question is that of the relative position of
the various parts of the world in terms of development. Just as within the society there is the strain
of rich and poor, and unless adjustments are made,
it is the biggest threat to long-term peace.

Asian diplomat

There is an increasing awareness of the developing
countries about their relative position vis-a-vis the
developed countries.

Latin American diplomat

Differences between countries are O.K., but we cannot accept them, if being different means occupying
an inferior place.

Middle Eastern diplomat

Each nation should equip itself for protection--mili-
tary strength is relative and determined by your relative position. . . . security depends on an equivalent
power position.

Asian diplomat

There is cooperation at the base, between smaller
states . . . if you go to the top it is more competitive. However, the top cooperates on different
things, for example, not on disarmament but arms
control . . . to keep their position.

East European diplomat

You realize that you are small when you are treated by
the Americans as a small country . . . they do not
understand that particular issues can be of great interest to you.

West European diplomat

In the international community there is a fight of
classes between developed and less developed countries.

Latin American diplomat

Nobody wants to be the underdog in security.

West European diplomat

> Sometimes we feel a sense of deprivation and humiliation as a small country.
>
> Middle Eastern diplomat

> . . . political independence without economic independence is a farce . . . real independence is very loved by third world countries.
>
> African diplomat

> Is the international system hierarchically structured? In principle, no; in practice, yes.
>
> European diplomat

> . . . poor countries who do not have resources are apprehensive about being at the bottom and envy the better positions . . . they want some sort of leveling . . . they find themselves below the level of respect.
>
> African diplomat

These observations indicate that the problem of international stratification is a matter of great concern in the world.

The growing apprehension of countries about their international position has been enhanced by the availability of better information, the communications revolution, group formation, and the impact of several recent international experiences. In the last ten years we have seen an improvement in the data base for cross-national comparisons. Each country's international identity card now contains such basic information as level of military power, economic development, degree of economic dependence and penetration, population growth, center versus periphery position, and so on. The United Nations, as producer and distributor of such information, has had a considerable impact on the positional awareness of its members. Further, at the level of the average citizen, the role of the modern means of mass communication has been enormous because it has amplified the perceived international inequalities among nations. The principal result of this comparison has been a group consciousness among nations whose positions in international stratification are homogeneous. As a consequence of such homogeneous group formation there has been an increase in political alertness, similarity of outlook, and sense of efficacy within these subgroups of nations. A final factor which has raised the expectations of countries occupying less-preferred positions and the apprehension of countries occupying more-preferred positions has been the impact of the oil crisis and the disentanglement of Vietnam from foreign intervention.

Both events demonstrated to all countries the impermanent state of international stratification and proved that positions can be successfully challenged and changed.

The purpose of this study is to inquire to what extent and in what respects diplomatic thinking varies as a function of the international position of a country. This chapter will examine the social-structural theory of social and political thinking in general and its application to the international system; will review the research done on foreign-policy thinking as a function of international position; and will discuss the dimensions of national position used and describe the procedures for calculating the national indicators needed to rank-order the countries whose diplomats were interviewed about these dimensions.

The basic assumption underlying the social-structural theory of thinking is that our conceptualizations--including our perceptions, values, strategic approaches, and even our cognitive modes (Mannheim 1936: 117)--can best be understood in their relationship to certain definable aspects of society. Where you are located in the hierarchy of status, power, and other relevant dimensions produces different perspectives on the environment. To put it less formally, "You stand where you sit."

Any review of the historical development of the theory inevitably pauses to pay respect to Karl Marx. Marxian theory argues that the observable expression of knowledge, belief, or ideology cannot be understood without uncovering their socioeconomic base. "His assertion that it is not the consciousness of men that determines their being, but on the contrary, their social being which determines their consciousness is not a philosophical proposition, but a statement about the genesis of ideological constructions, law, politics, religion, art and philosophy" (Bottomore and Rubel 1956: 24). To put it another way, the economic position of a social actor determines his specific manner of thinking about social reality.

In addition to studying the impact of economic position on thought, Marx also highlights two conditions which inhibit a scientific understanding of social reality. The first condition is the "parallel" study of cultural products, such as theories, belief systems, and images, and the study of socioeconomic systems. These theories, belief systems, and images, according to Marxian theory, constitute the principal stumbling block for scientific investigation, when they are considered in themselves, without taking into account the correlations which can be established between socioeconomic positions and those cultural products. In the study of international relations this condition is still present to a great extent. For example, the international system theory and the international image theory develop essentially in a parallel manner, and the studies which

focus on the mutual impact of cognitive and systemic variables are
scarce. Furthermore, there exists a subtle resistance in established academic milieux to make explicit or recognize the "positional"
bias of the theories of international relations that are current. The
second condition that concerned Marx was the tendency of a social
actor to believe that "his specific condition of existence and consciousness should be the general condition of existence and consciousness for all; and in fact that his own beliefs and knowledge are
the same beliefs and knowledge that all other persons have, regardless of their particular economic class position" (Sampson 1971: 194).
Marx noted that dominant classes feel that the conditions supportive
of their economic positions are the general conditions necessary for
the survival of everybody in the society. An example of the manner
by which a dominant group can determine the thinking that shapes the
consciousness of others can be found in a fascinating study by Pope
(1958). This tendency can sometimes also be detected in the study
of international relations, for example, in the "assumption of identity
of interests" made by early peace researchers (see Schmid 1968).
Although these two conditions can still be detected in the study of international relations, the growing interest in cross-national research
and the study of the relationships between cognitive and systemic
variables indicate an increased awareness of the inhibiting impact
of the presence of these two conditions on a better comprehension of
international relations.

The second figure who made sweeping contributions to the
social-structural theory of social and political thinking is Karl
Mannheim. In Ideology and Utopia (1936) he called into question
nearly all knowledge and ideological thought and did not restrict his
focus, as Marx had done, to the relationship between cognition and
economic position. In contrast, Mannheim urges social scientists
to question the validity of knowledge by checking the position of its
author along three different dimensions. First, authors must be
placed on the vertical dimension, which refers to the different strata
in a society, by inquiring about their economic well-being, political
power, academic status, and so on. Second, they must be placed on
the horizontal dimension, which distinguishes between different cultures, by establishing their cultural backgrounds. Third, they must
be placed on the time dimension, which distinguishes different points
or periods in history, by examining the historical context in which a
particular thought or idea originated.

What does this brief review of some of the principal sources
of variation in the thinking about social reality suggest about the
relevance of social-structural theory to the study of diplomatic thinking? I start with the assumption that the countries of the world can
be considered a large, interacting social system within which each

country occupies various positions. These positions can be ranked
in terms of such dimensions as power, economic stature, dependency
and penetration, security, and center versus periphery, which will
be discussed more extensively later in this chapter. Given this kind
of social system, several implications can be drawn from social-
structural theory.

First, the theory states that in a stratified social system, all
knowledge which is either political or involves a world-view is inevitably partisan. Therefore we can expect that, in this highly stratified world with extreme heterogeneity, we will find differences in the
diplomatic thinking of countries occupying different positions in the
international system. These diverse types of diplomatic thinking
could be seen as different modes of experiencing the same reality
and also, in a highly competitive world, as intellectual expressions
of conflicting groups defending or struggling for preferred positions.

Second, this approach stresses that, in the study of diplomatic
thinking, we need to be aware of the partial validity of each perspective. It reminds the researcher that opposing views and cognitions
are not infinite in number and are not products of arbitrary will, but
that they are complementary and that each is related to the systemic
position of its proponent. Therefore, if we want to understand fully
diplomatic thinking, we need to have a more comprehensive view of
the subject. This does not mean a generalization from one perspective or one mode of diplomatic thinking, nor averaging several perspectives, but instead the assimilation and transcendence of the limitations of particular points of view. In other words it means that
diplomatic thinking is characterizable only when one has taken into
account the different modes of diplomatic thinking of a sample of
diplomats representative of the relevant positions in international
relations and analyzed and compared them as a function of the international positions of their proponents.

Third, social-structural research of diplomatic thinking can
also inform us to what extent shifts in meaning and emphasis in diplomatic thinking can be used as sensitive indicators of present or
future changes in the structure of international relations. For example, conceptions of preferred world order could be called utopian
today, but also could become realities of tomorrow. Or as Lamartine
phrased it: "Utopias are often premature truths" (Mannheim 1936:
203). This is more the case when there is a close correlation between different forms of utopia and the social strata which are trans-
forming the existing order.

Finally, a better insight into the relations between diplomatic
thinking and its social base will improve our understanding about
"changing" diplomatic thinking. It can show us the conditions necessary for change and also, for example, the limits of "controlled

communication" (Burton 1969) as a means for changing the conceptual approach of the parties in an international conflict situation. Research in the field of social and political thinking indicates that changes in thinking do not occur independently from changes in the structural relations and that "it is not until their structural relations are gradually displaced by others, that the need for new theories and new orientations arises" (Mannheim 1936: 176).

MAJOR STRUCTURAL POSITIONS IN THE INTERNATIONAL SYSTEM

This section will look at some major structural dimensions of the international system and review the research findings about their relationship to foreign-policy thinking.

Center-Periphery

One of the primary dimensions in the international structure rank-orders countries according to their positions in the center versus the periphery of that structure. Most of the research on foreign-policy thinking as a function of international position was inspired by Galtung's (1964) ideas and findings on the center-periphery dimension in the study of national societies (see Table 3.1). Galtung's (1964: 207-08) model divides society into three parts: a decision-making nucleus, surrounded by the center of the social structure, which again is surrounded by the periphery: "The social center occupies positions that are socially rewarded, and the social periphery occupies positions that are less rewarded and even rejected. In the center are the topdogs of the society; in the periphery the underdogs. . . ." Galtung operationalizes his concepts of "center" and "periphery" through an index of social position which includes eight items: sex, age, education, income, ecological location, geographical location, occupational position, and occupational sector. He offers evidence that all eight components represent dimensions of rank or mobility preferences. Positions on these eight dimensions are combined into an additive index with total scores ranging from 0 to 8.

A parallel index rank-ordering countries instead of individuals was developed by Hveem (1972). The variables that he selected are shown in Table 3.1 along with the national index variables to which they correspond most closely (Hveem 1972: 70). This index was validated by use of an indicator of the international behavior of countries: Their frequency of absence from votes in the UN General

Assembly in 1962 and 1963. On the basis of his theory, Hveem predicted that center actors would tend to be present, while those on
the periphery would tend to be absent. He obtained a Spearman's
rank correlation of .68 between rank on the international social position index and the absence scores.

TABLE 3.1

Comparison of the Variables Included in the
Center-Periphery Index of Hveem and Galtung

| Types of Variables | Center-Periphery Index | |
	International (Hveem)	National (Galtung)
Attributive-ascriptive	Age Gross domestic product at factor cost Population	Age Income
Attributive-achievement	Industrialization Literacy level Gross domestic product per capita	Sector of occupation Educational level
Relational	Geographical centrality Memberships in international organizations	Place of residence: geographical

Source: Compiled by the author from his own research.

The general proposition underlying Hveem's theoretical model
is that the representatives of national actors perceive, feel, or generally behave as a function of the position of the national actor which
they represent in the international system. He predicts not only differences in foreign-policy thinking between center and periphery
countries but also greater variation within the periphery than within
the center. The differences in foreign-policy thinking between the
two groups are basically a reflection of the interests associated with
their respective positions. The explanation of the difference in the
range of attitudes and images within the two groups requires the

introduction of two additional variables into the model: asymmetric and symmetric penetration, and positive and negative reference groups. The first reason for greater similarity in foreign-policy thinking among center countries is the fact that they penetrate each other more than the periphery, whose individual units tend to remain more isolated. In other words, center countries interact with each other more and more on an equal footing (Hveem 1972: 72). Second, they also have more values to defend than the periphery nations.

> [They are] aware of being center nations, and this aware-
> ness creates a feeling of "responsibility" as well as a
> feeling of "we-ness," a feeling of community with other
> center nations. This "we-ness" may make the center
> nations view the periphery nations as an out-group,
> possibly a negative reference group. And it may make
> it especially responsive to other center nations (Hveem
> 1972: 72).

In addition to the above-mentioned two general predictions, Hveem also presents a list of hypotheses on what constitutes the typical thinking about foreign policy among center and periphery nations. To a large extent these hypotheses were adopted from the national center-periphery theory and related research findings (Galtung 1964; Halle 1966; Wiberg 1968). We will classify these hypotheses into two groups corresponding to the two components of diplomatic thinking—style of analysis and strategic approach—described in Chapter 2. Hveem proposes that the style of analysis of the center is characterized by a pragmatic rather than a moralistic way of looking at problems and also by a higher consistency in their perspectives than in the periphery. In their strategic approach, Hveem expects the center to follow the modern conservative change in order to preserve strategy and the periphery nations to be more radical. The center perspective on the international system is that present trends of development should merely be extrapolated into the future. It will accept deviations from these present trends and from the behavior compatible with them insofar as these deviations do not threaten the values of the position of the center nation (Hveem 1972: 75).

In this study we explored the impact of the center-periphery position of the diplomat's country on various aspects of his diplomatic thinking and, more specifically, we tested the set of hypotheses developed by Hveem. The index used is identical with Hveem's index with one exception: We substituted "degree of diplomatic representation of a country" for geographical centrality because we believe that the degree of diplomatic representation is a better indicator of the

intensity of communication between countries than physical distance.
The center-periphery position of the nation-states whose diplomats
we interviewed can be found in Table 3.2. Table 3.3 shows that the
distribution of diplomats was relatively even over the entire center-
periphery range. Our index of the center-periphery position of a
country is thus an additive index based on the following parameters:
age of the country, gross national product, population, industry output as a percentage of the gross national product, literacy level,
gross domestic product per capita, diplomatic representation, and
membership in international organizations. The relative weight attached to the three types of variables is: 11 to the attributive-
ascriptive variables, 11 to the attributive-achievement variables,
and 9 to the relational variables. This weighting is not so different
from Hveem's (3/8, 3/8, 2/8), is arbitrary, and has no theoretical
defense.

Selection of Other Relevant Positions

    Recognizing the multidimensionality of the international struc-
ture (Rummel 1966), we decided to look also at the impact, individually or jointly, of positions on some other relevant dimensions. Our
choice among several major dimensions of variation between countries was influenced by the answers of the diplomats to one of our
questions: "What factors account for differences in diplomatic thinking between countries?" Table 3.4 categorizes the factors mentioned
by the diplomats in response to this question. Looking at the five
factors mentioned most frequently, we find two that reflect the country's position on vertical dimensions: economic position and power
and security. In addition, respondents stressed the impact of historical experiences; tradition, culture and ideology; and the geographic position of a country. Though highly relevant to the understanding of diplomatic thinking, these three factors are not related
to our present concern with the effect of a country's position in the
international structure on diplomatic thinking.
    In order to explore the effect of economic position on diplo-
matic thinking, we developed four economic indexes: economic
development, overall penetration, economic interdependency, and
aid dependency--each of which measures an important aspect of
the economic position of a country. As measures of a country's
position on the power and security dimension, we developed two
indexes: military expenditure and the degree of security force investment of a country.

TABLE 3.2

Position of 116 Countries on the Center-Periphery Dimension

France	31	Colombia	21	Central African Rep.		
Great Britain		Egypt		Honduras		
Japan		Ireland		Ivory Coast		
Italy	30	Nigeria		Jamaica		
The Netherlands		Thailand		Liberia		
United States		Ecuador	20	Malaysia		
Argentina	29	South Africa		Malta		
Belgium		Uruguay		Nepal		
Canada		Indonesia	19	Zaire		
West Germany		Korea, South		Gabon		12
Switzerland		Philippines		Upper Volta		
Austria	28	Saudi Arabia		Jordan		11
Denmark		Pakistan	18	Burundi		10
Soviet Union		Bolivia	17	Dahomey		
Sweden		Dominican Rep.		Togo		
Spain		El Salvador		Missing Data		
Brazil	27	Iraq		Algeria		
Czechoslovakia		Panama		Bahamas		
Australia	26	Costa Rica	16	Bangladesh		
Chile		Ethiopia		Barbados		
Finland		Kuwait		Botswana		
Norway		Morocco		Chad		
Poland		Sri Lanka		Fiji		
Romania		Guatemala	15	Guinea		
Yugoslavia		Lebanon		Guyana		
Mexico	25	Nicaragua		Iceland		
Turkey		Syria		Lesotho		
Venezuela		Trinidad		Madagascar		
Bulgaria	24	Cyprus	14	Mali		
Greece		Ghana		Mauritania		
India	23	Kenya		Mauritius		
New Zealand		Paraguay		Niger		
Peru		Sudan		Oman		
Portugal		Tanzania		Qatar		
East Germany	22	Tunisia		Senegal		
Iran		Uganda		Sierra Leone		
Israel		Afghanistan	13	Singapore		
		Cameroon		Somalia		
				Taiwan		
				United Arab Emirates		
				Vatican		
				Zambia		

Note: The higher the score, the more central the country's position.
Source: Compiled by the author from his own research.

TABLE 3.3

Center–Periphery Distribution of Diplomats Interviewed

Center–Periphery Index	Number of Diplomats Interviewed	Relative Frequency (percent)	Adjusted Frequency (percent)	Cumulative Frequency (percent)
10	7	2.7	3.4	3.4
11	2	0.8	1.0	4.4
13	2	0.8	1.0	5.4
14	15	5.9	7.3	12.7
15	15	5.9	7.3	20.0
16	8	3.1	3.9	23.9
17	12	4.7	5.9	29.8
18	8	3.1	3.9	33.7
19	13	5.1	6.3	40.0
20	7	2.7	3.4	43.4
21	10	3.9	4.9	48.3
22	6	2.4	2.9	51.2
23	7	2.7	3.4	54.6
24	3	1.2	1.5	56.1
25	8	3.1	3.9	60.0
26	16	6.3	7.8	67.8
27	4	1.6	2.0	69.8
28	16	6.3	7.8	77.6
29	16	6.3	7.8	85.4
30	17	6.7	8.3	93.7
31	13	5.1	6.3	100.0
Missing	50	19.6	Missing	100.0
Total	255	100.0	100.0	

Source: Compiled by the author from his own research.

TABLE 3.4

Distribution of Factors Mentioned by Diplomats in
Response to the Question: "What factors account
for differences in diplomatic thinking between countries?"
(percents)

1	Economic position of a country	18.65
2	Historical experiences	15.67
3	Tradition-culture-ideology	14.67
4	Geographic location	12.68
5	Power-military security position	10.69
6	Age of a country	8.70
7	Size of a country	5.97
8	Synthesis of domestic power struggle	4.97
9	Group membership (for example, free world, Organization of African Unity, nonaligned)	3.98
10	Supreme pragmatism	1.99
11	International law	.99
12	Diplomatic talent	.99

Note: The percentage on the right-hand side indicates the
relative frequency with which that particular factor was mentioned,
if we add all the factors mentioned by the total sample of diplomats.
Source: Compiled by the author from his own research.

Economic Development Position

The importance of economic development as a determinant of
foreign-policy behavior is now well established. For a sample of
82 nations, Rummel (1966) found that the level of economic development was one of the two major factors (the other being size) account-
ing for the activity of nations. "The more economically developed
and larger a nation is, the more it will be active in the international
system" (Rummel 1969: 341). Economic development is also the
most important predictor of a nation's voting in the United Nations
(Vincent 1968: 493). Furthermore, Rummel (1969: 238) finds that
the more similar two nations are in their economic development,
the more congruent their UN voting will be. In our study we expect
to find significant effects of economic development, that is, wealth
of a country, upon the perspectives and values of its diplomats. We
shall also examine how strongly the country's wealth contributes to
the distinctive outlook that these diplomats bring to world affairs.

50108

The index used to rank-order countries along the economic development dimension combines measures of a country's gross national
product (GNP) per capita, percentage of the GNP that comes from
industry, and level of literacy. The rank-ordering on this index of
the countries whose diplomats we interviewed can be found in Table
3.5. Table 3.6 shows a satisfactory distribution of these diplomats
over the entire scale of economic development.

Overall Penetration Position

A second index which characterizes the economic position of
a country is its degree of economic penetration. According to
Rosenau (1966: 65) a penetrated system is "one in which nonmembers
of a society participate directly and authoritatively through actions
taken jointly with the society's members, in either the allocation of
values or the mobilization in behalf of its goals." The index of
penetration used in this study is developed by Hveem (1973: 336).
The theory behind this index describes and explains the world as
becoming a single system with global patterns of domination. "It
sees the development of an international hierarchical division of
labor where new levels and centers of control and accumulation are
developed whereas the structural constants--verticality, inegality,
and feudality--are retained" (Hveem 1973: 340). We expect that the
concerns of controllers and controlled in the international system
will differ and will be reflected in the thinking of their representatives. The index of penetration that is used in this study is not a
straight measure of "economic" penetration; it also contains information about military and political penetration. It is an additive index
based on the following parameters: stock of direct investments by
metropoles, imports from metropoles, and economic aid from
metropoles (these three measure economic penetration); military
alliance comembership with metropoles, and military aid received
from metropoles (military penetration). In addition it includes
voting agreement with the United States as an indicator of "political
penetration." On the other five parameters the metropole was operationalized as all Organization for Economic Cooperation and Development (OECD) countries. This index ranks the countries in terms
of the degree of penetratedness. It thus allows us to study the effects of degree of penetratedness on diplomatic thinking within our
subsample of periphery country diplomats. The list of periphery
countries whose diplomats we interviewed, classified according to
overall penetration by capitalist center countries, can be found in
Table 3.7. Distribution of the diplomats over the entire range of
penetratedness is presented in Table 3.8.

TABLE 3.5

Position of 116 Countries on the Economic Development Dimension

Austria	11	Jamaica		Ethiopia	
Belgium		Mexico		Ghana	
Czechoslovakia		Peru		Guatemala	
Finland		Saudi Arabia		Honduras	
East Germany		South Africa		India	
West Germany		Taiwan		Ivory Coast	
Great Britain		Bolivia	06	Jordan	
Japan		Colombia		Kenya	
The Netherlands		Costa Rica		Lesotho	
New Zealand		Dominican Rep.		Nepal	
Switzerland		Ecuador		Pakistan	
Argentina	10	El Salvador		Sudan	
Australia		Guyana		Togo	
Bulgaria		Iraq		Tunisia	
Canada		Korea, South		Uganda	
Chile		Lebanon		Upper Volta	
Denmark		Liberia		Bangladesh	03
Italy		Nicaragua		Burundi	
Kuwait		Nigeria		Missing Data	
Norway		Panama		Algeria	
Poland		Philippines		Bahamas	
Romania		Thailand		Barbados	
Soviet Union		Turkey		Chad	
Sweden		Zambia		Fiji	
United States		Botswana	05	Guinea	
Venezuela	09	Egypt		Ireland	
Greece		Indonesia		Iceland	
Israel		Malaysia		Madagascar	
Malta		Mauritius		Mali	
Portugal		Morocco		Mauritania	
Singapore		Paraguay		Niger	
Uruguay		Syria		Oman	
Yugoslavia		Sri Lanka		Qatar	
Brazil	07	Zaire		Senegal	
Cyprus		Afghanistan	04	Sierra Leone	
Gabon		Cameroon		Somalia	
Iran		Central African Rep.		Spain	
		Dahomey		Trinidad	
				United Arab Emirates	
				Vatican	

Note: The higher the score, the more developed the country.
Source: Compiled by the author from his own research.

TABLE 3.6

Economic Development Distribution of the
Diplomats Interviewed

Economic Development Index	Number of Diplomats Interviewed	Relative Frequency (percent)	Adjusted Frequency (percent)	Cumulative Frequency (percent)
3	5	2.0	2.3	2.3
4	37	14.5	16.9	19.2
5	24	9.4	11.0	30.1
6	32	12.5	14.6	44.7
7	19	7.5	8.7	53.4
8	11	4.3	5.0	58.4
9	9	3.5	4.1	62.6
10	42	16.5	19.2	81.7
11	40	15.7	18.3	100.0
Missing	36	14.1	Missing	100.0
Total	255	100.0	100.0	

Source: Compiled by the author from his own research.

Economic Interdependency Position

The third characteristic of the economic position of a country
is the degree of economic interdependency in the world system.
Economic interdependency could be defined as a relatively symmetrical exchange of goods and services, which are difficult to substitute
and vital for a country to keep its economic position.   To illustrate
this concept, let us look at the case of Belgium, a country that ranks
high on economic interdependency.   Because of the virtual absence
of essential natural resources within its boundaries, Belgium must
import large quantities of raw materials, finished goods, and foods;
to pay for these imports, it must maintain an equivalent level of
exports.   Thus the country's economic position depends to a large
extent upon the balance of foreign trade.   Belgium and Luxembourg
together lead all other countries in the per capita value of trade--
5,717 U.S. dollars in 1974.   This condition certainly explains the
disproportionately high diplomatic representation of Belgium abroad,
its traditional advocacy of freedom of trade among nations, and its

TABLE 3.7

Position of a Subset of Countries Who Are Penetrated

Penetration Index Score	Country
11	Bolivia, Peru
10	Gabon, Honduras, Panama, Venezuela
9	Central African Republic, Ivory Coast, Liberia, Mauritania, Chile, Costa Rica, Zaire
8	Argentina, Colombia, Dominican Republic, Ecuador, El Salvador, Guatemala, Nicaragua, Trinidad, Uruguay, Iran, Malaysia, Zambia
7	Algeria, Cameroon, Morocco, Niger, Senegal, Togo, Tunisia, Brazil, Jamaica, Paraguay, Kuwait, Philippines, Saudi Arabia, Taiwan, Turkey
6	Chad, Dahomey, Kenya, South Africa, Uganda, Malta, Israel, Thailand
5	Ghana, Guinea, Nigeria, Sierra Leone, Tanzania, Greece, Mexico, Iraq, South Korea
4	Ethiopia, Somalia, Upper Volta, Sri Lanka, Cyprus, Jordan, Pakistan
3	Burundi, Indonesia
2	Botswana, Lesotho, Mali, Sudan, Spain, India, Singapore
1	Yugoslavia

Note: The higher the score, the more penetrated the country.
Source: Compiled by the author from his own research.

consistent encouragement of the removal of trade restrictions by all countries. We believe that the degree of economic interdependency of a country has an effect on a country's sensitivity about the state of the international environment and consequently influences its diplomatic thinking. In our index of economic interdependency, we included information about import as a percentage of GNP, the per capita consumption of energy, and the percentage of the needed energy that has to be imported. The list of countries whose diplomats we interviewed, classified according to their position on the index of economic interdependency, can be found in Table 3.9. The distribution of the diplomats over the entire range of economic interdependency is presented in Table 3.10.

TABLE 3.8

Penetration Distribution of the
Diplomats Interviewed

Penetration Index	Number of Diplomats Interviewed	Relative Frequency (percent)	Adjusted Frequency (percent)	Cumulative Frequency (percent)
1	9	3.5	6.4	6.4
2	12	4.7	8.6	15.0
3	6	2.4	4.3	19.3
4	16	6.3	11.4	30.7
5	15	5.9	10.7	41.4
6	12	4.7	8.6	50.0
7	28	11.0	20.0	70.0
8	22	8.6	15.7	85.7
9	10	3.9	7.1	92.9
10	7	2.7	5.0	97.9
11	3	1.2	2.2	100.0
Missing	115	45.1	Missing	100.0
Total	225	100.0	100.0	

Source: Compiled by the author from his own research.

TABLE 3.9

Position of 116 Countries on the Economic Interdependency Dimension

Country	Score	Country	Score	Country	Score
Belgium	14	Spain		Argentina	06
		Togo		Gabon	
Iceland	13	Trinidad		Iran	
Ireland		Zaire		Mexico	
				Poland	
Denmark	12	Australia	08	Romania	
Malta		Burundi		Soviet Union	
Sweden		Cameroon		Venezuela	
Switzerland		Central African Rep.			
		Canada		Algeria	05
Austria	11	Chad		Bangladesh	
West Germany		Dominican Republic		Colombia	
Fiji		El Salvador		Iraq	
Finland		Guatemala		Malaysia	
France		Honduras			
Guyana		Israel		Afghanistan	04
Jamaica		Ivory Coast		Bolivia	
Lebanon		Kuwait		Ecuador	
Singapore		Mali		Egypt	
		Morocco		India	
Bulgaria	10	Nicaragua		Indonesia	
Cyprus		Philippines		Nigeria	
East Germany		Sri Lanka		Pakistan	
Great Britain		Sudan		Syria	
Italy		Tanzania		Tunisia	
Japan		Thailand			
Liberia		United States		Missing Data	
Norway		Upper Volta		Bahamas	
Portugal		Uruguay		Barbados	
Panama		Yugoslavia		Botswana	
				Korea, South	
Costa Rica	09	Brazil	07	Lesotho	
Czechoslovakia		Chile		Madagascar	
Dahomey		Ghana		Mauritania	
Greece		Guinea		Mauritius	
Jordan		Ethiopia		Nepal	
Kenya		Paraguay		Niger	
The Netherlands		Peru		Oman	
New Zealand		South Africa		Qatar	
Senegal		Saudi Arabia		Taiwan	
Sierra Leone		Turkey		United Arab Emirates	
Somalia		Uganda		Vatican	
				Zambia	

Note: The higher the score, the more interdependent the country.
Source: Compiled by the author from his own research.

TABLE 3.10

Economic Interdependency Distribution of
the Diplomats Interviewed

Economic Interdependency Index	Number of Diplomats Interviewed	Relative Frequency (percent)	Adjusted Frequency (percent)	Cumulative Frequency (percent)
4	24	9.4	10.9	10.9
5	12	4.7	5.4	16.3
6	17	6.7	7.7	24.0
7	20	7.8	9.0	33.0
8	51	20.0	23.1	56.1
9	31	12.2	14.0	70.1
10	23	9.0	10.4	80.5
11	22	8.6	10.0	90.5
12	11	4.3	5.0	95.5
13	5	2.0	2.3	97.7
14	5	2.0	2.3	100.0
Missing	34	13.3	Missing	100.0
Total	255	100.0	100.0	

Source: Compiled by the author from his own research.

Foreign Aid Received Position

The amount of foreign aid received is the final index of the economic position of a country used in this study as an independent variable. The receipt of aid by a country is a clear indicator of its asymmetric dependency position. Asymmetric dependency refers to a relationship between donor and recipient where the value exchanged is practically indispensable for the recipient and to a great extent dispensable for the donor. The aid issue has always been a very touchy matter in international relations, for aid carries a host of implications for the recipient's self-esteem, feelings of obligation, and evaluations of the donors (Kelman 1962; Gergen and Gergen 1974). The giving of aid does not always guarantee a positive response in terms of mutual respect, or efficient utilization of aid, because "the aid relationship necessarily casts its participants into a hierarchy: the independent donor has many sources, while the dependent recipient has a few. It's possible, in other words, that aid threatens the esteem of the recipient" (Gergen and Gergen 1974: 58). As periphery countries most often find themselves in the position of such dependency, we would like to find out to what extent this factor accounts for variations in diplomatic thinking within this subgroup of nations. In our study this subgroup will be limited to countries who receive aid from capitalist countries and multilateral institutions. The list of countries whose diplomats we interviewed, classified according to their position on the index of aid received, can be found in Table 3.11. The distribution of the diplomats on the index is presented in Table 3.12.

Military Expenditure Position

In addition to the economic position of a country, our diplomats stressed the importance of military power and security as significant sources of variation in diplomatic thinking. In other words, diplomacy cannot be understood outside the context of force, a fact underscored by Kissinger when he described diplomacy which is not related to a plausible employment of force as sterile (Graubard 1974: 83). The world seen from a position of strength differs clearly from the world as experienced from a position of weakness. For example, in conflict resolution the outcomes generally tend to be biased in favor of the actors possessing more power; the stronger parties impose their definition of the situation and seek to create conditions guaranteeing that they may not fight in the near future and that they may keep the advantages gained through force. The weaker powers are inclined to yield and express at least a tactical tolerance of their dictated situation. The purpose of our study is to find out how and to what extent their countries' positions of strength influence the thinking of diplomats. We defined the position of strength of a country in terms of the public expenditures that it devotes to military forces. The list of countries whose diplomats we interviewed, classified according to this index, can be found in Table 3.13. The distribution of the diplomats on the index is presented in Table 3.14.

Security Force Investment Position

Two motives for strengthening military force can be distinguished: one is to discourage aggression and enjoy peace and security; another is to improve the capability to impose oneself on neighbors and rivals and to guarantee an improved position in the world. Although these two motives are connected, for some countries

TABLE 3.11

Position of a Subset of Countries Who Receive Aid

				Missing Data
Bangladesh	4	Argentina	1	Australia
India		Bahamas		Austria
Indonesia		Barbados		Belgium
Korea, South		Burundi		Bulgaria
Pakistan		Costa Rica		Canada
Philippines		Dominican Rep.		Cyprus
Somalia		Ecuador		Czechoslovakia
		El Salvador		Denmark
Algeria	3	Fiji		Finland
Afghanistan		Guatemala		France
Brazil		Guinea		East Germany
Cameroon		Guyana		West Germany
Central African Rep.		Honduras		Great Britain
Morocco		Iran		Greece
Nigeria		Iraq		Iceland
Senegal		Jamaica		Ireland
Sri Lanka		Lebanon		Italy
Israel		Lesotho		Japan
Ivory Coast		Liberia		Kuwait
Jordan		Mauritius		Madagascar
Kenya		Mexico		Malta
Ethiopia		Nicaragua		Mauritania
Gabon		Panama		New Zealand
Ghana		Paraguay		Niger
Colombia		Qatar		Norway
Tanzania		Saudi Arabia		Oman
Thailand		Sierra Leone		Poland
Tunisia		Syria		Portugal
Zaire		Togo		Romania
		Trinidad		Taiwan
Bolivia	2	Uganda		South Africa
Botswana		Uruguay		Soviet Union
Chad		Venezuela		Spain
Chile				Sweden
Dahomey				Switzerland
Egypt				The Netherlands
Malaysia				Turkey
Mali				United Arab Emirates
Nepal				United States
Peru				Yugoslavia
Sudan				Vatican
Upper Volta				
Zambia				

Note: The higher the score, the more aid the country received.
Source: Compiled by the author from his own research.

TABLE 3.12

Foreign Aid Receipt Distribution of the Diplomats Interviewed

Aid Received Index	Number of Diplomats Interviewed	Relative Frequency (percent)	Adjusted Frequency (percent)	Cumulative Frequency (percent)
1	57	22.4	39.9	39.9
2	26	10.2	18.2	58.0
3	39	15.3	27.3	85.3
4	21	8.2	14.7	100.0
Missing	112	43.9	Missing	100.0
Total	255	100.0	100.0	

Source: Compiled by the author from his own research.

security may be the ultima ratio for strengthening their forces. For them especially, "to be without fear is a fate worthy of envy" (Aron 1966: 66). To compare countries according to the strength of their concern with security, we developed an index which we call degree of security force investment of a country. This index is an additive index based on the following parameters: military expenditure per capita, population per soldier, and internal security forces per 1,000 working age population. Whereas the index of military strength compares countries on the basis of their military expenditure irrespective of the size of their population, the index of security force investment controls for population and thus gives a better indicator of the extent to which a nation-state wants to invest in security. The list of countries whose diplomats we interviewed, classified according to their position on the index of security force investment, can be found in Table 3.15. The distribution of the diplomats on the index is described in Table 3.16.

CONCLUSION

In sum, this chapter has pointed out that diplomatic thinking cannot be fully comprehended unless, in addition to internal and external factors, the impact of systemic variables is taken into account. Seven systemic variables are included in this analysis: center-periphery, economic development, penetration, economic

TABLE 3.13

Position of 116 Countries on the Military Expenditure Dimension

Soviet Union	6	Bulgaria	2	Mali	
United States		Chile		Mauretania	
		Indonesia		Mauritius	
Canada	5	Ireland		Morocco	
France		Malaysia		Nepal	
West Germany		Mexico		New Zealand	
Great Britain		Peru		Nicaragua	
Japan		Syria		Panama	
Italy		Thailand		Paraguay	
India		Venezuela		Philippines	
		Finland		Senegal	
Australia	4			Sierra Leone	
Austria		Afghanistan	1	Singapore	
Belgium		Algeria		Somalia	
Brazil		Bangladesh		Sri Lanka	
Czechoslovakia		Bolivia		Sudan	
Egypt		Burundi		Tanzania	
East Germany		Cameroon		Togo	
Iran		Central African Rep.		Trinidad	
Israel		Chad		Uganda	
The Netherlands		Colombia		Upper Volta	
Poland		Costa Rica		Uruguay	
Spain		Cyprus		Zambia	
Sweden		Dahomey		Zaire	
		Dominican Rep.		Tunisia	
Argentina	3	Ecuador			
Denmark		El Salvador		Missing Data	
Greece		Ethiopia		Bahamas	
Iraq		Gabon		Barbados	
Korea, South		Ghana		Botswana	
Nigeria		Guatemala		Fiji	
Norway		Guinea		Iceland	
Pakistan		Guyana		Lesotho	
Portugal		Honduras		Madagascar	
Romania		Ivory Coast		Malta	
Saudi Arabia		Jamaica		Niger	
South Africa		Jordan		Oman	
Switzerland		Kenya		Qatar	
Taiwan		Kuwait		United Arab Emirates	
Turkey		Lebanon		Vatican	
Yugoslavia		Liberia			

Note: The higher the score, the higher the military expenditure of a country.

Source: Compiled by the author from his own research.

TABLE 3.14

Military Expenditure Distribution of
the Diplomats Interviewed

Military Expenditure Index	Number of Diplomats Interviewed	Relative Frequency (percent)	Adjusted Frequency (percent)	Cumulative Frequency (percent)
1	97	38.0	42.4	42.4
2	24	9.4	10.5	52.8
3	33	12.9	14.4	67.2
4	32	12.5	14.0	81.2
5	33	12.9	14.4	95.6
6	10	3.9	4.4	100.0
Missing	26	10.2	Missing	100.0
Total	255	100.0	100.0	

Source: Compiled by the author from his own research.

TABLE 3.15

Position of 116 Countries on the Security Force Investment Dimension

Country	Score	Country	Score	Country
Bulgaria	12	Malaysia		Honduras
		New Zealand		India
Israel	11	South Africa		Indonesia
		Spain		Ivory Coast
France	10	Switzerland		Mali
West Germany				Mauretania
Greece		Afghanistan	05	Philippines
Jordan		Bolivia		Sri Lanka
		Brazil		Sudan
Czechoslovakia	09	Chile		Tanzania
The Netherlands		Dominican Rep.		Togo
Portugal		Gabon		Uganda
Singapore		Guyana		Upper Volta
Soviet Union		Jamaica		Venezuela
United States		Japan		
		Nicaragua		Missing Data
Australia	08	Pakistan		Austria
Belgium		Somalia		Bahamas
East Germany		Trinidad		Bangladesh
Great Britain		Tunisia		Barbados
Iraq				Botswana
Italy		Cameroon	04	Costa Rica
Norway		Ghana		Egypt
Sweden		Kenya		Fiji
Syria		Lebanon		Finland
Taiwan		Morocco		Iceland
		Nigeria		Kuwait
Ethiopia		Peru		Lesotho
Korea, South		Senegal		Madagascar
Paraguay		Zaire		Malta
Poland		Zambia		Mauritius
Romania		Thailand		Mexico
Yugoslavia				Nepal
		Argentina	03	Niger
Algeria	06	Burundi		Oman
Canada		Central African Rep.		Panama
Colombia		Chad		Qatar
Cyprus		Dahomey		Saudi Arabia
Denmark		Ecuador		Sierra Leone
Ireland		El Salvador		United Arab Emirates
Iran		Guatemala		Uruguay
Liberia		Guinea		Turkey
				Vatican

Note: The higher the score, the more a country invests in security force.

Source: Compiled by the author from his own research.

TABLE 3.16

Security Force Investment Distribution of
the Diplomats Interviewed

Security Force Investment Index	Number of Diplomats Interviewed	Relative Frequency (percent)	Adjusted Frequency (percent)	Cumulative Frequency (percent)
3	44	17.3	22.2	22.2
4	20	7.8	10.1	32.3
5	29	11.4	14.6	47.0
6	28	11.0	14.1	61.1
7	11	4.3	5.6	66.7
8	33	12.9	16.7	83.3
9	20	7.8	10.1	93.4
10	10	3.9	5.1	98.5
11	2	0.8	1.0	99.5
12	1	0.4	0.5	100.0
Missing	57	22.4	Missing	100.0
Total	255	100.0	100.0	

Source: Compiled by the author from his own research.

42

TABLE 3.17

Correlation Matrix of the Positional Variables

	Center-Periphery	Economic Development	Penetration	Economic Interdependency	Aid Receipt	Military Expenditure	Security Force Investment
Center-periphery	X	.85	.16	.31	.08	.83	.55
Economic development	(205)	X	.22	.56	-.37	.66	.62
Penetration	(118)	(126)	X	-.02	-.18	.11	.11
Economic interdependency	(200)	(206)	(127)	X	-.34	.16	.38
Aid receipt	(109)	(121)	(122)	(134)	X	.21	.03
Military expenditure	(204)	(215)	(136)	(217)	(132)	X	.62
Security force investment	(180)	(186)	(119)	(189)	(113)	(198)	X

Note: Numbers in parentheses represent the number of cases. The other numbers are the correlation coefficients.

Source: Compiled by the author from his own research.

interdependency, aid receipt, military expenditure, and security force investment. Although conceptually distinct, these dimensions are not empirically independent, as we can see from the correlation matrix in Table 3.17. For example, we find the center-periphery dimension strongly correlated with economic development and military expenditure. The first link is not unexpected, as part of the center-periphery index consists of measures of the economic development of a country. The fact that these two indexes overlap in meaning and data base would allow us to substitute the one for the other. This is, however, not the case with military expenditure, which is conceptually totally distinct and has a different data base. The existence of a statistical relationship between the center-periphery and the military expenditure dimension (and of course also between other dimensions) must be considered in the interpretation of the partial correlation coefficients which we will use to examine the combined effects of all our independent variables. To assess the relative effects of our systemic variables on the dependent variables (diplomatic thinking), we must regress each dependent variable on our independent variables. The partial correlation coefficient obtained for each independent variable can be interpreted as the correlation between the independent variable and the dependent variable, while holding constant the independent variables which were previously introduced in the step-wise regression analysis (Ezekiel and Fox 1959: 192-96). Having defined and operationalized our independent variables, Chapter 4 will review the methods used for studying the dependent variables on diplomatic thinking.

4

The Study of
Diplomatic Thinking

The methodological premise of this study is that the best way to study the thinking of diplomats is to talk with them and listen carefully. However, because of time constraints and the consequent need for more efficient data collection, questionnaires, despite their flaws, were also considered a very useful tool to complement the open-ended interviews. From January 1975 to August 1975 I collected information from 266 diplomats representing 116 countries in the world, most by means of semistructured interviews, which lasted somewhat more than one hour each. In addition, most diplomats responded to written questionnaires. The analysis of these interviews and questionnaires provides the empirical basis for this study. This chapter describes national and international contexts of the study, the sample, the interviews, the questionnaires, the coding of the interview responses, and the data analysis procedures.

THE CONTEXTS

The Diplomatic Delegations

Nowhere is the logic of comparative inquiry more important than in the description and analysis of diplomatic culture, yet nowhere has it been more ignored. The literature on diplomacy has by and large been so concerned with the uniqueness of national diplomacies or, conversely, with the universal principles of diplomacy, that there have been relatively few attempts to place these different diplomatic cultures along common dimensions, so that one could see how, and to what extent, they are distinct. To take an example to which we will return in Chapter 5, some observers of international relations tend to speak about the international climate, implying that one and the same international climate prevails for all countries. But is it true that the perceptions of the international environment are identical for all countries and, if not, how do they differ? Does speaking about the international climate contain a fallacy based on an egocentric bias—namely, a tendency to treat our own perceptions as accurate and to discount the possibility that they may be colored by our own historical experiences, our positions, and so on (Gamson and Modigliani 1974: 90)? Such questions can not be answered without carefully constructed comparisons.

A comparative study like this one runs risks, of course, because certain methodological difficulties increase with the number of diplomatic delegations studied. Not the least agonizing of the difficulties is the need for sensitivity to the idiosyncrasies of diplomats from diverse delegations or countries. In several ways the present study does not do justice to the idiosyncrasies of each country's diplomatic thinking, but if we are to comprehend the full complexity of diplomatic culture, the benefits of explicit cross-national comparison far outweigh the costs. One factor that makes the objection less applicable to our study is that it focuses on comparisons not between single countries, but rather between groups of countries. The decision to obtain interviews from diplomats of as many countries as possible requires no defense, since we wanted to have a reasonable number of diplomats distributed along the seven systemic dimensions described in Chapter 3. The countries represented in our sample of diplomats are listed in Table 4.1, along with the number of diplomats from each country from whom data were obtained. The total number does not add up to 266 because 12 diplomats failed to indicate the names of their countries on their questionnaires.

The Period

The year 1975 was a turning point for the United States and by implication for a great part of the world. The Watergate scandal and the Vietnam war were put aside. The termination of the war was sudden and unpredicted. The victory of Vietnam brought into question the strength of the commitment of the United States to its allies around the world and U.S. Secretary of State Kissinger felt compelled to assure both allies and foes that the United States intended to keep all its mutual pledges. The Middle East showed another year of intransigence; the only progress was the initialing of an agreement between Egypt and Israel providing for Israeli withdrawal from portions of the occupied territory in the Sinai Peninsula.

TABLE 4.1

Countries Represented in the Sample of Diplomats

	Number of Diplomats Interviewed		Country	Number of Diplomats Interviewed
Country				
1 Afghanistan	2	59	Lebanon	2
2 Algeria	1	60	Lesotho	1
3 Argentina	2	61	Liberia	1
4 Australia	3	62	Madagascar	2
5 Austria	4	63	Malaysia	2
6 Bahamas	1	64	Mali	1
7 Bangladesh	4	65	Malta	1
8 Barbados	2	66	Mauritania	2
9 Belgium	5	67	Mauritius	1
10 Bolivia	2	68	Mexico	2
11 Botswana	2	69	Morocco	3
12 Brazil	4	70	Nepal	2
13 Bulgaria	1	71	New Zealand	2
14 Burundi	1	72	Nicaragua	1
15 Cameroon	2	73	Niger	1
16 Canada	3	74	Nigeria	2
17 Central African Republic	1	75	Norway	2
18 Chad	1	76	Oman	2
19 Chile	2	77	Pakistan	3
20 Colombia	2	78	Panama	1
21 Costa Rica	2	79	Paraguay	2
22 Cyprus	3	80	Peru	2
23 Czechoslovakia	1	81	Philippines	2
24 Dahomey	2	82	Poland	2
25 Denmark	4	83	Portugal	2
26 Dominican Republic	2	84	Qatar	2
27 Ecuador	2	85	Romania	2
28 Egypt	2	86	Saudi Arabia	1
29 El Salvador	2	87	Senegal	2
30 Ethiopia	2	88	Sierra Leone	2
31 Fiji	1	89	Singapore	1
32 Finland	2	90	South Africa	2
33 France	5	91	Soviet Union	2
34 Gabon	1	92	Somalia	2
35 East Germany	2	93	Spain	2
36 West Germany	7	94	Sri Lanka	3
37 Ghana	1	95	Sudan	2
38 Great Britain	4	96	Sweden	4
39 Greece	2	97	Switzerland	2
40 Guatemala	1	98	Syria	2
41 Guinea	1	99	Taiwan	2
42 Guyana	2	100	Tanzania	2
43 Honduras	1	101	Thailand	2
44 Iceland	2	102	The Netherlands	4
45 India	3	103	Togo	2
46 Indonesia	5	104	Trinidad	2
47 Iran	2	105	Tunisia	1
48 Iraq	1	106	Turkey	3
49 Ireland	3	107	Uganda	2
50 Israel	2	108	United Arab Emirates	2
51 Italy	8	109	United States	8
52 Ivory Coast	1	110	Upper Volta	1
53 Jamaica	2	111	Uruguay	2
54 Japan	4	112	Vatican	1
55 Jordan	2	113	Venezuela	3
56 Kenya	2	114	Yugoslavia	1
57 Korea, South	2	115	Zaire	1
58 Kuwait	2	116	Zambia	2

Total diplomats interviewed: 254

Source: Compiled by the author from his own research.

In Europe, Portugal's leadership swung to the far left. Britain, in an unprecedented referendum, voted in favor of the Common Market, but, unable to curb high inflation and declining productivity, its future was a serious concern for its European partners and other capitalist countries. A conference in Helsinki gave its final approval to the post-World War II division of Europe. There was also a spectacular symbolic display of detente with the first linking of U.S. and Soviet space ships in orbit.

Population growth and hunger continued to be critical issues despite the world food conference in Rome, which seemed to be long on outlining the difficulties inherent in achieving an equitable distribution of resources but short on solutions.

The question of sharing the world's wealth became a major issue in 1974-75, as the developing countries began to demand what was considered a fairer share, and this increased the world's polarization along the North-South axis. The new strength of the Third World countries became apparent in the United Nations to the great discomfort of the major Western powers, as could be heard through the loud and eloquent voice of U.S. Ambassador Patrick Moynihan.

There was slow progress toward control of long-range nuclear missiles, but rapid acceleration of the international trade in conventional weaponry. Sales of arms and nuclear power plants and a slowdown in the fight against pollution were rationalized as economically necessary in a world of energy crises and economic stagflation.

In addition to Southeast Asia and the Middle East, other hotspots were Lebanon, Ethiopia, Cyprus, and Angola. In 1975 we also observed some growth in the number of nations. In the eight months of my interviewing, four new countries joined the family of nations: Comoro Islands, Mozambique, Cape Verde, and Sao Tome.

Diplomats, like most people, live in a world with a short-term perspective, and when talking about international politics they tend to focus on today's priorities, or yesterday's or tomorrow's. It is fair to assume that their perceptions of the world, their styles of thought, and their value patterns or strategic approaches do not change markedly from day to day, but the issues to which they apply their thinking do change. It is therefore important to note that the events in the period of data collection were not radically different from the period before or after the interviewing. It was, by and large, a period of "diplomatic relations as usual."

The Setting

Diplomacy is carried on all over the world in the capitals of countries or headquarters of international organizations. They are very different places and it is necessary for the reader to keep in mind the location of the interviewing. We collected the bulk of our data in Washington, D.C. (226), and the remainder in New York at the United Nations (18), Ottawa, Canada (12), and Cambridge, Massachusetts from fellows at the Center for International Affairs at Harvard (10). There are essentially two reasons why the interpretation of the findings must take into account where the diplomats are stationed: one is related to the impact of the location on the thinking of the diplomat, and the other to the selection of different types of diplomats by their respective foreign offices for different locations. One of the long-standing problems that plague each foreign office is what Macomber (1975: 138) calls "localitis." It basically refers to the tendency of some diplomats to develop an interest and sympathy for the country to which they have been assigned and their consequent propensity to allow this to color their judgment about their own country's interests. The impact of the host country on the thinking of the diplomat was illustrated by a Latin American diplomat when referring to his colleagues who served in the Middle East: "I know colleagues and other diplomats sent to Arab countries to become pro-Arab, and the ones sent to Israel to become pro-Israeli." It is a fact that the flow of information, patterns of contact, and new roles characteristic of a particular location provide new experiences that affect the thinking of diplomats (Alger 1965).

Another reason why information about the interview location is relevant to the analysis is the fact that foreign offices tend to select different diplomats for different places. Washington is considered by all diplomats interviewed as a top diplomatic assignment, not only because of its function as the political capital of a Western superpower, but also because it houses four major organizations of the monetary world: International Monetary Fund, International Bank for Reconstruction and Development, International Development Association, and International Finance Corporation. For a major embassy, very good diplomats tend to be selected. However, this does not mean that all diplomats in major posts are of high quality, for, "as you have larger Embassies, people of lesser quality can more easily be included" (West European diplomat). Although we do not have systematic research about the selection of diplomats for different places and the impact of the station on diplomatic thinking, we should keep these two variables in mind when interpreting the data and considering the best way to make generalizations on the basis of these specific findings.

THE SAMPLE

Washington, D. C.

Not counting military attachés and American diplomats at the State Department, there reside in Washington approximately 1,600 foreign diplomats representing 130 countries. I contacted all of the embassies, with the exception of the Baltic States—Latvia, Lithuania, and Estonia—which still represent pre-World War II nations, and those of Vietnam and the Khmer Republic, which closed their doors during my stay in Washington. Embassies contacted but which did not grant personal interviews were Burma, Grenada, Haiti, Hungary, Laos, Luxembourg, The People's Republic of China, Rwanda, Swaziland, and Yemen. However, the delegation of The People's Republic of China did send an ample amount of written documentation that "would answer all my questions." Responding to questions about personal opinions was not considered part of the role description of the Hungarian diplomat. The embassies of Luxembourg and Grenada had only one officer each, who were out of town most of the time. The embassies of Burma, Haiti, Laos, Rwanda, Swaziland, and Yemen expressed strong reservations. Thus we obtained information from approximately 13 percent of the diplomats stationed in Washington and 87 percent of the countries represented there. Of the 226 diplomats in Washington, 218 were interviewed, and 178 filled out a questionnaire.

United Nations-New York and Ottawa, Canada

To increase the sample of diplomats, in June 1975 I sent questionnaires to all the UN embassies in New York and in Ottawa, Canada. I received 18 questionnaires (15 percent) from New York and 16 (16 percent) from Ottawa.

Cambridge, Massachusetts

Before going to Washington, I was able to try out the final version of my questionnaire and interview questions on 10 diplomats who were fellows at the Center for International Affairs at Harvard University.

Sample Data

The primary aim was to obtain as many interviews and questionnaires from as many countries as possible, so that we would end up with a large enough number of diplomats, fairly evenly distributed over the seven systemic dimensions. The distribution of diplomats came out satisfactorily. As for the sample size, we recognize that samples in social science are always too small, but we feel that our sample is respectable, particularly in view of the difficulties of interviewing and of the use of questionnaires in diplomatic environments and the limits of our logistic support. The number of respondents from whom the data were collected gives us a sufficient basis for a thorough exploratory study of diplomatic thinking and allows the use of moderately sophisticated statistical tools. Moreover, the main findings are sufficiently clear that the size of the sample does not constitute a major handicap.

In selecting the sample I tried to avoid being channeled only to younger diplomats or cultural attachés. Instead, I aimed for diplomats working in the chancery, fairly evenly distributed across the dimensions of rank and influence, age, experience, and sex. Table 4.2 shows the distribution of the final sample along these variables. The rank distribution shows a high representation of high- and mid-level diplomats in the sample. This makes our data more valuable in that they reflect the thinking of diplomats with greater influence in their own foreign office. The data on the age of diplomats were collected mainly to explore possible differences in diplomatic thinking between age cohorts. According to age-cohort analysts, different generations tend to have diverse, sometimes radically so, socializations and experiences (Puchala 1971: 43). The basic structure of thinking about political issues is assumed to be laid down early in a person's professional training or at the point at which he becomes concerned with policy issues. Steinbruner (1973: 171) believes that the powerful formative experiences of the young person in his twenties or early thirties in his professional training are the sources of his operative thinking about politics. Looking at the age distribution in Table 4.2, we note that most of the diplomats (76.5 percent) fall between the ages of 30 and 50. The younger half (30-40) had their formative experiences in the 1960s, a period of tensions within and between the power blocs, of the beginning of peaceful coexistence, of further emancipation of Africa and conflicts around new states, and of tensions and local wars in Asia. The older half (40-50) were socialized in the 1950s, a period characterized by some attempts at coexistence, but basically a continuation of the cold war; some of the major events in that period were the insurrections in Poland and Hungary, tensions around Berlin, tensions in the Near and Middle East, the emergence of The People's

Republic of China as a new power pole in world politics, further economiciintegration of the West, and the beginning of the emancipation of Africa.

TABLE 4.2

Composition of the Sample of Diplomats by Rank, Age,
Experience, and Sex
(percents)

Rank (N = 255)	
Ambassador	14.1
Minister	8.6
Minister counselor	9.8
Counselor	28.2
First secretary	21.2
Second secretary	9.0
Third secretary	3.1
Attaché	6.0
Age (N = 247)	
61 and over	2.8
51 to 60	14.6
41 to 50	37.2
31 to 40	39.3
Less than 30	6.1
Number of years of experience (N = 102)	
20 and over	16.7
16 to 20	11.7
11 to 15	16.7
6 to 10	20.6
1 to 5	34.3
Sex (N = 251)	
Female	4.0
Male	96.0

Source: Compiled by the author from his own research.

The number of years of diplomatic experience is another major force that shapes the thinking of diplomats. In Table 4.2 we see that the diplomatic experience varied from 1 to 50 years. The average, 12 years, permits us to say that our findings are based on a great deal of diplomatic experience.

A last variable about which we collected information was the sex of the respondents. Our sample included 4 percent female diplomats. The diplomatic corps comes close to being an all-male body and may be another example of Lionel Tiger's thesis (1969) on the importance of male bonding on the higher levels of society.

THE INTERVIEWS AND QUESTIONNAIRES

Arrangements

Each of the ambassadors in Washington was sent an introductory letter (see Appendix B) explaining the study in general terms, stressing its academic and confidential character, and asking for the opportunity to meet with two diplomats from his embassy—preferably the ambassador himself and another member of his staff. In the letter I also mentioned that I would call their office on a particular date to establish contact and arrange the appointments. An average of five calls was required to set a final appointment with each of the 226 diplomats in the Washington sample. The difficulties in arranging interviews were partly caused by the understaffing of some embassies, resulting in tight schedules for the diplomats, and by their frequent attendance at conferences and travels around and outside of the country. At some embassies I was helped by personal introductions from diplomats whom I knew at the Center for International Affairs at Harvard. Most of the interviews were held on the premises of the embassy, ordinarily in the diplomat's office or in a reception room. Sometimes, however, I had the pleasure of being invited for lunch in one or another restaurant. I conducted all the interviews myself.

The Questions

Questions were introduced in the form of both elite interviews and questionnaires. Riesman (1964: 528) defines an elite interview as an interview with any interviewee who is given special nonstandardized treatment, stressing the interviewee's definition of the situation, encouraging the interviewee to structure the account of the situation, and letting the interviewee introduce to a considerable extent his own notions of what he regards as relevant, instead of relying upon the investigator's notions of relevance. The choice of the elite interview approach was based essentially on three considerations. First, elite interviewees dislike a steady flow of questions, especially if they are of a closed-ended nature. "They would prefer a discussion or still more, perhaps, something which sounds like a discussion but is really a quasi-monologue stimulated by understanding comments" (Dexter 1970: 56). Second, this technique had been used before in the study of belief systems and images of elites and had been successful in yielding communicative and responsive interviewees (Deutsch et al. 1967; Isaacs 1958; Heradstveit 1974). Isaacs (1962: 29) noted during his interviews that there is generally no more fascinating subject to a person than what he himself thinks or feels:

> A serious inquiry into this subject is an honest kind of flattery, and there are few so utterly self-contained as not to respond to it. With notably few exceptions, the individuals interviewed proved responsive, communicative, candid, and often quite stimulated by the unfamiliar experience of self-examination in the particular matters.

Third, in keeping with the exploratory nature of the research, we wanted to give the fullest possible freedom to the interviewee to define relevant concepts and values, and to apply his own way of thinking to the topics introduced in the course of the interview situation.

The interview opened with questions about the general role of the diplomat in international relations and his influence on the outcome of foreign policy making in his country. This was followed by a more specific question about his likes and dislikes in diplomatic life. We then focused on issues of international peace. Topics successively included the "essential characteristics" of peace, the three or four most important problems which cause dissatisfaction and are a threat to peace in the world today, means for alleviating these strains, and an assessment of the success of their implementation. After an extended discussion of the issue of peace, we asked the interviewee his opinion about the use or misuse of conventional and nuclear weapons. Subsequently, we explored the diplomat's ideas about his preferred world order, the practical changes that would be necessary to achieve that kind of world, and the likelihood of its realization. The final questions asked about the extent to which the present period of international politics could be considered a turning point in the history of international relations, about factors that influence diplomatic thinking, and about the frankness of diplomats. Time constraints frequently made it impossible to cover all questions in every interview, and therefore certain questions were asked only of random subsamples. All questions in the interview schedule are reproduced in Appendix C.

The interviews lasted an average of 80 minutes, but there was considerable variation. The minimum time (because the respondent was unavailable for longer) was 35 minutes, while a few interviews lasted three hours. At the conclusion of each interview I asked the respondent to complete a four-page written questionnaire, which I picked up at a time of his or her convenience. The decision to use a questionnaire in addition to the interview was made after a pilot study done during the fall of 1974. Although the elite interview technique provided most of the data we were looking for, we found that some specific information could be collected more efficiently in written form, that some information could be evoked without the use of a structured set of questions, and that the use of scales would be an important aid in comparing particular aspects of diplomatic thinking.

To measure perception of the international environment, we used a semantic differential scale with 28 polar attributes. For the evaluation of a set of peace proposals we used a set of 24 Likert-type items. The third part of the questionnaire consisted of 28 Likert items, measuring the opinions of diplomats on a variety of issues such as the degree of dependency and penetration of their respective countries, the future of the international system, the role of ideology in international politics, diplomatic behavior, and so on. The questionnaire is reproduced in Appendix D. We used an English and French version. Of the diplomats with whom I spoke in Washington, 78 percent completed the questionnaire. Of the questionnaires mailed to New York and Ottawa, 15 and 16 percent, respectively, were returned. The response rate to the mail questionnaires was as expected. The return rate of previous studies of diplomatic elites using mail questionnaires averaged around 13 percent (Jacobson 1967). The higher yield of completed questionnaires in the Washington sample can largely be explained by three factors: personal rapport had been established with the respondents, the interview and the questionnaire were designed as a single unit of information, and the completed questionnaires were collected personally.

The Responses

To reduce error in the recording of answers, we took down verbatim all of the essentials. Also we transcribed our notes into a more readable format on the same day.

Most of the diplomats seemed to enjoy the opportunity to reflect on their diplomatic experience and the nature of international relations. Of the interviewees, 57 percent explicitly agreed to a second visit, if necessary, at another time. In general the rapport with the diplomats was good and their responses were invariably frank. The degree of frankness, of course, varied for different respondents and different questions. To assess the degree of frankness of an interviewee we have to examine the interview situation—more specifically, the questions and the questioner. From the viewpoint of the majority of interviewees, few if any of the questions were potentially sensitive. There were, however, some items in the questionnaire that a small number of diplomats preferred to evade, such as, for example, "In disputes with other countries my country is usually right. Its ideals and standards are usually wise." A second factor which determines the frankness of answers is the interviewee's perception of his audience. An interview situation is basically a transaction, where the interviewer is a set of stimuli that evokes role conceptions in the interviewee and consequently determines how he answers the questions (Dexter 1970: 144). In the letter asking for an interview I tried to influence this transaction by stressing that my interests were strictly academic, that the interviews were off the record and no statement would be associated with the name of the diplomat or the name of his country, and that their views were of great relevance in our effort to learn how international relations are perceived by diplomats from different countries in the world. Frequently, I found it necessary to elaborate on these points prior to the interview, or at the end of an interview when I presented the questionnaire. In addition I also indicated my nationality and the fact that I was a doctoral student. My student status was suggestive of a discussion between two persons, reflecting about international politics and diplomacy, in which the interviewer—as the less-experienced person—would be deferring to the expert and learning from him. The fact that I am a Belgian national and the interviewee's awareness of this fact probably also affected his degree of confidence and frankness, although I am not certain about the nature and extent of its impact. One possible influence of this fact on the respondent's answers can be illustrated by the following observation of one of the diplomats: "If you were an American, I would not have told you what I told you now. Diplomats always think: What person is he? What does he want? If you were an American he could assume that you were on a fishing expedition; trying to find things out." My general impression was that most diplomats were cooperative and frank. Neither the questions nor the questioner in this research seem to have evoked special apprehensiveness. At the end of each interview I judged the respondent's relative frankness. Table 4.3 shows how the diplomats were distributed along this dimension. This evidence, of course, does not demonstrate the veracity of the answers, but it does indicate the overall impression of the interviewer. On balance, I think, we can trust these interviews.

TABLE 4.3

Interviewer's Ratings of Frankness
(in percents)

Very frank and open	23.6
Basically frank	72.1
Basically reserved	4.3
Very closed and reserved	0.0

Source: Compiled by the author from his own research.

In general, the majority of the diplomats took the questionnaire seriously and expressed an interest in seeing the results. I will illustrate this general positive response by quoting two covering letters attached to the questionnaires:

I have received many questionnaires of this sort during my time in the United States. It is a very American type of approach. This is the first I have taken seriously. I thought the questions were intelligent and subtle and I should be interested to see the results.

Many of your questions cannot be answered satisfactorily according to the methods described. However, on the whole they were enlightening and I enjoyed answering them to the best of my ability, given my limited knowledge of the state of the world.

Despite the general acceptance of the questionnaire and the relatively high response rate, some resistance to the request was expressed by a minority of respondents and, of course, by the non-responders. There were several reasons that diplomats gave for not filling out the questionnaire or for complying only with reluctance. Two diplomats from different delegations sent variations of the following notice:

I am sorry to tell you that it is not the custom in our diplomatic service for individual officers to make statements of their personal views in relationship to inquiries such as yours.

In one of these delegations I knew that the ambassador had imposed the rule not to play the "game of the academicians." In the second case it was apparently the individual's personal decision because he was insecure in his position or just not interested, since two of his colleagues had previously filled out a questionnaire. The second category of reservations was based on status considerations. We learned that some diplomats were inclined to resent the notion of a survey of opinions using standard questions. One diplomat told me that his son, who attended a U.S. school, came home from time to time with similar types of questionnaires and that it was not the appropriate way of inquiring into the opinions of diplomats, that the approach was too American and that he did not believe in schemas of this sort.

Another objection, more commonly shared by the diplomats who expressed some reservations about filling out the questionnaires, was the "generality" of the questions, especially of the items in the third part (for example, "the relations between nations are basically governed by international law"). This objection was expressed in different ways, from "All questions are too general," to "This is how McNamara handled the Vietnam war. International relations is situational and concrete. Each case has to be judged on its own merits." In more technical terms, what created discomfort was the absence of a statement of the conditions or a definition of the specific context to which the set of items applied. This reservation was not totally unexpected, as I was warned by Roetter (1963: 84), in his article on the art of diplomacy, that the foreign office professionally distrusts generalizations. But while these objections are valid, in that the specific context influences diplomatic thinking, our aim in this study was to identify generalized patterns of diplomatic thinking across situations. This was the explicit purpose of the set of items in the third part of the questionnaire.

The focus of the fourth group of objections was the semantic differential, which was designed to measure the diplomat's perception of the international environment. The main complaint here was that the semantic differential requests answers that are not analytic but synthetic, in the sense that the diplomat is asked only for the end product of his thinking, that is, his perception of the international environment. No information is solicited about the diplomat's definition of the international environment, nor the way he analyzes it, nor why he perceives the international environment in his particular way, nor what the relative importance is of the factors that he considers in his overall evaluation of the system. I can understand that for assertive persons with an analytic mind this kind of synthetic questioning can be quite irritating. Therefore the respondents' willingness to complete this part of the questionnaire is doubly appreciated.

Another point of contention was the straitjacket effect of the questionnaire on the respondent. One diplomat told me that my approach was influenced by the German way of thinking, that it was too formalized and attempted to preorganize the interviewee's responses. "What you have created is a set of categories unfit to fit international relations. International relations is too complex for a mathematical approach." This comment is to the point but needs to be qualified. Despite its limitations, we believe that the questionnaire is a very efficient tool for probing certain components of diplomatic thinking and that findings gained through this technique might stimulate in-depth followups through the more elaborate technique of elite interviewing. It is interesting that most of the diplomats who expressed this particular reservation also offered to fill out the questionnaire in my presence and qualify their answers. Such occasions were very informative and contributed considerably to my understanding of diplomatic thinking.

A sixth criticism pointed to the lack of definition of particular items, especially the term "peace" in the second part of the questionnaire, which asked the diplomats to evaluate a set of proposals in relation to their importance for international peace. One respondent remarked that "since the definitions of peace vary with every interview no conclusions could be drawn from the responses." This remark is unfounded for the simple reason that the purpose of this second part is to infer the respondent's definition of peace from his evaluation of the set of proposals. For some other terms, such as "socialism" or "enlightened egoism," the criticism is more warranted, since there is a great deal of variation in their meaning. Socialism could refer to any of the various economic and political theories advocating collective or governmental ownership and administration of the means of production and distribution of goods. But since I believe that hints and suggestions are important at this stage of understanding the thinking of diplomats, we will include such data in our analysis, but always with the explicit understanding that their meaning lacks some precision.

Several diplomats indicated in no uncertain terms a reluctance to express themselves in moral categories. Instead of indicating, by means of a check mark, their perception of the international environment as just or unjust, and as honest or hypocritical, some of them substituted the following comments:

It is not just or unjust. It just is.

The function of public relations is to convert power into morals.

One might give moral reasons to rationalize policies taken.

Our decisions are not moralistic, but are effective stands; we provide options and expectations about their effects.

There are hypocrites who are not realizing it and some honesty is worse than robbery.

I don't believe in dualism. I am a monist. Your approach is too Western—nothing is good or bad.

These answers indicate a difference in the propensity to use moral categories. In Chapter 7 we will look at this aspect of the style of analysis more carefully.

Finally, the eighth category of objections was related to the following item: "In its disputes with other countries my country is usually right. Its ideals and standards are usually fair and wise." This item, which measures the respondent's attitude to his own country (one might say the degree of natiocentrism), has the lowest response rate. The reasons expressed for leaving this question unanswered vary from "This is an unfair question to ask diplomats" to "In the question containing the words 'my country is usually right . . . usually fair and wise,' it was the rather self-righteous phraseology of the question that disturbed me; I would not wish to relate to such a question positively or negatively." In addition to being unfair or self-righteous, it is also fair to assume that this question is a sensitive one and therefore increases the inhibition to respond to it. In Chapter 7 we will analyze the responses to this item.

From my experience with the questionnaires I am inclined to conclude that, taking into account some of the above-mentioned limitations, they yield extensive data on delicate subjects, which could not have been collected in the same time span by the use of elite interview techniques.

THE ANALYSIS

Coding

Having elicited responses from our sample of diplomats, how do we extract from them an understanding of diplomatic thinking? In this study we made use of four different coding procedures (classification borrowed from Putnam 1973). The first procedure, which could be called automatic coding, applies to the questionnaire items that required the respondent to choose among a fixed set of alternatives. If the person agrees strongly, for example, with the statement, "Those countries that usually get ahead, get ahead at the expense of others," he is automatically classified as "high on zero-sum thinking." Apart from administrative errors, the reliability of this procedure is perfect. The validity of responses, however, is much more uncertain, for it is not always clear that the "responses" to close-ended questions accurately measure the presumed under-lying dimension of diplomatic thinking.

The second type of coding classifies answers to explicit and open-ended questions. An example would be the question asking the interviewee what he thinks are the three or four most important problems in the world today that cause dissatisfaction and tension. The reliability of this kind of coding is high and is a function of the quality of the classification system. In the coding of these answers we based our judgment not merely on the explicit answer, but also on what the respondent seemed to mean, taking into account his entire discussion of the topic. Coding reliability is found to be very high when these two bases of judgment are combined (Putnam 1973: 242). There is every reason to believe that the validity of explicit coding is quite high and is even higher when the coding is based on the broader judgment.

The third type of coding that we used is called "latent feature" coding. Suppose we want to know not what a diplomat thinks about population growth, but how he thinks about it; or, to what extent he analyzes international relations in structural terms. The reliability of such coding is, of course, lower than coding of manifest responses to explicit questions. However, the results that are presented in Chapters 7 and 8 illustrate that the use of a carefully defined set of categories can produce relatively high levels of agreement among independent judges.

The validity of latent feature coding must be demonstrated in any given case. But there are some theoretical concerns that re-quire this kind of coding; analytic style is a good example. Asking the diplomat whether he is a "moralizer" may produce a reliable codable response, but that answer tells you virtually nothing about this analytic style. The results based on latent feature coding are generally easy to interpret, for in most cases they are based on a quite specific section of the interview and on precise and explicit coding criteria. Interpretation is not always as easy in the fourth type of coding procedure, which requires the coder to make a global judgment about certain characteristics of respondents based on the interview as a whole. To discover certain aspects of diplomatic thinking, this type of coding is useful. For example, if one wants to know "the extent to which the diplomat applies to the overall discussion a single conceptual or explanatory frame of analysis," global coding is essential. This type of coding is not easy because the criteria for the judgment are not easily made explicit nor the basis of judgment easily specifiable. The coder reliability data are presented in Chapter 7. These variables, though important, must always be treated with caution, because of the questionable validity of the judgments on which they are based.

The guide for analyzing the interviews in the present research is given in Appendix A. Perusal of the codebook will give the reader an idea of the judgments that the coders had to make in each of the above-mentioned types of coding.

Statistical Analysis

To let the data speak better for themselves, we will treat them with a variety of statistical methods. The statistics we used fulfill essentially five purposes. First, to describe the main variables and their comparative importance, statistics such as means and percentages will be used. For example, we will use means to indicate the degree of fit between six ideal types of moral political environments and the present state of the international environment as perceived by the diplomats. Second, we want to know how different groups of diplomats—for example, center versus periphery—differ in their degree of satisfaction with the present state of international relations, or in their rank-ordering of necessary conditions for peace, or in their responses to many other issues in diplomatic thinking. To indicate the direction and strength of these differences, we employed Pearson correlations; to establish the significance of the differences between the respective means of the groups that we want to compare, t-tests were used. A third function, for which we used factor analysis, is data reduction. The 28 variables of our semantic differential, for example, are obviously a bit cumbersome, and factor analysis can reduce this large number of variables to a smaller number of composite variables or dimensions. With a smaller number of variables, one can more easily analyze the relationship between the systemic variables and our dependent variables. In addition to reducing the number of variables, factor analysis with varimax rotation gives us an idea about the number of independent dimensions and the dimensional structure of our data. To examine the impact of each single independent variable on the dependent variables, we calculated r squares; to study their combined effect, each of the dependent variables was

regressed on all seven systemic variables. For the assessment of
the combined effect we chose the procedure of forward stepwise
inclusion of our independent variables in the multiple regression
analysis. In this procedure the computer enters the variable that
explains the greatest amount of variance in the dependent variable
first; the variable that explains the greatest amount of variance in
conjunction with the first, second, and so on. This procedure was
chosen because of our wish to isolate a subset of variables that
would yield an optimal prediction with as few variables as possible.
In the following chapters each of the above-mentioned statistical
methods will be discussed in greater depth.

Finally, I would like to make clear that for analyzing and
understanding each of the four components of diplomatic thinking,
we will draw on data from questionnaire items, from open-ended
interview questions, and from various types of judgments by the
coder. Rather than relying on one source of data for studying "the
diplomat's image of peace," for example, we will draw data from
different parts of the interview and questionnaire and different
modes of response and coding. The main reason for adopting this
method of analysis is that our study concerns basic patterns or
tendencies in diplomatic thinking, and that theoretically these tendencies should demonstrate the responses of the interviewee to
various probes. Therefore, if responses to independent measures
tend to be congruent, we have a good reason for assuming the existence of a common underlying pattern or tendency. Another reason
for using multiple sources of information is that it can increase
considerably the confidence in the reliability and validity of one's
findings (Cook and Selltiz 1964). Chapter 5 will highlight some aspects of the world of the diplomat.

5

International Climate

DEFINITION OF INTERNATIONAL CLIMATE

Among the multitude of concepts used in international relations, the concept of international climate is not firmly established. To most students of international relations, the vagueness and ambiguity of the term is a difficult hurdle to surmount. The term has been used in many contexts, from the description of different perspectives in the international arena to the study of the rise of secular symbols of universal claim and aspiration, such as nationalism, proletarianism, or racism (see Lasswell 1965). Clearly, before research on the international climate can be undertaken, it must be defined in some manageable manner. Another factor that inhibits the study of the international climate is the tendency to use evocative language in the description of this phenomenon. Lasswell (1965: 342) cites this fact as one explanation of why recent psychologists have had comparatively little to say about the international climate: "They have been embarrassed by the seeming necessity of adopting literary language to do it." The problem here is that most writers have used impressionistic methods for analyzing climate and failed to apply the tools at the disposal of the behavioral sciences, which make these phenomena increasingly accessible to systematic study. Among the tools now available are, for example, the methods of content analysis developed by Robert North and his associates (1963), interview and questionnaire procedures, and the semantic differential method which is used in this study.

To facilitate the systematic study of the international climate, we shall propose a better definition of the term, present a systematic way for distinguishing different international climates, and describe a method for measuring to what extent reality conforms to these distinctions. We will then assess the usefulness of the concept of international climate by linking it with other aspects of diplomatic thinking, thereby generating empirically testable hypotheses. Finally, we will present our data and discuss to what extent they support the usefulness of the concept of international climate to an understanding of diplomatic thinking.

The term "international climate," as used in our study, refers to the quality of a relatively enduring international environment that is perceived by the occupants, influences their behavior, and can be described in terms of attributes of the international environment. We use "climate" to accentuate the subjective character of the phenomenon and also that we are focusing not on sharply defined images of the international environment but on perception of the highly generalized content of the international context.

The definition of international climate as used in our study overlaps only partly with Lasswell's use of the term. Both definitions are similar in the sense that they stress the subjective and generalized content of the international climate. They differ, however, in their designation of the elements that make up the international climate. Lasswell includes both attitudes and perceptions, with an emphasis on the attitudinal or "generalized value orientation" aspect of the climate. In this study we restrict the term international climate to the perception of the international environment. Our decision to exclude attitudes from the definition is based on the recognition that perceptions and attitudes are theoretically distinct entities, which should not be confounded in one term if we want to contribute to better understanding of diplomatic thinking. To be sure, the realities these terms grasp are often interrelated, but the concepts should be kept analytically independent. Furthermore, we believe that, where a term is borrowed from another field, in this case from meteorology, the overall meaning of the term should be kept intact in order to preserve it as a tool for efficient communication. In meteorology the term "climate" refers to the observation and the study of weather patterns and not attitudes of people toward the weather. Finally, it should be made clear that the decision to exclude attitudes from the definition does not imply that attitudes are to be considered less important than perception. They are equally important and some of the diplomats' attitudes will be highlighted in this study.

USE OF THE SEMANTIC DIFFERENTIAL AS A METHOD FOR COLLECTING DATA

The bulk of the data on which we base our analysis of the diplomat's perception of the international environment was collected by means of a semantic differential. The semantic differential technique was developed by Charles Osgood and his colleagues (Osgood et al. 1957) and consists essentially of a number of seven-point rating scales that are bipolar, with each extreme defined by an adjective; for example, static/dynamic, rational/irrational. We attempted to construct an exhaustive list of characteristics used by diplomats, students of foreign affairs, foreign policy makers, diplomatic correspondents, and so on, in their descriptions of the international environment. Each reader perusing the list that we made up (Appendix D) will no doubt have a candidate that has been ignored, and some may feel that certain aspects have been over-represented. But since the study of international climate is in its infancy, there is no generally agreed-upon list. To collect data concerning the diplomat's perception of the international environment, we then translated the list into a semantic differential. The respondent was given this set of scales and asked to rate the present international relations environment on every scale in turn. Osgood offers valuable evidence on the validity, reliability, and sensitivity of his scales for assessing the subjective semantic world of the individuals.

In addition to the information collected by means of this semantic differential, we also analyzed the diplomat's responses to three questionnaire items. His perception of the role of international law in international relations was measured by his response to the statement: "The relations between nations are basically governed by international law." The diplomat's perceived degree of pene-tratedness of his country was inferred from his responses to these statements: "Our defense system is to a great extent controlled by another country," and "My country's economy is significantly influenced by foreign investors."

THREE APPROACHES FOR STUDYING
THE INTERNATIONAL CLIMATE

Having collected the raw data, how do we proceed to describe different international climates in a systematic way? In our study we used three approaches.

The first approach started with a set of ideal types of international climates and proceeded to inquire to what degree reality conformed to them. This approach is clearly inspired by Weber. Weber perceives reality as an endless fabric of meaningful and meaningless factors and says that, in order to apprehend it, we require constructed concepts which are not reality themselves but technical instruments of investigation by which to approach reality. He calls these constructed concepts "ideal types." Ideal types are means by which we measure reality, in order to get a "pregnant formulation of it, and in order to bring out clearly the elements that do not conform to them. They are not the goal of investigation, not the laws of the process, but means by which to gain the clearest awareness of the specific characteristics of the human reality in question." Later in this chapter we will give some examples of ideal types or models that exist in international relations studies and will describe the ideal types whose reality we will test in this study.

In contrast to the first approach, the second approach is inductive. Instead of testing a preconceived set of ideal types, we factor-analyzed the 28 variables of our semantic differential in order to find out if they were clustered in an intelligible pattern and if these clusters or dimensions would form a basis for developing a multidimensional model of the international climate. This approach is much more exploratory in nature than the former method. The results of this approach will be presented later in this chapter.

In the last approach, we singled out for emphasis distinctive features of the international context—for example, predictability or security—and analyzed data about the diplomat's perception of these specific characteristics. Our findings about these distinctive features will also be described.

IDEAL-TYPE APPROACH

Overview of Some Models of the International Environment in the Study of International Relations

In international studies several ideal types or models exist for describing the international environment. The oldest model could be called the traditional model, which looks at the world as an aggregate of sovereign states living in an international state of nature or a condition of mutual competition and conflict. This model of international relations is used by a large number of international-relations theorists, ranging from Hobbes to Aron and Hoffmann. One pungent statement of this model is Aron's (1966: 8) assertion that the essential characteristic of international relations is the "absence of an entity that holds a monopoly of legitimate violence." For Hoffmann (1961: 206), also, the simple and banal point of departure for thinking about international relations remains "the permanent possibility of free and legitimate recourse to violence among countries."

A second model of the perceived international environment can be found in the writings of classical international lawyers. For them, international relations is not a naked struggle for power, but a struggle tempered by moral and legal norms. Their view of anarchy is similarly modified, and it resembles Locke's relatively peaceful and orderly state of nature rather than Hobbes' state of perpetual hot and cold war (Lijphart 1974: 50). An exponent of this perception of the international environment is, for example, Grotius, because he considers the international normative consensus strong and pervasive enough to render the image of the state of nature inappropriate.

A third model is embodied in nineteenth-century liberal thought. It is basically a vision of a preferred international environment, characterized by a natural harmony of states, governed by democratic regimes. This model was never shared by a great number of students of international relations and its influence was only minor.

The fourth model is embodied in theories about international stratification and imperialism. The world is perceived as a global dominance system composed of different countries, which occupy various positions within the system. Some of these countries exercise control and accumulate value from other countries (Hveem 1973). This perception of the world is held by a group of peace researchers and by several Third World students of international relations.

A final model is shared by a great number of behaviorists. This model differs from the traditional one in several ways. Whereas the traditional model emphasizes the fundamental difference between the domestic and the international environment, the behaviorists implicitly regard the similarities between international and domestic policies as more significant than their differences. The second difference consists in the elimination of the traditional notion of anarchy. Deutsch (1957: 5-6) was one of the first to attack this traditional notion of anarchy by introducing a conceptual distinction between an amalgamated community, which has "one supreme decision-making center," and a security-community, in which there is "real assurance that the members . . . will not fight each other physically." This means that the state of nature is dissociated from the state of war, actual or potential, and the correlation between war and anarchy, taken for granted by the traditionalists, is here reduced to the level of a hypothesis.

This sketchy overview of the models is meant to indicate that different scholars of international relations practice their trade in different worlds. They are all looking at the same world, but in some areas they see different things, and they see them in different relations to each other. A second observation is that these different models are used rather exclusively and even viewed as incommensurable.

Description of Six Types of International Climates

Instead of testing to what extent these above-described separate models are current among diplomats, we developed a typology of international climates, within which the models are more meaningfully related. We postulated that the moral political qualities of the international climate can be classified in terms of ideal-type constructions parallel to the moral stages developed by Kohlberg (1971). Accordingly, we distinguished six types of international climates, which are defined in terms of the perceived moral-political qualities of the international environment and are ranked in order of preference for the moral quality of the relations between nations, envisaged in these different types of international climate. I consider it fair to assume that higher levels of the international climate typology are more preferred than the lower levels.

Hobbesian Climate

The first international climate that we distinguish may be referred to as Hobbesian. Such an environment could be characterized as a very rudimentary power interaction between countries pursuing their self-interests and indifferent to the fate of others. The absence of recognition of a higher authority forces them to live in a condition of international anarchy, distrust, strong concern with security, and permanent possibility of free recourse to violence among states. To inquire to what degree the perceived international reality of the diplomat conforms to our description of the Hobbesian climate, we developed an index that includes information about all the above-mentioned characteristics. More specifically, we added and divided by eight the scores given on eight 1-7 scales of the semantic differential (see Appendix E).

Examples of the perception of the international environment as Hobbesian are the following observations made by some of the diplomats:

The whole thing is based on survival. (African diplomat)

It is not the Gods, but might that makes right. (West European diplomat)

Real politicians don't follow ideas, but take into account the raw distribution of power. (East European diplomat)

Sovereign states are selfish in nature. (Asian diplomat)

> International politics are about power. (Asian diplomat)

> War is still the natural state of the world. (West Euro-
> pean diplomat)

Marxian Climate

The second international climate in our typology is labeled
Marxian. In terms of moral preference, however, it is on the same
level as the Hobbesian climate. Both perceive the world as violent,
except that in the Marxian climate, violence is perceived in structural terms. People for whom this is the dominant climate perceive
the international environment not as anarchic, but as a highly structured system with topdogs and underdogs, the former having control
over and exploiting the latter. Illustrative of the perception of the
international environment as Marxian are the following quotes
selected from interviews with the diplomats:

> Due to the fact that the political structure is controlled
> by foreigners, culture shrinks and the economy is
> raped. (African diplomat)

> You could speak of economic classes in the international
> arena exactly as it was in the nineteenth century on the
> national level. (Asian diplomat)

The index that we use for testing the presence of this perception in
the minds of diplomats includes information about perceived degree
of exploitation, polarization, and hierarchical organization in international relations (see Appendix E).

Instrumental Exchange Climate

The third type of climate we call instrumental exchange.
Kohlberg (1971: 164) would characterize a situation in which this
climate dominates as a situation where

> right action consists of that which instrumentally satis-
> fies one's needs and occasionally the needs of others.
> Human relations are viewed in terms like those of a
> market place. Elements as fairness, or reciprocity,
> and of equal sharing are present, but they are always
> interpreted in a physically pragmatic way. Reciprocity
> is a matter of "you scratch my back and I'll scratch
> yours," not of loyalty, gratitude or justice.

It is a world where good diplomacy must ignore feelings and has no friends or enemies as such; it does not regard the latter as worse than the former, because it is based on enlightened egoism. The following quotations of diplomats are indicative of their perception of the international environment as instrumental-exchange oriented:

> Diplomacy is a question of recognizing the needs and aspirations of others, not in moral terms, good or bad, but in order to do business together.
> (Latin American diplomat)

> The best way to serve is self service. (Latin American diplomat)

> To work for the common interest is trying to do something for your own country. (African diplomat)

> International relations are based on economics and are profit oriented. (Latin American diplomat)

Our index of the instrumental exchange climate contains information about the above-mentioned characteristics. The procedure for calculating the index can be found in Appendix E.

We-ness Climate

The next climate that we distinguish is referred to as we-ness. The term is applicable to international relations characterized by a growing feeling of we-ness on a global level, as can now be observed in subgroups of countries, such as the rich man's club, the European Community, the Group of Nonaligned Countries, the free world, the Arab League, and so on. Each of these groups makes an effort to achieve consensus about their problems and ways to cope with them. In addition to the existence of a feeling of we-ness and consensus, we also consider the perceived degree of integration, cooperation, supportiveness, and responsiveness of countries as indicators of this climate. Most of the statements by our diplomats implying the existence of a we-ness climate are made in relation to regional organizations or other subgroups of nations. Among the few statements indicative of the recognition of we-ness characteristics on a global level are:

> There is a gradual acceptance of the need for a global solution. (African diplomat)

> There is an increased awareness about questions which
> affect the overall world situation.   (Latin American
> diplomat)

The we-ness climate index contains information about all the above-
mentioned characteristics. The procedure for calculating the index
can be found in Appendix E.

International Law Climate

The fifth climate could be called international law. In such an
international climate, international law is perceived as the attribute
of the international community. Here relations between nations are
seen as basically governed by international law, which defines their
boundaries, the limits of their sovereignty, and their reciprocal
rights and duties where jurisdictions overlap. Very few statements
of the diplomats refer to this kind of world, and most statements
about the role of international law are indicative of its weaknesses:

> One cannot base his policy on it; any law is as good as
> the people who make it.   (East European diplomat)

> International law has an effect on minor issues, and
> none when important issues are at stake. (Latin
> American diplomat)

> Nobody knows what international law is. (Asian diplomat)

> International law is still valid, not dead; it exercises a
> restraining influence on the situation. (East European
> diplomat)

The calculation of the index of international law climate is based on
the diplomat's sources of agreement or disagreement with the following item: "The relations between nations are basically governed
by international law. "

Shared Principled Agreement Climate

The last international climate could be referred to as shared
principled agreement. This somewhat ponderous term describes an
international arena where decisions are made by mutual consent,
without sacrifice of one or the other party. This mutual consent is
based on reciprocity of the partners and equality between them prior
to the agreement. The international system here is characterized
by coordinative rather than subordinative relationships. It also

requires a considerable tolerance for diversity and a willingness to take action through conciliation even when the power to act unilaterally would be available. Comments made by our diplomats in reference to this climate were practically all normative in nature and were mostly evoked by the question about their preferred world order. As for the present state of the world, diplomats recognize the existence of a plethora of shared principles democratically arrived at but feel that these are espoused only at the abstract level or when their implementation would enhance national interests. The index that we used for testing the presence of this perception in the minds of diplomats contains information about the perceived degree of democracy, tolerance for diversity, principledness, morality, cooperation, justice, and global thinking in the world. The procedure for calculating this index can be found in Appendix E.

Some Propositions about the Nature of the International Environment

Proposition 1

The five levels of the moral-political climate form a universal rank order of preference in the minds of diplomats. On the basis of this assumption, we predict that higher levels of international climate will be more positively correlated with indicators of preference, such as satisfaction or justness, than lower levels. We also expect this preference rank-order to be valid across different groups of diplomats indicating its universal validity.

Proposition 2

In terms of applicability to the reality of international relations, the five levels form a rank-order of diminishing relevance. In other words, we predict that the degree to which diplomats consider the first-level climate applicable will be significantly higher than the next one, and so on; the least applicable level we expect to be the shared principled agreement climate.

Proposition 3

The content of the international-environment perception varies as a function of the observer's attention scope. This scope could be defined in terms of system-level. In our inquiry we contrasted the perception of the international environment on the global international and regional levels. As an example of a regional-level system, we selected the European Community. We predict that the perceptions of the two environments will differ significantly and that in the latter the lower-level climates will receive lower evaluations and higher climates higher evaluations than in the global international environment.

Proposition 4

The perception of the international environment is a function of the position of the diplomat's country in the international stratification. We predict that the systemic position of the diplomat's country will have an effect on some aspects of his perceived international environment. For example, we would expect that diplomats from countries who are less in control of their economic conditions would perceive the world as more distrustful than their colleagues from countries that have greater economic power. This prediction is based on Solomon's (1966) experimental findings that people tend to engage in more trusting behavior when they have greater control over their economic position. It should be understood that we do not consider the position of the country as the main determinant of diplomatic thinking, but as an important component of it. We predict that the social-structural variables will, in combination, account for a not unimportant percentage of the variance of our dependent variables.

In the next section we will check the validity of each of the propositions.

Description of the Results

Let us now look at the international environment from the vantage point of the diplomat. The analysis will be described in the following sequence: First we will find out to what extent the six ideal-type climates are reflected in the diplomat's perception of the international environment. As we believe that the perception of the international environment varies as a function of the position of the observer in the international system, and also as a function of the scope of his perception, we will test the impact of the latter through comparing the perceptions of the global international environment with the perception of a part of the international system, the European Community, and the impact of position, through comparing the perceptual differences between diplomats from developed and developing countries. We also will look at the correlations of the other systemic variables with the perception of the international environment. Finally, we will present data relating to the combined predictive power of all our systemic variables.

A schematic overview of the results of the inquiry into the diplomat's perception of the global environment can be found in Figure 5.1. In that figure are presented the mean scores of the whole sample of diplomats for all the variables which are included in the indexes of the six different moral-political climates. Examining this figure reveals that as we move to the right, the mean scores tend to become smaller, indicating a descending order of realism attributed to the five different levels. (We consider the Hobbesian and Marxian climates as variables of level 1.) The descending order is even more evident when we look at the indexes themselves, rather than at their component variables (see Figure 5.2).

The climates which seem to predominate in the thinking of the diplomats are at level 1, namely, the Marxian and the Hobbesian climates. Following in terms of importance are the instrumental exchange climate, and then levels 3 to 5. With respect to the last three levels we notice two unexpected findings: the importance of level 4 is higher than level 3, and there is no clear difference between levels 3 and 5. This small difference could be explained by the high correlation (.741) that we found between these two indexes (see Table 5.1). This suggests that to a great extent both indexes measure a similar climate. The fact that the international law climate has markedly higher scores than the we-ness and the shared principled agreement climates suggests that the high presence of either climate is not a precondition for international law to be perceived as operative in international relations.*

As a statistical measure of differences in importance assigned to each of the ideal-type climates, we used t-tests (see Appendix F). On level 1 we found a significant difference between the Marxian and the Hobbesian climates $(t = 4.88, p < .001)$. The perception of the world as a hierarchic system, polarized and exploitative, seems clearly to predominate the worldview of the diplomats. Next in line is the Hobbesian climate. Of interest here is the fact that two of the component variables of the Hobbesian climate index, nationalism and power-orientedness, have a higher mean score than any of the component variables of the Marxian climate index. This finding corroborates the traditionalist view of the world as a power struggle

---

*To measure the international law climate we used a 1-5 (strongly disagree-strongly agree) scale. To compare the mean of the international law climate with the means of other climates, we converted the mean of the international law climate as follows:

$$[(2.9 - 1) \times 1.5] + 1 = 3.85$$

FIGURE 5.1

Typology of International Political-Moral Environments

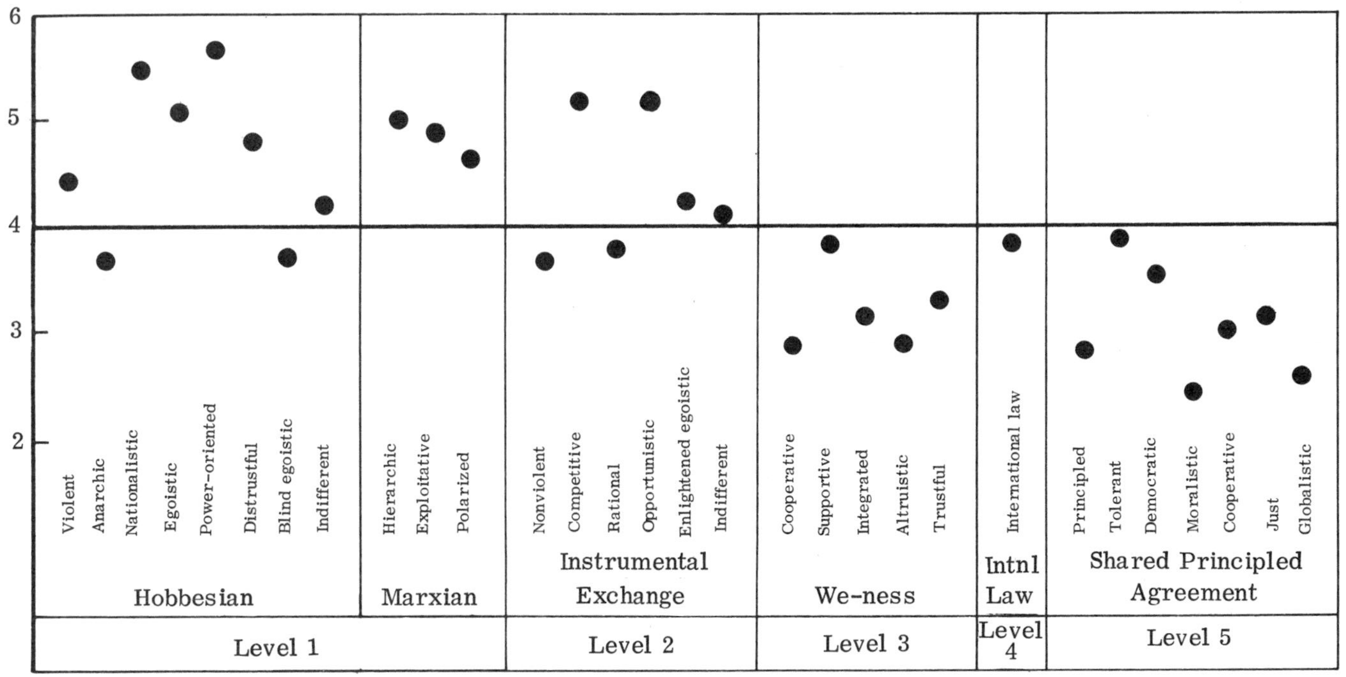

Note: The dots indicate the average scores of each variable included in the indexes of the six climates—the minimum score is 1 and the maximum is 7.

Source: Compiled by the author from his own research.

76

FIGURE 5.2

Comparison of the Moral-Political Climate of the Global
International Environment and the European Community

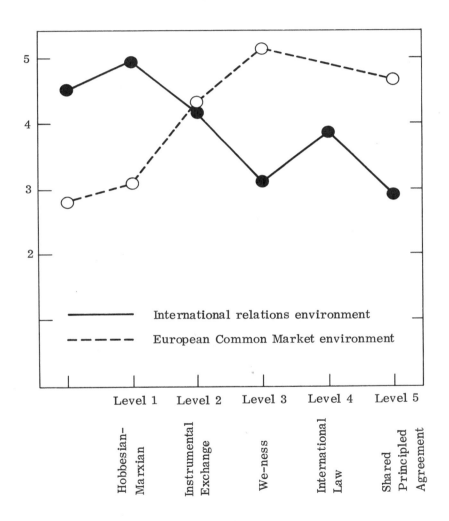

Note: The dots indicate the means of the total sample for each
climate. The scale has a minimum of 1 and a maximum of 7.
Source: Compiled by the author from his own research.

TABLE 5.1

Correlations between the Ideal-Type Climates

	Hobbesian	Marxian	Instrumental Exchange	We-ness	International Law	Shared Principled Agreement
Hobbesian		0.36 (146) S = 0.001	-.00 (151)	-.84 (154) S = 0.001	-.33 (150) S = 0.001	-.81 (147) S = 0.001
Marxian	0.36 (146) S = 0.001		0.21 (149) S = 0.004	-.52 (150) S = 0.001	-.05 (155)	-.39 (148) S = 0.001
Instrumental exchange	-.00 (151)	0.21 (149) S = 0.004		-.28 (154) S = 0.001	-.03 (153)	-.20 (148) S = 0.006
We-ness	-.84 (154) S = 0.001	-.52 (150) S = 0.001	-.28 (154) S = 0.001		0.25 (154) S = 0.001	0.74 (148) S = 0.001
International law	-.33 (150) S = 0.001	-.05 (155)	-.03 (153)	0.25 (154) S = 0.001		0.23 (152) S = 0.001
Shared principled agreement	-.81 (147) S = 0.001	-.39 (148) S = 0.001	-.20 (148) S = 0.006	0.74 (148) S = 0.001	0.23 (152) S - 0.001	

Source: Compiled by the author from his own research.

between national actors. The fact that both Marxian and Hobbesian climates have a high weight suggests that they are not mutually exclusive. They are two dominant and complementary aspects of the diplomat's worldview. If we compare the means of the Hobbesian and Marxian climate indexes with the instrumental exchange index, we find quite significant differences (t = 5.23, p < .001 and t = 10.12, p < .001, respectively). Despite the relatively lower weight assigned to this climate, it should be considered as another important aspect of the diplomat's perception of the world for two reasons. First, if we look at the curve in Figure 5.2, we observe that the sharpest drop occurs between the mean of the instrumental exchange index and the we-ness index; in other words, the mean score of the instrumental exchange climate is much closer to the score of the level 1 climate (4.83) than to the scores of the climates at the other three levels. This means that, relatively speaking, the instrumental exchange climate occupies a quite salient place in the diplomat's world.

Second, the perception of the international environment as a place where instrumental exchange is the norm could be considered as a constant in the diplomat's perception of the world. Table 5.2 shows that the standard deviation of scores on the instrumental exchange index is considerably lower than that for any of the other indexes. Agreement among diplomats is greatest with respect to this aspect of international relations. Further, if we compare the perceptions of the global international environment and the environment of the European Community (Figure 5.2), we observe that the weights assigned to the instrumental exchange climate are almost identical. Thus we find a high degree of constancy, not only between diplomats, but also between their perceptions of different environments, with respect to the weight assigned to the instrumental exchange climate.

TABLE 5.2

Standard Deviations of the International Climate Indexes

International law	1.007
Marxian	.807
Shared principled agreement	.780
Hobbesian	.716
We-ness	.713
Instrumental exchange	.407

Source: Compiled by the author from his own research.

In view of the sharp drop between the mean scores of the instrumental exchange and the we-ness climate, it is not surprising that the difference between these scores is statistically highly significant (t = 15.41, p < .001). The difference between the we-ness and the shared principled agreement climates (.18) is not significant. These results clearly indicate that in comparison to the level 1 and 2 climates, these two climates have a relatively low profile in the diplomat's perception of the international environment.

Concerning the differences between the mean scores of the international law climate and the other climates, we have no t-test scores available. However, when we look at the size of the mean score differences between the international law climate and the level 1, 2, 3, and 5 climates, we observe prominent differences. These differences indicate that the importance of the international law climate is markedly less than the level 1 and 2 climates, and clearly more important than the climates of levels 3 and 5. A fair conclusion seems to be to qualify the international law climate as an important but not central feature in the diplomat's perception of the international environment.

Comparison of Global and Regional Environments

Having described the diplomat's perception of the highest level of the international relations system, namely the global international environment, we can now ask to what extent these findings can be generalized to other levels of the international system, for example, to the level of a regional organization. To provide an empirical answer to this question, we asked ten diplomats, representing member countries of the European Economic Community (EEC), to complete the same semantic differential used to describe the international system (to the other diplomats), but this time with the European Common Market as the object.* A schematic overview of the results can be found in Figure 5.2. It seems that the findings for the global international environment are rotated 180 degrees around the instrumental exchange point. As indicated above, the only similarity in both perceptions is in the weight assigned to the instrumental exchange climate. Both environments are relatively high on the dimensions of nonviolence, competitive, rational, opportunistic, indifferent, and enlightened egoistic. Let us now look at the contrasts. First, we observe the predominant level of the global

---

*It must be kept in mind that the conclusions drawn from such a small sample are highly tentative.

international environment to be the least salient level in the perception of the EEC. The differences are rather striking, and they could be explained partly by the fact that since World War II no violence has been experienced within the EEC, a fact that makes the Hobbesian climate less applicable. Also, in terms of international stratification, there are no great discrepancies between the positions of its members, a reality that reduces the applicability of the Marxian model.

The second contrast consists in the movement of levels 3 and 5 (we did not collect data concerning level 4) from least salient for the international system to most salient for the EEC. In the European environment the instrumental exchange climate is tempered by high we-ness and shared principled agreement climates. The European environment is very high on the dimensions of tolerant for diversity, trustful, democratic, just, integrated, supportive, and cooperative. These data clearly indicate the existence of two different work environments for diplomats. Of the two, the European is also perceived as most satisfactory. On the unsatisfactory-satisfactory scale of the semantic differential, the mean for the EEC is 5; for the global international environment 3.23 (see Appendix G). This difference in the attribution of satisfaction to the various environments corroborates our assumption about the positive correlation between moral-political levels and the degree of preferredness. Finally, the results of this comparison clearly point out that results collected about the global environment cannot be transferred to another international system level, and vice versa, without great risks. The remainder of the analyses will focus only on the perception of the global international environment.

Impact of Systemic Variables

The study of the impact of systemic variables on the international climate will begin by contrasting the perceptions of diplomats from developed and developing countries. For a schematic overview of the results, see Figure 5.3. The perceptions of these two groups differ least in their view of the world as a place where instrumental exchange is the rule of the game; on the other hand, they differ most with respect to description of the world as a dominance system. Whereas the difference between the means of the instrumental exchange climate is practically zero (.018) and nonsignificant, the difference between the means of the Marxian climate indexes is more sizable and significant (.25, $p < .05$). The perception of the world in terms of topdogs and bottomdogs or as a hierarchic structure of control and accumulation capacities is a more salient aspect in the world of the diplomat representing less-developed countries. There is also a difference in the presence of the Hobbesian climate

FIGURE 5.3

Contrasts between the Perceptions of the Moral–Political
Climate in the World of Diplomats from
Developed and Developing Countries
(means)

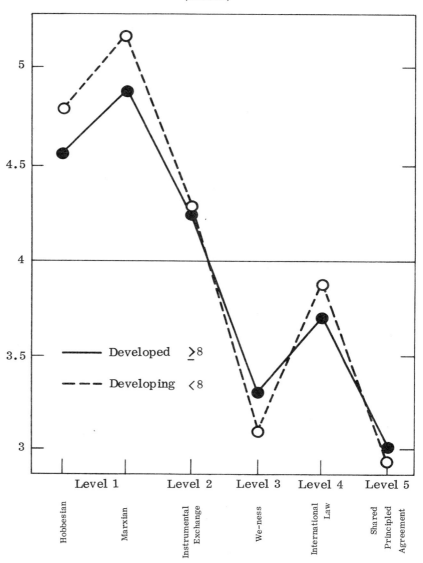

Source: Compiled by the author from his own research.

in their worldviews, although it is not highly significant (p < .10). For the diplomat of the developed country the world is somewhat less Hobbesian. This finding is consistent with our expectation that there would be a positive correlation between the degree of control a country has over its welfare and the likelihood of placing trust in its environment. This expectation was based on the experimental findings of Solomon (1966), supporting the hypothesis that an actor is more likely to engage in trusting behavior the greater control he has over his economic situation.

We also observe some small and nonsignificant differences in relation to the last three levels. Diplomats from developed countries assign greater weight to the we-ness and shared principled agreement climates. If we look at the attribution of importance to international law we observe that diplomats from developing countries assign a somewhat greater role to it. This result could partly be explained by Friedheim's (1968: 182) finding that often delegates from developed countries do not concede any necessary relationship between law and international politics; they see "law as an abstract perfectable entity, divorced from the compromises required by the politics of compelling interests." On the other hand, he found delegates from developing countries to be unable to differentiate between political and legal reality. For them it was very much "a cloak, a set of ideas to camouflage self-interest, the domination of the few by the many" (p. 172). In other words, diplomats of developing countries tend to perceive international law more as an active agent in international politics than their colleagues from developed countries. As noticed before, these last three differences are relatively small and should be treated with caution. But, since I believe that hints and suggestions are important at this stage of understanding diplomatic thinking, we include them in the focus of attention.

Though we have focused on the differences between scores on the levels of the political-moral climate, we should note the preponderant overall similarity of diplomats from developed and developing countries in their patterns of weights assigned to the different levels. It seems clear that the work environments of both groups of diplomats are more similar than different. The similarity is found with respect to the comparative saliency of the different climates in their worldview and their new unanimity in viewing international relations in the instrumental exchange terms of a marketplace. They differ, however, in the assignment of weight to the Hobbesian and Marxian climate; the diplomat of a developing country tends to discern in the present world a higher degree of structural violence, distrust, lack of organization, indifference, power orientedness, natiocentricism, and violence than the diplomat from a developed country.

Let us now examine the impact, single and in combination, of all the systemic variables on the diplomat's perception of the moral-political climate of the world. A schematic overview of the data on which we base the following discussion can be found in Table 5.3. The first column presents the single correlations between our dependent and independent variables. The second and third columns present the results of a regression analysis. We regressed each dependent variable on all our independent variables, with one exception: the center-periphery variable was excluded from the regression analysis because of its high correlation with degree of development and military expenditure (.85 and .83, respectively). The degree of development index can be considered as a valid substitute for the center-periphery index of a country. We entered the independent variables stepwise into the analysis. This means that the variable which accounts for most of the variance in the dependent variable will be entered first; the variable that accounts for the greatest amount of variance in conjunction with the first will be entered second, and so on. In other words, the variable that explains the great amount of the variance unaccounted for by the variables already in the equation enters the equation at the next step. The multiple correlation values in the second column reflect the total variation of the dependent variable that is explained by the variables included. We prefer to use the term R^2 because of its straightforward interpretation, as the percentage of the variation in the dependent variable that is explained by the included variables operating jointly. For example, if we look at the findings in relation to the Hobbesian climate, we see that the six systemic variables entered jointly have an R^2 of .15, indicating that 15 percent of the variation of the Hobbesian climate can be predicted if we enter information about the position of the diplomat with respect to the six structural dimensions.

Hobbesian Climate

The variable which has the strongest single correlation (.25, $p < .008$) with this index is the degree of aid received by the diplomat's country; the more aid received, the greater the tendency to experience the world as a Hobbesian environment. Consistent with this finding is the negative correlation (-.12, $p < .07$) found between the degree of economic development and Hobbesian climate. In other words, the less-developed countries tend to perceive the world as a less-hospitable place. Not significant, but meaningful, is the positive correlation of our dependent variable with the degree of security force investment, indicating that the more security-minded countries also perceive the world as a less-secure habitat.

TABLE 5.3

Relationships between the Systemic Variables and the Different Climates

Climate	Pearson Correlation	Multiple R	R square
Hobbesian			
Aid receipt	.258[b]	.258	.066
Penetration	.023	.290	.084
Security force investment	.103	.311	.096
Economic development	-.123	.380	.144
Economic interdependency	-.069	.385	.148
Military expenditure	.007	.397	.157
(Center-periphery)	-.007		
Marxian			
Military expenditure	-.232[c]	.232	.053
Aid receipt	.159	.315	.099
Economic development	-.164[a]	.373	.139
Economic interdependency	.010	.376	.141
Security force investment	-.139	.379	.144
Penetration	.043	.380	.144
(Center-periphery)	-.204[b]		
Instrumental exchange			
Penetration	.084	.084	.007
Security force investment	-.075	.106	.011
Aid receipt	.020	.120	.014
Economic interdependency	.033	.143	.020
Economic development	-.001	.144	.020
Military expenditure	-.042	.146	.021
(Center-periphery)	-.003		
We-ness			
Aid receipt	-.287[c]	.287	.082
Penetration	-.003	.313	.098
Security force investment	-.124	.339	.115
Military expenditure	.028	.399	.159
Economic interdependency	.016	.402	.162
Economic development	.098	.406	.165
(Center-periphery)	.014		
International law			
Security force investment	-.174[b]	.174	.030
Aid receipt	-.115	.205	.042
Penetration	-.031	.230	.053
Economic interdependency	.019	.236	.056
Economic development	-.121[a]	.245	.060
Military expenditure	-.133	.260	.067
(Center-periphery)	-.148[a]		
Shared principled agreement			
Aid receipt	-.234[b]	.234	.054
Penetration	-.030	.268	.071
Military expenditure	.075	.292	.085
Security force investment	-.001	.311	.097
Economic interdependency	.052	.313	.098
Economic development	.116		
(Center-periphery)	.048		

[a] $p < .05$.   [b] $p < .01$.   [c] $p < .005$.

Source: Compiled by the author from his own research.

Together all the systemic variables are able to predict 15 percent of the variance of the Hobbesian climate.

Marxian Climate

The degree of military expenditure is here the single strongest predictor of the perception of a Marxian climate (-.23, $p < .005$); the weaker powers tend to perceive the world as a place marked by greater structural violence. Also, the diplomats of countries with a low degree of security force investment view the world as more Marxian than the countries on the opposite side of the scale. The second most important predictor is the center-periphery position of a country (-.20, $p < .01$); periphery countries express greater awareness of the existence of structural violence in the world. The importance of economic position on the perception of a Marxian climate is further underscored by the negative correlation with economic development (-.16, $p < .15$), and the positive correlation with the amount of aid received (.15, $p < .15$). Fourteen percent of the variation can be accounted for by the six systemic variables in combination.

Instrumental Exchange

As expected, this variable, which was earlier described as practically a constant in the diplomat's world, has no significant predictors. None of the small amount of variation that we found in the diplomats' perception of the world as an instrumental exchange place can be accounted for by any of the systemic positions.

We-ness Climate

The two systemic positions which individually account for most of the variation are aid received (-.28, $p < .004$) and the degree of security force investment (-.12). Diplomats whose countries receive a high amount of aid or are big security spenders tend to detect less of a we-ness atmosphere in the world. Sixteen percent of the variance is predicted, if we include our systemic variables in the prediction equation.

International Law

Differences in the attribution of importance to the role of international law are most strongly correlated with the degree of security force investment (-.17, $p < .01$). Greater concern with security goes with a tendency to perceive international law as a less-potent factor in international relations. The six systemic variables combined account for 6 percent of the variance.

Shared Principled Agreement

The single strongest predictor here is the degree of aid received by the diplomat's country (-.23, p < .005). This indicates that a diplomat whose country is more dependent on aid has a lesser propensity to view the world as democratic, tolerant for diversity, principled, moralistic, cooperative, globalistic, and just than does his colleague who represents a country that is less-economically dependent and exerts greater control over its economic welfare. This systemic variable alone accounts for 5 percent of the variance of the climate. Together, the six variables predict 9 percent of the variance.

The empirical results of this section demonstrate the relationships between systemic and perceptual variables. The relations are not strong, but they clearly indicate that the diplomat's perception of the world cannot be fully understood and predicted without knowing more about the link between systemic and perceptual variables. This positive finding would at least encourage further analysis of this link and utilization of the systemic variable as a component in the comparative study of foreign policy and diplomatic thinking.

INDUCTIVE APPROACH

Factor Analysis as a Method

The previous section examined the perceptions of the diplomat deductively; we started with constructed concepts which we then confronted with the data to see to what extent the perceived reality conformed to them. Now we will inquire into the diplomat's perception in a more inductive way. We will look at the original variables and study how they are correlated and clustered into meaningful patterns. To ease this task, one can reduce the set of variables to a smaller number of composite variables by using factor analysis. What results is a series of "dimensions" or composite variables, each dimension being formed by a series of highly correlated variables. The original variables which we intend to factor analyze are the 28 variables of our semantic differential. Since an attempt was made to construct an exhaustive list of attributes used to describe the international environment, we can say, with some reservation, that the resulting factor structure reflects the main dimensions of the perceived world of the diplomat. Table 5.4 identifies the first eight factors derived from a factor analysis pooling the data from all the diplomats in the sample. The number of factors extracted was determined by the specification of a minimum eigenvalue of 1.0.

TABLE 5.4

Dimensions in the Perception of the International Environment Derived from Factor-Analysis

Dimension 1: State of nature		Dimension 5: Progressive interdependency	
Blind egoistic	.649	Dynamic	.585
Unconscious	.577	High interdependency	.478
Irrational	.454	Progressive	.476
Undemocratic	.430	Tolerant for diversity	.351
Unjust	.384		
Indifferent	.359		
Intolerant of diversity	.321	Dimension 6: Preconventionalism	
		Opportunistic	.631
Dimension 2: Equity		Distrustful	.628
Moralistic	.616	Unjust	.509
Unexploitative	.457	Anarchic	.492
Relaxed	.360	Unstable	.436
Rational	.338	Short-term oriented	.392
Tolerant for diversity	.337	Hypocritical	.388
Altruistic	.311	Indifferent	.378
Cooperative	.302	Power-oriented	.316
Dimension 3: Degree of comfort		Dimension 7: Democratization of the international structure	
Stable	.637		
Satisfactory	.496	Egalitarian	.583
Nonviolent	.488	Democratic	.406
Has a bright future	.477		
Relaxed	.360	Dimension 8: Degree of unpredictability	
Organized-orderly	.369		
		Unpredictability	.592
Dimension 4: Global thinking			
Globalistic	.899		
Cooperative	.377		
Integrated	.369		

Note: Entries are loadings of perceived international environment characteristics on factors. The cutoff point for the loadings was $\geq$ .30. Varimax rotation used.

Source: Compiled by the author from his own research.

88

Each factor can be interpreted in terms of the perceptual characteristics most closely related to it—in technical terms, those that
load most heavily on it.

Description of the Dimensions

Dimension 1 represents the clustering of seven primary characteristics: blindly egoistic, unconscious, irrational, undemocratic,
unjust, indifferent, and intolerant of diversity. This dimension
conveys the content of what people mean by the "state of nature";
therefore, we will refer to it as the state of nature dimension. Most
of the labels that we will attach to the several dimensions are open
to discussion; we hope to express through them the essence of the
dimension and consider them as means for easing communication.

Dimension 2 brings out the mutual linking among seven variables: moralistic, unexploitative, relaxed, rational, tolerant of
diversity, altruistic, and cooperative. It seems plausible to call
this dimension the degree of perceived equity.

Dimension 3 indicates that the next clustering of perceptual
characteristics includes stability, satisfaction, nonviolence, re-
laxation, order, and optimism about the future. This dimension
should probably be termed degree of comfort, since a high score on
it implies a comfortable feeling about the state of the world, while
those who score low refer instead to those characteristics that are
normally associated with a feeling of discomfort.

Dimension 4 reflects a tendency for some diplomats to talk
about the world as less nationalistic and more globally oriented,
cooperative, and integrated; other diplomats tend consistently to
talk about the world as polarized, competitive, and natiocentric.
The clustering of these variables I shall call degree of global
thinking in the world.

Dimension 5 indicates a clustering of such perceptual characteristics as dynamic, high interdependent, progressive, and
tolerant of diversity. We would like to call this dimension degree
of perceived progressive interdependency.

The characteristics that form dimension 6 are opportunistic,
distrustful, unjust, anarchic, unstable, short-term oriented, hypocritical, indifferent, and power–oriented. All these characteristics
could be seen as typical of a preconventional world or, in other
words, a world that lacks the necessary ingredients of convention
such as principles, trust, consensus, order, stability, long-term
orientation, honesty, altruism, and morality. We will attach to
this dimension the label preconventional. This dimension is very
similar to the state of nature dimension.

Dimension 7 consists only of two variables, both indicating structural qualities of the international system, namely, equality and democracy. For some diplomats the world is high on equality and democracy and low on structural violence; for others we find the opposite perception. We elect to label this dimension degree of democratization of the international structure.

Finally, on dimension 8, only one variable loads heavily, namely, predictable-unpredictable. We will refer to this dimension as degree of unpredictability.

The simple primary conclusion to be drawn from the results of this factor analysis is that the perceptual world of the diplomat is multidimensional and diplomats differ in their perceptions of the world with respect to all of these dimensions.

To develop scores for the eight dimensions derived from the factor analysis, we included only those variables that had a loading higher than .30 on a particular factor. Each diplomat was then given a score on each dimension, based on the sum of these variable scores, each weighted by its factor score estimate. The factor score estimates used and generated by the Statistical Package for Social Sciences (SPSS 1975) are essentially partial regression co-efficients of the variables regressed upon the factor (see Green 1976). For example, on the state of nature dimension, a diplomat's conscious-unconscious score was multipled by .255. A diplomat's score for every other variable that loaded above .30 was likewise multiplied by the factor score estimates of that variable, and the sum of all weighted variable scores was used to obtain the dimension score for state of nature. (For calculations of all dimensions see Appendix H.) Using these scores, we will now examine how these eight dimensions relate to our six ideal-type environments. A schematic overview of the correlations can be found in Table 5.5.

Relation between Ideal Climates and Dimensions

A perusal of the correlation matrix shows that most of the dimensions tend to divide our ideal-type environments into two groups: those above the dividing line are negatively correlated with the dimension and those below positively correlated, or vice versa. Excluding dimension 8, we see that two dimensions have the dividing point after level 1 (Hobbesian and Marxian climate) and five dimensions after level 2. We also see an overall trend in the change of strength in the correlations as they move from level 1 (Hobbesian and Marxian climate) to level 5 (shared principled agreement). For example, in dimension 3, the correlations with the six ideal-type climates are as follows: -.60, -.26, .13, .49, .22, .51. In most

TABLE 5.5

Matrix of the Correlations between the Ideal Climates and the Perceptual Dimensions

	Hobbesian	Marxian	Instrumental Exchange	We-ness	International Law	Shared Principled Agreement
State of nature	.73 (144)	.18 (146)	-.31 (147)	-.57 (147)	-.30 (147)	-.68 (146)
Equity	-.76 (149)	-.46 (151)	-.03 (150)	.66 (151)	.21 (153)	.81 (151)
Comfort	-.60 (152)	-.26 (155)	.13 (154)	.49 (155)	.22 (161)	.51 (152)
Global thinking	-.57 (154)	-.28 (156)	-.23 (155)	.56 (157)	.09 (160)	.61 (154)
Progressive interdependency	-.33 (142)	-.17 (148)	-.10 (145)	.33 (145)	.10 (152)	.42 (146)
Preconventionalism	.82 (148)	.30 (146)	.16 (149)	-.72 (150)	-.29 (148)	-.77 (148)
Democratic international structure	-.33 (145)	-.55 (157)	-.02 (148)	.27 (149)	.20 (156)	.47 (150)
Unpredictability	.31 (152)	-.03 (158)	-.03 (155)	-.24 (156)	-.23 (166)	-.21 (154)

Note: The N for each correlation is in parentheses.
Source: Compiled by the author from his own research.

other dimensions a similar trend is found. These findings indicate a tendency of lower-level climates to be negatively associated with characteristics in the international environment which are generally considered positive (equity, degree of comfort, global thinking, progressive interdependency, and democratic international structure), and positively associated with negative characteristics (state of nature and preconventionalism). The higher-level climates tend to show the opposite pattern. What stands out is a dichotomy, with the Hobbesian and shared principled agreement climates as poles. Of all the climates the Hobbesian is related most strongly: negatively to dimensions 2, 3, 4, and 5, and positively to dimensions 1, 6, and 8. Shared principled agreement, with the exception of its relation to dimension 8, shows precisely the opposite pattern. A climate which is very similar, in terms of strength and pattern of relationships to the dimensions, is we-ness. This suggests that both refer to climates that are not so different and could be considered as substitutes for each other to describe one pole of the dichotomy.

What we now have is a continuum with two distinct poles. On the left pole we have the Hobbesian climate, and on the right pole the shared principled agreement/we-ness climate. The pattern of correlations of the Marxian climate closely approximates that of the left pole (the only exception is dimension 8), while the international law climate persistently follows the pattern of correlations of the right pole. The instrumental exchange climate is located somewhere around the middle of the continuum.

A last point of interest concerns the correlations of the climates with dimension 3 (degree of comfort). If we consider degree of comfort as a preferred quality of the international environment, then the pattern of correlations suggests that our ideal-type climates form an order of preferredness from negative to positive. In other words, we could say that the more an environment approximates a higher-level environment, the higher its propensity of being perceived as a more comfortable place to live. Let us now look at the relations between each ideal-type climate and the dimensions.

The Hobbesian climate has its highest positive correlations with dimension 1, referred to as the state of nature (.73), and dimension 6, referred to as degree of preconventionality (.82). The Hobbesian climate could be considered as a composite variable of both dimensions. Its correlations with all other dimensions, with the exception of dimension 8, are negative.

The Marxian climate has its highest correlation with dimension 7, called degree of democratization of the international structure (-.55). This correlation is, of course, as we expected and therefore meaningful.

The instrumental exchange climate has no strong presence in any of the eight dimensions. The highest correlation it has is with dimension 1 (-.31). The meaning of this correlation is that the perception of the international environment as a place for instrumental exchange tends to go together with a reduction in the perception of state-of-nature characteristics.

The we-ness climate is most strongly represented in the equity (.66) and global thinking dimensions (.56). It also has a strong negative correlation with the preconventional dimension (-.72). These correlations are also very meaningful and consistent with what we would have expected.

The international law climate has no strong presence in any of the dimensions. It has positive correlations with dimensions 2, 3, 4, 5, and 7, and negative correlations with 1, 6, and 8.

The shared principled agreement climate is most strongly represented in the equity dimension (.81).

This brief scanning of the links between our ideal-type climates and the dimensions was meant to assess further the validity of the typology. The results show that, first, the we-ness and the shared principled agreement climates are very similar and can be substituted for each other; second, that the climates are positioned on a continuum with its two poles being the Hobbesian and the shared principled agreement/we-ness climates. On this continuum the climates are rank-ordered as follows: Hobbesian, Marxian, instrumental exchange, international law, and shared principled agreement/we-ness. Higher-level climates tend to be positively associated with characteristics of the international environment which are considered as positive, and lower-level climates are associated positively with negative characteristics. Further, the results show that the rank-order among the different environments also reflects a real preference expressed by the diplomats for certain international climates.

Impact of Systemic Variables

As we did for the ideal-type climates, let us now compare diplomats from countries with different economic positions (developed and developing countries) on their perceptions of the world along the eight dimensions. More specifically, we will contrast the means of diplomats from countries with a position of 8 or higher on economic development with the means of the diplomats from countries with a lower position. For a schematic presentation of the results, see Figure 5.4. Of the eight comparisons, we find half to

FIGURE 5.4

Contrasting Perceptions of the International Environment by
Diplomats from Developed and Developing Countries

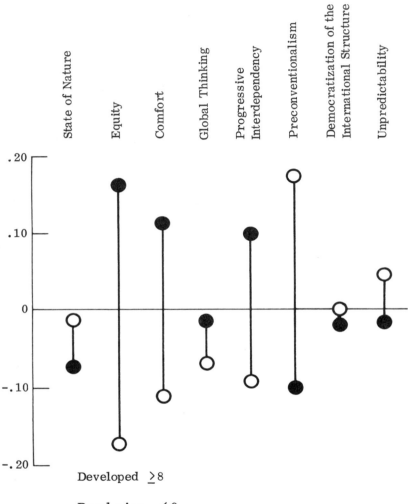

Developed ≥8

Developing <8

The means are based on standardized scores

be significant: the diplomat's perception of the degree of equity, comfort, progressive interdependency, and preconventionalism. On the equity dimension, the difference between the means is .33 (p < .01), with diplomats from developed countries tending to perceive the world as a more equitable place than their colleagues from developing countries. On the third dimension, referred to as degree of comfort, the difference is .22 (p < .05). Not unexpectedly, diplomats from less-developed countries perceive the world as a somewhat less comfortable habitat than diplomats from wealthier countries. The third difference, in perception of the world as progressive and interdependent (.20, p < .05), indicates that diplomats of developed countries see the world as more dynamic, higher in interdependency, more progressive, and more tolerant of diversity, while diplomats from developing countries see it as more static, lower in interdependency, more reactionary, and more intolerant of diversity. The last significant difference is found in the sixth dimension or degree of perceived preconventionalism (-.27, p < .05), indicating that for developed countries the world has more ingredients necessary for a conventional international order, such as principles, trust, consensus, order, stability, long-term orientation, honesty, altruism, and morality, than for developing countries.

All these dimensions, although statistically independent, could also be seen as different measures of the perceived positiveness or negativeness of the international environment. If this is true, then our findings clearly indicate that the overall perception of the international environment by diplomats from developed countries is more positive, and the perception of their colleagues from developing countries more negative.

We will now look at the effects of all systemic variables, singly and in combination, on variation in the eight dimensions. A schematic overview of the data on which the following descriptions are based can be found in Table 5.6.

Dimension 1: State of Nature

The two variables which have the strongest single correlation with this dimension are the degree of security force investment (.20, p < .01) and the amount of aid received (.18, p < .05). Diplomats from countries that spend a great amount on military security and countries that are highly dependent on aid tend to perceive the world more in negative terms and as closer to the state of nature than diplomats from countries that are less security-minded or have more power over their economic condition. Ten percent of the variance of the first dimension can be explained by the six systemic factors in combination.

TABLE 5.6

Relations between the Systemic Variables and the Eight Empirically Derived Dimensions

Dimension	Pearson Correlation	Multiple R	R square
1 State of nature			
Security force investment	.20[b]	.20	.04
Economic development	-.01	.27	.07
Aid receipt	.18[a]	.28	.08
Penetration	-.06	.30	.09
Economic interdependency	.03	.31	.09
Military expenditure	.06	.31	.10
(Center-periphery)	.04		
2 Equity			
Aid receipt	-.25[b]	.25	.06
Military expenditure	.15	.33	.10
Penetration	-.06	.36	.13
Economic interdependency	.06	.37	.13
Security force investment	.09	.37	.14
Economic development	.20[b]	.37	.14
(Center-periphery)	.14[a]		
3 Degree of Comfort			
Aid receipt	-.20[a]	.20	.04
Penetration	-.14	.32	.10
Security force investment	-.07	.33	.11
Economic development	.08	.39	.15
Economic interdependency	.03	.40	.16
Military expenditure	.05	.40	.16
(Center-periphery)	.06		
4 Global thinking			
Aid receipt	-.28[b]	.28	.08
Penetration	-.04	.33	.11
Economic interdependency	-.01	.35	.12
Military expenditure	.04	.38	.14
Economic development	.03	.42	.18
Security force investment	.02	.43	.18
(Center-periphery)			

Dimension	Pearson Correlation	Multiple R	R square
5 Progressive interdependency			
Aid receipt	-.22[a]	.22	.04
Military expenditure	.10	.27	.07
Economic interdependency	.03	.28	.08
Penetration	.14	.29	.08
Economic development	.17[a]	.31	.09
Security force investment	.09	.32	.10
(Center-periphery)	.11		
6 Preconventionalism			
Aid receipt	.17[a]	.17	.03
Penetration	.05	.22	.05
Economic development	-.14[a]	.25	.06
Security force investment	.08	.37	.14
Military expenditure	-.04	.38	.14
Economic interdependency	-.08	.39	.15
(Center-periphery)	-.06		
7 Democratization of the international structure			
Penetration	-.15	.15	.02
Aid receipt	-.09	.22	.05
Economic interdependency	.00	.23	.05
Military expenditure	.00	.23	.05
Economic development	-.01		
Security force investment	.01		
(Center-periphery)	-.04		
8 Degree of unpredictability			
Aid receipt	.21[a]	.21	.04
Economic interdependency	-.11	.21	.04
Security force investment	.03	.22	.05
Military expenditure	.00	.23	.05
Economic development	-.06	.25	.06
Penetration	-.05	.26	.06
(Center-periphery)	.06		

[a]$p < .05.$ [b]$p < .01.$

Source: Compiled by the author from his own research.

Dimension 2: Equity

The two variables which are most strongly correlated with the degree of perceived equity in the world relate to a country's economic position, namely, the amount of aid received ($-.25$, $p < .01$) and the degree of economic development ($.20$, $p < .009$). This indicates that the less developed and the more dependent on aid a country is, the greater the propensity of its diplomats to perceive the international environment as inequitable. The six variables combined predict 14 percent of the variance.

Dimension 3: Degree of Comfort

The two variables with the highest correlation are the amount of aid received ($-.20$, $p < .02$) and the degree of penetratedness ($-.14$). These correlations demonstrate that diplomats from countries with high control over their economic and military conditions tend to perceive the world as more comfortable than their colleagues from countries with less control. Information about the six systemic variables enables us to predict 16 percent of the variance in expressed degree of comfort.

Dimension 4: Global Thinking

The systemic index most highly correlated with this dimension is the amount of aid received by the diplomat's country ($-.28$, $p < .003$). The diplomats from countries high in received aid perceive less global thinking, cooperation, and integration in the world than their colleagues from those receiving less aid; instead they perceive more nationalism, competition, and polarization. To explain 18 percent of the variance we need information about the amount of aid received, penetration, economic interdependency, economic development, military expenditure, and security force investment.

Dimension 5: Progressive Interdependency

The two highest systemic correlations of this dimension are the amount of aid received ($-.22$, $p < .02$) and the degree of economic development ($.17$, $p < .02$). Diplomats from developed countries tend to see the world as more progressive and interdependent than their colleagues from less-developed countries, and especially those who receive a high amount of aid. Ten percent of this variance can be explained by the six systemic variables.

Dimension 6: Preconventionalism

The amount of aid received and the degree of economic development are the only two systemic variables which are significantly correlated with dimension 6 (.17, p < .05, and -.14, p < .05). Diplomats from countries high on the amount of aid received and low on economic development tend to view the world as more opportunistic, distrustful, unjust, anarchic, unstable, short-term-oriented, hypocritical, indifferent, and power-oriented than their colleagues whose countries occupy a stronger economic position in the world. Together with the degree of penetration and degree of security force investment, these variables account for 14 percent of the variance.

Dimension 7: Democratization of the International Structure

This dimension has its highest correlation with the degree of penetratedness and amount of aid received (-.15 and -.09). This indicates, not unexpectedly, that diplomats from countries that are bottomdogs in the international relations structure tend to perceive the world as less egalitarian and democratic than their colleagues from topdog countries. Together the six systemic variables predict 5 percent of the variance.

Dimension 8: Degree of Unpredictability

This dimension measures the perception of the predictability of international relations. The systemic variable with the strongest single correlation is the amount of aid received (.21, p < .02). This correlation suggests that diplomats whose countries are high on aid receipt tend to be less sure about the future of international relations than their colleagues from countries low on aid receipt. The amount of variation explained by all the systemic variables is 6 percent.

The results described in this section demonstrate relationships between the perceptual dimensions and the systemic variables. The most consistent predictors of these perceptions on most of the dimensions are the aid receipt variable and, to a lesser extent, the economic development variable. The other systemic variables which have an impact, but only on one dimension, are security force investment and center-periphery; they affect the state of nature and equity dimensions, respectively. The correlations are not strong but clearly indicate that this perceptual component of diplomatic thinking cannot be fully comprehended or predicted if the impact of the systemic position on the diplomat's thinking is overlooked.

SPECIFIC ASPECTS OF THE DIPLOMAT'S
PERCEPTION OF THE WORLD

Unsatisfactory-Satisfactory

For the last section of this chapter, we have singled out for emphasis some distinct aspects of the diplomat's perception of the world. The first aspect on which we want to focus is the diplomat's degree of satisfaction with the present international system and some correlates of satisfaction. An overview of the data used in this discussion can be found in Table 5.7. As indicated by the overall mean (3.23), most diplomats express relative dissatisfaction with the international system. To understand the meaning of this dissatisfaction, we must know what criteria have to be fulfilled or what conditions have to be present in the international system for the diplomat to express satisfaction. Relevant information can be obtained by looking at some of the correlates of satisfaction. Among the highest positive correlates we find stability and order, justice, international democracy, absence of violence, honesty, trust, and long-term orientation. The two most-wanted conditions of satisfaction are stability (.45) and justice (.44). The absence of these and the other characteristics explains the rather low degree of expressed satisfaction with the present international system. It should be noted here that, although the characteristics associated with satisfaction are shared by all diplomats, their ordering in terms of priority is not the same across subgroups of diplomats. In Chapter 6 we will look at some of these differences, in their rank-ordering of preferred conditions, between different groups of diplomats.

Let us now look at the correlations of our six ideal-type environments with expressed satisfaction. As we move from level 1 to level 6, the degree of satisfaction tends to rise. There is only one exception: the international law climate (level 5) shows a lower correlation than we-ness (level 4). This could be explained by the fact that the presence of international law is not always valued per se, but it is often valued to the extent that it serves specific interests. It would be fair to say that the differences between diplomats in degree of satisfaction are a function not only of the presence of international law (as measured by our index), but also of the extent to which international law is perceived as serving national interests. This pattern of correlations of the ideal-type climates with the satisfaction index underscores our assumption that the six climates are rank-ordered in terms of preference.

How is satisfaction related to the eight empirically derived dimensions? It is positively correlated with degree of comfort (.69), equity (.35), democratization (.31), global thinking (.23), and

TABLE 5.7

Mean, Standard Deviation, and Correlates of the Degree
of Satisfaction with the International System

Correlations with	
Perceived international characteristics	
Stable	.45[a]
Just	.44[a]
Democratic	.40[a]
Nonviolent	.35[a]
Long-term oriented	.34[a]
Trustful	.31[a]
Honest	.30[a]
Orderly/organized	.30[a]
Ideal type international climates	
Shared principled agreement	.42[a]
We-ness	.31[a]
International law	.23[a]
Instrumental exchange	.13[c]
Marxian	-.25[a]
Hobbesian	-.40[a]
Dimensions of perceived international environment	
Degree of comfort	.69[a]
Equity	.35[a]
Democratization of international structure	.31[a]
Global thinking	.23[a]
Progressive interdependency	.14[a]
Unpredictability	-.19[b]
State of nature	-.40[a]
Preconventionalism	-.41[a]
Systemic position of the diplomat's country	
Military expenditure	.05
Economic interdependency	.00
Economic development	-.01
Security force investment	-.04
Penetration	-.05
Center-periphery	-.06
Aid receipt	-.27[b]

Unsatisfactory-satisfactory (N = 172) 1 . . . . . 7.
Mean: 3.23.
Standard deviation: 1.38.
[a]$p < .001$.
[b]$p < .01$.
[c]$p < .05$.
Source: Compiled by the author from his own research.

progressive interdependency (.14); it is negatively correlated with preconventionalism (-.41), state of nature (-.40), and degree of unpredictability (-.19).

Finally, let us look at the relationship of satisfaction or dissatisfaction with systemic variables. The systemic position which is most significantly correlated with degree of satisfaction is the amount of aid received (-.27, $p < .004$). Diplomats with the highest dissatisfaction index tend to come from the poorest countries as indicated by the amount of aid received.

Perceived Justice

A second salient aspect of the international system is its legitimacy or perceived justness. The mean of the perceived justness of the world (3) is even lower than the expressed satisfaction with the world. In order to understand the source of this perceived unjustness, let us look at the conditions that are associated with justness in the minds of the diplomats. A schematic overview of the data on which this discussion is based can be found in Table 5.8. The number of conditions that are associated with a just environment is rather large. Fifteen characteristics have correlations greater than or equal to .30 with our unjust-just index. All the characteristics which were highly correlated with satisfaction also appear in this list, although their rank-ordering in terms of size of correlation differs. For example, stability is highest among the correlates of satisfaction but only the tenth-ranked correlate of justice. The additional characteristics can be categorized in three groups: the presence of moral principles (moralistic, principled), the presence of cooperation (cooperative, supportive, altruistic), and the presence of rationality (rational, enlightened-egoistic). The three highest correlates are democratic, trustful, and supportive.

How are the ideal-type, moral-political climates rank-ordered with respect to their correlations with attribution of justice? From the Hobbesian climate to the shared principled agreement climate, the correlations vary from strong negative to high positive (-.60, -.29, .00, .54, .14, .69). The only exception in the trend is international law. A possible explanation of this discrepancy was offered previously.

The rank-order of the empirically derived dimensions is basically the same as for satisfaction, with the exception of a reversal among the first two. For the justice index, equity tops the list and is followed by degree of comfort. Diplomats from states high on security force investment tend to see the world as more unjust than their colleagues from countries that spend a smaller amount of the

TABLE 5.8

Mean, Standard Deviation, and Correlates of the Degree
of Perceived Justice

Correlations with	
Perceived international environment characteristics	
(only correlations .30 are listed)	
Democratic	.49*
Trustful	.48*
Supportive	.45*
Satisfactory	.44*
Principled	.44*
Orderly/organized	.42*
Moralistic	.40*
Altruistic	.39*
Enlightened egoistic	.39*
Stable	.38*
Cooperative	.34*
Long-term oriented	.34*
Rational	.33*
Nonviolent	.30*
Honest	.30*
Ideal-type international climates	
Shared principled agreement	.69
We-ness	.54
International law	.14
Instrumental exchange	.00
Marxian	-.29
Hobbesian	-.60
Dimensions of perceived international environment	
Equity	.59
Degree of comfort	.51
Democratization of international structure	.39
Global thinking	.23
Progressive interdependency	.07
Degree of unpredictability	-.11
State of nature	-.64
Preconventionalism	-.69
Systemic position of the diplomat's country	
Military expenditure	.09
Center-periphery	.07
Economic development	.06
Penetration	.06
Economic interdependency	-.02
Aid receipt	-.07
Security force investment	-.13

Unjust-just (N = 169) 1 . . . . . 7.
Mean: 3.00
Standard deviation: 1.21.
*p < .001.
Source: Compiled by the author from his own research.

budget on internal and external security. Also, for high aid recipients the world is a less-just habitat. Finally, there is also an indication (.09) that diplomats from greater powers tend to view the world as more just than their small-power colleagues.

Predictability

A principal characteristic of the international environment is its degree of predictability. The impact of degrees of predictability on the occurrence of certain kinds of processes or decisions in foreign policy has been documented (Hermann 1969).

As can be seen in Table 5.9, the perceived predictability of the international system in the present sample is 3.5, which indicates that the world is perceived as more unpredictable than predictable. Predictability is associated with perceived stability, altruism, consciousness, trustfulness, and enlightened egoism. All of these conditions could be interpreted as preconditions of predictability, that is, as characteristics that tend to enhance the predictability of the system. The only significant systemic variable associated with predictability is the amount of aid received (-.21, $p < .02$). This would suggest that diplomats whose countries are highly dependent on aid tend to see the world as less predictable than do those who are not dependent on aid.

Pessimism-Optimism

The more predictable a diplomat's perceived environment, the more optimistic he tends to be about the future of that environment (.19, $p < .01$). Predictability is, however, not the main correlate of optimism. As shown in Table 5.10, among correlates higher than .26 are order and stability, absence of tension and violence, honesty, cooperation, satisfaction, and rationality. An environment characterized by such qualities tends to evoke a more optimistic view about its future state. The types of moral-political climate that evoke the most optimism are the we-ness and shared principled agreement climates (.43 and .37). On the other hand, the ones that evoke the most pessimism are the Marxian and Hobbesian climates (-.18 and -.41). The predominant positive correlate among the eight dimensions is the degree of comfort (.61). Turning to systemic positions, we find that pessimistic diplomats tend to come from countries that are high on penetration, security force investment, military power, and peripheral status.

TABLE 5.9

Mean, Standard Deviation, and Correlates of the Degree
of Perceived Predictability

	Correlations with
Perceived international characteristics	
Stable	.25[a]
Altruistic	.22[b]
Conscious	.22[b]
Trustful	.22[b]
Enlightened egoistic	.21[b]
Systemic position of the diplomat's country	
Economic interdependency	.11
Economic development	.06
Penetration	.05
Military expenditure	-.00
Security force investment	-.03
Center-periphery	-.06
Aid receipt	-.21[c]

Unpredictability-predictability (N = 172) 1 . . . . . . 7.
Mean: 3.57.
Standard deviation: 1.49.
[a]$p < .001$.
[b]$p < .01$.
[c]$p < .05$.
Source: Compiled by the author from his own research.

Perceived Penetration

The final aspect of the diplomat's perception of the international environment to be considered is his view of his own country's
degree of penetration. The data used to measure perceived penetration are the diplomats' responses to the following statements:

> Our defense system is to a great extent controlled by
> another country.

> My country's economy is significantly influenced by
> foreign investors.

TABLE 5.10

Mean, Standard Deviation, and Correlates of the Degree of
Optimism about the Future of International Relations

Correlations with	
Perceived international environment characteristics	
Stable	.35[a]
Honest	.31[a]
Orderly/organized	.28[a]
Relaxed	.28[a]
Cooperative	.27[a]
Nonviolent	.27[a]
Satisfaction	.27[a]
Rational	.27[a]
Ideal-type international climate	
We-ness	.41
Shared principled agreement	.37
International law	.03
Instrumental exchange	.01
Marxian	−.18
Hobbesian	−.41
Dimensions of perceived international environment	
Degree of comfort	.61
Equity	.35
Progressive interdependency	.23
Global thinking	.19
Democratization of international structure	.11
Degree of unpredictability	−.19
State of nature	−.34
Preconventional	−.38
Systemic position of the diplomat's country	
Economic interdependency	.03
Center-periphery	.02
Economic development	−.01
Aid receipt	−.08
Military expenditure	−.08
Security force investment	−.13
Penetration	−.20[b]

Pessimism-optimism (N = 169) 1 . . . . . 7.
Mean: 3.93.
Standard deviation: 1.23.
[a]$p < .001$.
[b]$p < .05$.
Source: Compiled by the author from his own research.

The purpose of including this variable in our analysis was to examine how objective positions are reflected in the perceptions of the diplomat. This variable provides a measure of what we could call positional awareness of the diplomat and also provides a means of validating one of the objective measures. The correlation of the objective measure of penetration with the measure of perceived penetration was found to be .28 ($p < .003$). This result demonstrates a significant level of positional awareness, at least in this particular case, and also supports the validity of the objective measure.

CONCLUSION

One of the purposes of this chapter has been to analyze and describe systematically the diplomat's perception of the world. To distinguish different views of the world, we used two classificatory schemas: a theoretically derived ideal-type classification of moral-political climates, and an empirically derived multidimensional scheme of the diplomat's perception of the international environment. The multidimensional model was arrived at by factor analyzing the diplomats' scores on judgments of 28 characteristics of the international system. The empirical results demonstrate that the perceptual world of diplomats is multidimensional and that a comprehensive report of the diplomat's environment must provide information concerning all these dimensions.

Our results also suggest that the typology of moral-political climates taps several dimensions of the diplomat's perceived world and ranks the climates in order of preference. That is, their order of preference in the minds of our total sample of diplomats corresponds, more or less, to the theoretically based ordering of the five levels of moral-political climates. We had no time to check whether the rank-ordering also holds across subgroups of diplomats. Such a comparison could be considered a better test of the universal validity of the preference rank-order.

In proposition 2 we stated that, in terms of the present applicability to the reality of international relations, the five levels form a rank-order of diminishing relevance, and we predicted that the weight assigned to each consecutive level would decrease. With the exception of the rank-order of international law, this prediction was unequivocally validated. Our original placing of international law in the rank-order was based on the rather unsubstantiated assumption that international law is per se a highly preferred state. The results, however, indicate that the preferredness of international law is not only a function of its presence but also of the extent to which it satisfies particular national interests. Aside from the description of the diplomats' perception of their work environment, we were also interested in the sources of its variation. First we wanted to indicate that the perception of the global international system on which most of our analyses focused differs strongly from perceptions of subsystems of the international system, such as the European Community, and that the findings about perceptions on one system level cannot be transferred to another system level. The data strongly indicated significant differences between the perceptions of the global and the regional international environment. Our prediction that in the latter environment the lower-level climates would receive lower evaluations and higher climates higher evaluations than in the global international environment was found to be valid.

A second determinant of the perception of the diplomat is the international position of his country along several salient systemic dimensions. We were able to check the saliency of only one of these positions, penetration. Our results showed a significant positive correlation between the objective indicator and the perceived penetratedness index. Examining the effects of certain systemic attributes on the diplomat's perception, we found the results positive; the amount of variance of the dependent variables that could be predicted by the systemic variables is not insignificant. The most consistent predictor of the variance of the diplomat's perception of the international environment is aid receipt and, to a lesser extent, the economic development variable. The other systemic variables which have an impact, but only on a few climates or dimensions, are, in order of importance, center-periphery, security force investment, and military expenditure. In general we consider our findings of this exploratory inquiry positive and encouraging for further analysis and utilization of this approach in the comparative study of diplomatic thinking.

Having established the measurable existence of perceived international climate, we must address ourselves to the question of relevance. Therefore, let us now look at the international climate as an independent variable and study how consequential it is or, in other words, what implications it has for international behavior. The social-psychological reality of the international climate concept is not unrelated to what Merton calls the Thomas theorem: "If men define situations as real, they are real in their consequences." One of the consequences relates to the impact of the international climate on the level of moral thinking in international relations. Several students of moral thinking support the idea that the social environment plays an important role in determining the level of moral thinking of the actors. A strikingly explicit statement of this point of view is Jaspers' (1951: 105) assertion that "our humanity is not, properly speaking, real, but exists only under certain conditions, and when these are in abeyance the savagery of animal selfishness manifests itself as life seeking to maintain itself at any cost to others."

An interesting study testing this model in a prison environment was done by Peter Sharf (1971). In his study, Sharf found that the level of moral thinking of the prisoners varied as a function of the moral atmosphere in which the prisoners lived. Extrapolating this finding to the international arena, we could say that different international moral-political climates will evoke different patterns of moral thinking about international relations. We further base this thesis on the assumption that a national actor who wants to survive and maximize his valued international position (or at least have control over his position) has to adapt his thinking to the principles which govern the international system. For a national actor, Rousseau's saying, "To be sane in a world of madness is itself a kind of madness," summarizes an important principle of foreign politics. An example of such madness for a nation would be to be moral in an immoral world. It is even fair to apply Roussea's principle to the world of moral behavior; we could say that "to be moral in an immoral world is itself a kind of immorality." In our study we found the observations made by diplomats about the moral principles governing international relations to be very congruent with their perceptions of the moral-political climate of the international environment. An overview of the statements that pertain to moral behavior in international relations can be found in Table 5.11.

In addition to having an effect on the value component of the diplomat's thinking, we also expect that his perception of the international environment has an impact on his style of analysis. For example, we expect that diplomats who perceive the world as more Hobbesian or Marxian would also be more prone to analyze it as a zero-sum game, whereas diplomats higher on a we-ness climate would be more prone to analyze the world in nonzero terms. Moreover, we expect to find an effect of the perceived international environment on the diplomatic strategic approach. For example, diplomats who perceive a greater presence of structural violence in the world should tend to favor a strategy of self-determination and self-sufficiency, structural change, and less gradualism. All of the implications considered until now refer to the effects of perceived international climate on other components of diplomatic thinking. We opted not to discuss the links between international climate and diplomatic behavior, not only because of their complexity, but also because of limitations of space. It is very likely, however, that the perceived international environment is a matter of some significance for foreign policy. As Frankel (1973: 66)

TABLE 5.11

Observations Made by Diplomats about the State
of International Morality

International policy is a very rudimentary power interaction	21
There is nothing right or wrong, only things that are in your interests	14
You could speak of economic classes in the international arena	9
The world is a mess	2
People are very closed minded	2
The world is not peaceful; leadership is basically concerned with the maintenance of order	2
In order to succeed in the world, you have to have a competitive nature	2
Humanitarian understanding doesn't exist very much	2
"Just" is a Third World word	2
Conflict is a part of the nature of the world	1
In relations between nations there is no confidence; this is universal	1

Note: This table classifies the observations about international morality made by a sample of 58 diplomats. Each statement intends to capture the essence of a group of observations (number indicated on right-hand side) which are very similar in content.

Source: Compiled by the author from his own research.

points out, "Serious differences between the psychological environments of individual states frequently occur, giving rise to corresponding differences in foreign policy."

The perception of the international environment is only the
first of four components of diplomatic thinking that we intend to
discuss. The second component pertains to the diplomat's aspirations. More specifically, Chapter 6 will examine the diplomat's
thinking about peace and his vision of a preferred world order.

6

Values in Diplomatic Thinking:
Peace and Preferred World Order

To understand diplomatic thinking, we need information not only about the work environment, but also about the value systems of diplomats. To evaluate or orient himself toward his environment, the diplomat, like any other decision maker, must relate it to his values. Hence, if we want to understand his response to the international environment, we need to investigate the criteria by which he judges international conduct. In this chapter we will inquire into two major values: international peace and preferred world order. To gain some understanding of diplomatic value systems, we will group the diplomats according to the degree of economic development of their countries and study the differences in their value operationalizations. We decided to compare the diplomats in relation to only one systemic position to stay within the space limitations of this study. But before we focus on the diplomat's thinking about peace and preferred world order, we would like to say a word about each of these issues: the ambiguities and paradoxes inherent in peace thinking in general, different conceptions of peace in the relevant literature of international relations, the linkage between the concept of peace or other international values and international relations, and the advantages of systemic study of international values, such as peace and preferred world order.

AMBIGUITIES AND PARADOXES IN PEACE THINKING

Today, to contribute to peace is the declared goal of all countries in the world. What does this declared goal mean? An operational definition of it would significantly enhance our understanding of international behavior. The study of this phenomenon turns out to be an inquiry into paradoxes. Peace is undoubtedly one of the most frequently used words in the vocabulary of diplomats; yet it is also one of the most ambiguous and least communicative words. Furthermore, there is a pluralism of concepts of peace; rather than wanting peace, men want "peaces." Finally, when the record of diplomatic dialog is weighted against the record of international events, it looks as if peace is at one and the same time the most wanted and the most elusive state of international affairs. "The central paradox in the study of peace lies in its continuing appeal for lasting peace and the actuality of continuing war" (Puchala 1971: 141).

These paradoxes and the conceptual ambiguity of peace could be accounted for by several factors. First, the vagueness of the term allows it to be used as a cover. This particular use was recognized by Dulles (1955: 6) when he attacked the kind of peace that can "be a cover whereby men perpetrate diabolical wrongs." Second, the use of unclear language makes it possible to evade critical problems. This function was well described in Janik and Toulmin's (1973: 269-73) analysis of political language in Austria before 1914. They claim that there was a consistent attempt to evade the social and political problems of Austria by the debasement of language--by the invention of "bogus language games" based on the pretense that the existing norms of life were different from what they really were. The authors perceive the present scene as not so different from the pre-World War I Austria. "Nowadays as much as in the years before 1914, political dishonesty and deviousness quickly find expression in debased language. . . . Counterargument is no weapon against this tactic, since issues are always blurred by translation into officialese" (Janik and Toulmin 1972: 269). Third, an international environment characterized by competition and distrust does not help in making values or interests explicit. Not only political considerations, but also cultural factors account for the low quality of conceptualization of international peace. In the field of social science there has been, for a long time, a "flight from tenderness" (Rubin 1973: 11-12). In the research and theorizing of social scientists, much more attention tends to be devoted to the study of aggressive, hostile, and conflictual behavior, at the expense of so-called softer behaviors, such as cooperation, peace, and justice, which are equally important ingredients of international life. Peace research is a very recent arrival in the study of international relations. A more important explanation of the relative uselessness of the term peace in international dialog is the natiocentric tendency in peace thinking, evidenced by each country's claim to having the only true definition of peace. Nations tend to claim a universally recognized patent for their operational definition and conceive any other definition as highly improper. A final explanation of misunderstandings

in the dialog about international peace are the differences in meaning associated with the universally used symbol of peace. This explanation recognizes and accepts a pluralism in definitions, and it
agrees with the fact that men's values and judgments are likely to
differ, especially when their interests are engaged (Rawls 1971:
196-97).

DIFFERENT CONCEPTIONS OF PEACE

Having traced some of the sources of lack of consensus in the
conceptualization of peace, let us now look at some of the differences
in peace thinking. We will scan the relevant literature on peace in
international relations to see which different concepts of peace can
be distinguished and how these can be organized into a useful taxon-
omy. To compare different conceptions of peace in terms of their
unique contents, we shall use a general schema for describing the
cognitive structure of the concept of peace. The assumption is that
the same cognitive structure is applicable to all concepts of peace,
regardless of their specific contents. The basic units of conceptual
structure are the dimensions or attributes used to define a given
object--in this case, international peace. Conceptual differentia-
tion, then, is a function of the specific location of the object in a
multidimensional space. This approach to the comparative analysis
of peace concepts has also been used in the social-psychological
study of international images (Scott 1965). Several dimensions are
needed to define most of the concepts of peace that have been pro-
posed.

Domain of Peace

This dimension refers to the size of the geographic area to
which a particular peace arrangement applies. Over the course of
history, Aron (1966: 232) observed a progressive widening of the
domain of peace. "If we consider wars down through history, we
cannot fail to see in them the elasticity of movement, more precisely, of the progressive widening of the zones of sovereignty, hence
the zones of peace." Another example of a reference to domain can
be found in the concept of Pax Africana: the specifically military
aspect of the principle of continental jurisdiction, which explicitly
asserts that peace in Africa is to be assured by exertions of Afri-
cans themselves (Mazrui 1967: 203).

Basis of Peace

This dimension classifies different peace arrangements according to the degree of agreement about the conditions for peace between the parties to the arrangement. On one end of the continuum we would place imposed peace, that is, a peace agreed upon in an asymmetrical conflict situation where the stronger power imposes its interpretation of peace on the weaker or defeated party. On the other end of the continuum, agreement on peace is characterized by consensus based on mutual satisfaction. A good example of an imposed peace was the peace legitimized by the League of Nations after World War I: "The League was not so much to keep peace, but to keep a specific peace--to legitimize and stabilize a particular world settlement based upon victory" (Claude 1959: 49). All peace arrangements based upon power can be placed here. Aron distinguishes three forms of peace based on power. The first is peace by equilibrium, which can also be called peaceful coexistence or cold peace. This type of peace refers to a prolonged absence of active hostility among states that are, however, so suspicious and dissatisfied with each other that they continuously engage in hostile activities short of actual war. A variant of peace by equilibrium is peace by terror or impotence.

> The combined progress of techniques of production and destruction introduces a principle of peace, different from power, which usage has already been baptized. Peace by terror is that peace which reigns (or would range) between political units each of which has (or would have) the capacity to deal mortal blows to the other. In this sense, peace by terror could also be described as peace by impotence (Aron 1966: 159).

The second form of peace based on power is peace by hegemony. In this case the asymmetry between the parties is such that "the unsatisfied states despair of modifying the status quo, and yet the hegemony state does not try to absorb the units reduced to impotence. It does not abuse the hegemony, it respects external forms of state-independence, it does not aspire to empire" (Aron 1966: 151). This form of peace is also very much alive and part of the present state of international relations. The third kind of peace based upon power is imperial peace. Over the course of human history we found such arrangements as Pax Romana, Pax Brittanica, Pax Germanica, Pax Americana, Pax Russica, and so on. In each of these cases the terms of peace were dictated by the imperial power. The aims of imperial peace were very pungently expressed by Joseph Chamberlain in 1897:

In carrying out this work of civilization we are fulfill-
ing what I believe to be our national mission, and we
are finding scope for the exercise of those faculties
and qualities which have made us a great governing
race. In almost every instance in which the rule of the
queen has been established and the great Pax Britannica
has been enforced, there has come with it greater security to life, and property, and material improvement in
the condition of the bulk of the population (Bennett 1953:
138).

Hitler explained his recipe for peace even more blatantly:

Who really would desire the victory of pacifism in this
world, must work with all his power for the conquest
of the world by the Germans. . . . Actually the paci-
fist humanitarian idea will perhaps be quite good,
when once the master-man has conquered and sub-
jected the world to a degree that makes him the only
master of the world (Kohn 1942: 141-42).

Value of Peace

Here we are looking at the comparative value of peace, defined
as the absence of physical violence. The relevant question is: Does
the author give the highest priority in his value scale to the preservation of life? Deutsch (1972: 9), for example, in a strikingly explicit
statement, affirms the absence of physical violence as the predominant value in international relations since all other values are meaningful only among the living: "There is no pursuit of values among
the dead. If mankind does not survive, discussions about how to
make life freer, nobler, most just, or more aesthetically satisfying,
would become worse than academic." There are, however, other
thinkers about peace who think otherwise. For Karl Jaspers (1976),
freedom has priority, for neo-Marxists, justice, and for classical
peace theorists, the protection of a power position.

Peace as a Normal or Abnormal State
of International Relations

Distinctive beliefs about the nature of international peace are
another source of variation in peace thinking. In his book The
Troubled Partnership, Kissinger (1965: 244) criticizes the belief

held in the United States that peace is natural and crises are caused by personal will and not by objective conditions. Instead he warns that "no idea could be more dangerous than to assume that peace is the normal pattern of relations among states. A power can survive only if it is willing to fight for its interpretation of justice and its conception of vital interests."

Peace as Means or End

For some, peace is considered as a means; for others it is the goal of foreign policy. The conception of peace as a means is clearly illustrated in the following statement by Ben-Gurion in 1936:

An agreement with the Arabs is necessary for us, not in order to create peace in the country. Peace is indeed vital for us. It is not possible to build up a country in a situation of permanent war, but peace for us is a means. The aim is the complete and absolute fulfillment of Zionism. Only for this do we need an agreement (Chomsky (1974: xii).

At the other end of the dimension we find peace conceptualized as the main goal toward which international relations should be directed. The description of the purpose of the United Nations in its Charter (1945) illustrates this approach to peace:

The purposes of the United Nations are . . . to maintain international peace and security, and to that end: to take effective collective measures for the prevention and removal of threats to peace, and for the suppression of acts of aggression or other breaches of peace, and to bring about by peaceful means, and in conformity with the principles of justice and international law, adjustment or settlement of international disputes or situations which might lead to a breach of the peace.

Scope of Peace

This dimension distinguishes different peace concepts in terms of the range of conditions that have to be present in order to define a situation as peaceful. At one end of the scale we would locate the definition of peace as the absence of physical violence, which is sometimes referred to as negative peace. Here peace is defined as the absence of war, and peace policy is aimed at the prevention of wars. Peace seen in this light is primarily concerned with questions of strategy, balance of power, peace keeping, pacification, arms races, formation of alliances, and collective security systems. Research aiming at offering a solution to the problems of war and peace concentrates primarily on the conditions of war, giving only minimal attention to the conditions of peace: "A mentality prevails which tends to neglect the possibility that wars may result, not from factors present in the war situation, but from the absence of factors safeguarding peace" (Levi 1964: 23). A second blinder of the negative peace definition is its built-in conservative bias. Negative peace is the kind of peace that is envisaged by the law-and-order-oriented person (Schmid 1968: 223). As Galtung (1967: 2) has noted, peace research defined solely in terms of negative peace

> will therefore easily be research into the conditions of maintaining power, of freezing the status-quo, of manipulating the underdog so that he does not take up arms against the topdog. This concept of peace will obviously be in the interests of the status-quo powers at the national and international level, and may equally easily become a conservative force in politics.

In summary, we could say that negative peace is a quite narrow definition, treating qualitatively different situations as peaceful as long as no symptoms of physical violence are observed.

At the other end of the scale we find concepts of peace that arose in protest to the confining character of the "negative peace" paradigm. Hveem (1973) distinguishes three schools, each of which proposes an alternative definition of peace. The first school, which he calls "early protest peace research," adds positive peace to the absence of violence as an ingredient of the concept. The term "positive peace" refers to the unification of mankind into a cooperative enterprise on a world scale (Rapoport 1971: 92). In this school of peace thinking, the absence of war still has priority over the positive component of the definition. Military force is still considered the conditio sine qua non for the achievement of positive peace. The primary means advocated for the achievement of positive peace are impartial mediation, nonviolent strategy, peace expertise, and conflict management or resolution. In contrast to the two other concepts that we will discuss below, the term "positive peace" is defined in subjective, rather than in structural, terms. The definition of positive peace as cooperation on a world scale or brotherly harmony of all humankind seems to be devoid of meaning and allows people to endow it with their own subjective values.

A reaction against this subjective character of the concept of peace was crystallized in the "constructivist school of peace" researchers. They defined peace as the absence of physical as well as structural violence. Structural violence refers to a "structure which perpetuates a situation where some members of society are permitted to realize their aspirations at the same time as others are dying from nonexistent health facilities, lack of protein or generally the most basic standards necessary for staying alive" (Hveem 1973: 106). To put it in other terms, structural violence is inequality, in the distribution of power and resources. Therefore, for this school of thought, peace making implies structural transformations, mediation in symmetrical conflicts, and support for the underdogs in asymmetrical conflicts. The supporters of this structural definition of peace are split on two issues: the objects of their primary loyalty and their strategic approach. The "constructivists" take the individual in world society and the victims of violence as their objects of loyalty and nonviolence as their strategy. The "neo-Marxians" take the proletariat of the world as their main object of loyalty and do not see violence as a priori negative. They argue that violence can play a dual role: a reactionary one and a progressive one. That is why Marxists reject all theories or views that categorically repudiate violence: "Marxism recognizes the justification of the use of violence provided such use is relevant to historical progress. At the same time, however, Marxism rejects all theories that overestimate the role of violence in history, notably its sharpest form--war" (Kara 1968: 4-5).

One of the most recent contributions to peace research is characterized by an enlargement of the scope of peace and greater stress on the existence of different international perspectives in peace research. This new strand of research is represented most heavily in the World Order Model Project (Mendlovitz 1975). Participants in the project believe that peace cannot be realized unless improvements are made with respect to poverty, social justice, ecological instability, and alienation or identity crises. Apart from recognizing the mutual impact of these five values, they also stress that the weights attached to these values vary as a function of the social class of the proponent (Mendlovitz 1975: 296). In the growth process of the project, "it became increasingly clear that while peace, in the sense of elimination of international violence, might have a very high priority with individuals in the industrialized sector of the globe, economic well being and social justice received a much higher rating in the third world (Mendlovitz 1975: x). Therefore, instead of defining their object of study as "peace" they chose to inquire into preferred world orders. This concept implies the recognition of multiple values and of the existence of different preferences.

A preferred world order is defined as "the relevant utopia, selected by a proponent because it is most likely to realize his or her goals" (Mendlovitz 1975: xiv).

Peace as a Perpetual Process or as an End State

Peace at one end of the dimension is equated with a relatively well-defined world order. People who subscribe to this kind of peace thinking believe that the realization of a particular world order would bring peace. For them, peace is a specific end state that should be realized. At this end of the dimension we could locate, for example, most of the world government models of world order.

At the other end of the dimension, peace is perceived as a relative concept; not as a particular end state, but as a continuous process. In contrast to the rather static quality of the first peace-research group's definition of peace, the definition of the latter is much more dynamic. For them, the content of peace is always susceptible to change, and its realization is a perpetual task of all the partners involved. They also reject all abstract normative formulas for peace, which they consider to be unrealistic. Instead they recognize the existence of different levels of peace and propose that the achievement of one level generates claims for a new level of peace (t'Hart 1955).

Use or Nonuse of Physical Violence to Achieve Peace

People concerned with the phenomenon of peace can also be distinguished according to their attitude toward the use of violent or nonviolent strategies in its realization. Fanon is an example of a believer in physical violence as necessary to abolish structural violence and bring about peace of mind. He clearly prefers victory to survival and sees violence as a cleansing force: "It frees the native from his inferiority complex and from his despair and inaction; it makes him fearless and restores his self-respect" (Fanon 1968: 94). At the other end of the dimension we find proponents of nonviolence basing their argument on moral grounds, together with nonviolence strategists as, for example, Sharp (1973).

The foregoing set of dimensions does not do justice to all the variations in peace thinking, but it gives us an idea of the pluralistic approaches in the field. The next section will look at some effects of the existence of different conceptions of peace on the state of international relations.

CONCEPTIONS OF PEACE AND
INTERNATIONAL RELATIONS

The impact of different conceptions of peace is clearly indicated by several students of international relations. First, these
conceptions account for the unstable state of the international system. The precariousness of world order is not a mere temporary
de facto failing, but rather follows from divergent conceptions of
that order. Hoffmann (1968: 16) points out clearly that the order of
the world is a product of man's creation, and that "the diversity of
conceptions, that is, of value preferences, concerning the ultimate
directions and purposes accounts for the fragility of our order; and
the existence of common directions accounts for its possibility."
Further, differences in the conceptualization of peace account for
the existence of opposition. The quotation from Mo-ti, a classic
Chinese author, selected by F. Northrop as an epigraph for his
book, The Meeting of East and West (1946), still retains its validity:
"Where standards differ, there will be opposition."

Third, the existence of different ideas about peace and what
constitutes a right world order accounts for the fact that any world
order that is not based on the consensus of all the interested parties
has no insurance for permanence. This is in part due to the various
ideas about what constitutes the right world order (Gadamar 1968:
325). All of these authors agree that some measure of agreement
is a prerequisite for a viable human community. In the absence of
some degree of consensus on what is peaceful and not peaceful, just
and unjust, it is clearly more difficult for countries to coordinate
their plans effectively and insure that mutually beneficial arrangements are maintained.

ADVANTAGES OF A SYSTEMATIC
STUDY OF INTERNATIONAL VALUES

The linkage between the concept of peace or other international
values, such as preferred world order and international relations,
suggests the importance of knowing the precise content of different
conceptions of peace and different visions of a preferred world order.
Let us highlight some advantages for a systematic description of the
content of differing conceptions of peace and their comparative
analysis. (The same considerations apply to the description of different visions of a preferred world order.) First, concepts of
peace can be used as indicators in the study of international relations. Changes of concepts of peace could reflect changes in international relations. We would expect a world where most diplomats

defined peace as the absence of structural and physical violence to be different from one in which peace was predominantly defined as the continuation of struggle by other means. Second, concepts of peace could be used as criteria for the evaluation of the performance of the international systems. A better knowledge of peace thinking in the diplomatic world could help us understand, for example, the different appraisals of the performance of the United Nations, expressed by different countries or groups of countries. A third contribution of conceptual clarification is elimination of the frequent dialog between the deaf in international relations: "Peace is so emotive a term, one which lends itself so easily to political propaganda and abuse, that if it is to be used as a tool in intelligent discussion—especially international discussion—it must be precisely defined" (Howard 1971: 225). Fourth, a clarification and recognition of differences in the operationalization of the value of peace would promote a more pluralistic attitude. "Pluralism encourages both scepticism and innovation and is thus inherently subversive of the taken for granted reality of the traditional status-quo" (Berger and Luckmann 1966: 125). Fifth, a comparative study of peace would enhance the understanding of the phenomenon. The object of thought becomes progressively clearer with the accumulation of different perspectives on it (Mannheim 1936). Sixth, information about differences on the concepts of peace or preferred world order can be used in the assessment of the future of international relations. To determine the feasibility of alternative international or supranational structures, it is useful to know the precise content of different aspirations for the world and the images of the future which they generate. Having highlighted some of the advantages of studying international values, let us now look at how an important group of international actors, the diplomats, operationalize two prime international values: peace and preferred world order.

PEACE AND PREFERRED WORLD ORDER

Data on the conceptions of peace and visions of preferred world order among the diplomats will be presented in four parts: In the first part we shall explore the indicators used by diplomats for assessing the existence of peace in international relations. To that end, we analyzed the diplomat's answers to the following question posed during the interview:

> The term peace is one of the most loosely used terms in international relations; to you personally, what conditions do you think have to be present in order to call

international relations peaceful--or in other words,
what do you consider as indicators of peace?

We will review the answers given by the total sample, and then contrast the indicators of peace used by diplomats from developing and
developed countries. We will focus on differences in the rank-
ordering of the indicators and test the significance of these differences. In the second part we shall turn to the diplomats' views of
peace in the present state of international relations. Analyses are
based on the question:

What are the three or four most important problems in
the world today which cause dissatisfaction and tension,
and are directly or indirectly a threat to peace?

This question was intended to elicit a more concrete definition of
peace, in terms of conditions in the world today, that the diplomats
perceived as inhibitors of the realization of a peaceful world order.
In the third part we shall examine the diplomats' views on the possi-
bilities for peace. We presented the diplomats with a representative
set of peace proposals and asked them to evaluate each in terms of
its importance for international peace and its probability of being
carried out in the short or long term. In contrast to the analysis in
the second part, where we looked at the inhibitors of peace, here
we inquired into the factors the diplomats considered to be conducive
to peace. We will focus first on the results for the total sample and
then contrast the responses of the diplomats from developed and developing countries. Among the variables to be compared are the
rank-ordering of the proposals in terms of importance, the most-
and least-trusted proposals, the level of orientation (global, interregional, intraregional, national, subnational/individual), and the
degree of incongruence between the importance assigned to the proposals and the assessment of the probability of their being realized.
The final set of data is relevant to what we consider to be a necessary condition for the creation of a satisfactory international peace:
namely, a consensus about a preferred world order among all countries. Information about the diplomats' visions of a preferred world
order was evoked by the question:

How would the world you'd like to see for your children differ from that of today, or, how would you
describe your preferred world order?

Some Propositions

In our data we will check the validity of the following six propositions:

Proposition 1: There is no consensus among diplomats on such basic values as peace or preferred world order. In other words, these two values cannot be considered as universal values, at least not at this stage in the history of diplomatic thinking.

Proposition 2: Values held by a particular diplomat are a function of the systemic position of his country. For example, we would expect the "absence of structural violence and the feeling of deprived status or atimia" (Lagos 1963) to be more central in the thinking about peace among diplomats from developing countries than among those from developed countries.

Proposition 3: The gap between the present state of international peace and the ideal state is considerable. Hence we predict a marked difference between the optimal and realistic peace profiles of the diplomats. The term "optimal peace profile" refers to the diplomat's ranking of a set of peace proposals in terms of their importance for the realization of peace; the term "realistic peace profile" refers to the ranking of the same proposals according to whether or not they might be carried out in the long or short term.

Proposition 4. The systemic position of a country does not affect or affects only marginally the assessment of the likelihood of a peace proposal being carried out; it does, however, have an impact on the rank-order of peace proposals in terms of their importance or preference.

Proposition 5. The discrepancy between optimal and realistic peace profiles is greater for diplomats from developing countries than from developed countries. This proposition is based on the following two expectations: that both groups of diplomats will differ less with respect to their assessment of what they can get (realistic peace profile) than in relation to their wants (optimal peace profile), and that diplomats from developing countries will tend to articulate a greater number of wants than diplomats from developed countries.

Proposition 6. Middle-range peace proposals (proposals about changes at the interregional and intraregional level of the international system) tend to be more trusted and hence perceived as operational than proposals at the global or national or subnational levels.

Indicators of Peace

Responses to the question about what the diplomat would consider as indicators of peace--as conditions that must be present if international relations are to be called peaceful--were grouped into meaningful categories in Table 6.1. This table presents the categories into which the indicators were grouped and rank-orders them according to the frequency of responses in each category for the total sample of diplomats.

TABLE 6.1

Indicators of Peace for Total Sample of Diplomats
(frequencies)

Absence of violence	114
International cooperation	47
No domestic interference	37
Absence of structural violence	33
Economic welfare	28
Understanding	26
Respect and dignity	24
Justice	22
Symmetrical relations	22
Detente	21
Military security	21
New economic order	18
Equality	17
Stability and order	15
Dialog	13
Conflict management	13
Friendly relations	13
Arms control and disarmament	11
Existence of common interests	10
Pluralism	9
Empathy	9
Freedom	9
Integration	9
International law	5
Ecology	2

Source: Compiled by the author from his own research.

The predominant indicator of peace was, not unexpectedly, the absence of violence. It topped the list of the total sample and of the two subsamples. A t-test for the significance of the difference between the means on this indicator for the two groups of diplomats yields a t-value of 2.07 (p < .02). This finding suggests that, despite the fact that the absence of violence is most salient for both groups, on a comparative basis it is significantly more salient for diplomats from developed than for those from developing countries. We would also expect diplomats from those countries to place greater emphasis on "stability and order" among their indicators of peace, along with the absence of violence. As Johan Galtung (1967: 2) has noted: "This concept of peace will obviously be in the interests of the status-quo power at the national and the international levels, and may equally easily become a conservative force in politics." This expectation was corroborated by the finding that the stability and order indicator ranks third among indicators for the developed countries and is not among the top ten indicators for developing countries. A t-test for the means of this indicator yields a t-value of 1.74 (p < .05), indicating a significantly higher salience of this indicator for diplomats from developed than from developing countries.

The second-ranking indicator for the total sample of diplomats was international cooperation. All responses that referred explicitly to cooperation or coordination in different areas were placed in this category. This indicator ranks high for both groups of diplomats--in second place for developed, and in fourth place for developing countries. Further, the difference between the two groups, although large, falls short of significance. This finding indicates that diplomats from both developing and developed countries perceive the existence of patterns of cooperation as important indicators of peace. The meaning of the international cooperation indicator is less clear than the meaning of the absence of violence or stability and order indicators, because we lack information about the terms of cooperation. However, we could say that this indicator enriches the definition of peace of the diplomats by adding a component that is positively valued by all.

The indicator on which the diplomats from developing and developed countries differ most significantly is called absence of structural violence. Examples of responses that were so categorized are peace is the absence of exploitation, economic imperialism, colonialism, imperialistic and hegemonistic attitudes, or a dominated race in the world. All of these statements explicitly affirm a negative association between the existence of an exploitative hierarchical structure and peace. What distinguishes diplomats from developing countries most from their colleagues from developed countries is the high saliency of the absence of structural violence indicator.

The t-test between the means of the two groups yields the highest t-value (see Table 6.2), with a significance level of less than .005. Further, the absence of structural violence indicator ranks second in the list for developing countries and is not among the top ten indicators for developed countries. This implies that a world with built-in structural violence, but also characterized by absence of physical violence and by cooperation, would be perceived as less peaceful by diplomats from developing countries than their colleagues from better-off countries.

Consistent with the high ranking of the absence of structural violence (2nd) by diplomats from developing countries is the almost equally high saliency of no domestic interference for them (rank 3). Comparison of the means for developed and developing countries yields a t-value of -1.78 (p < .05). To clarify the meaning of no domestic interference, let us illustrate some of the responses that were placed in this category. The included statements that peace means noninterference in internal affairs of countries; respect for sovereignty; self-determination; abstaining from criticizing the internal policy of other countries; and live and let live. The high saliency of this indicator among diplomats from developing countries could be explained by their greater sensitivity to and dissatisfaction with the experience of being asymmetrically penetrated. "Center countries are comparatively better off than periphery nations in avoiding strong asymmetric penetration" (Hveem 1972: 72).

Having highlighted some of the most important indicators of peace, let us now quickly look at the other indicators and their similarities or differences in saliency among the two subsamples of diplomats. In the top-ten list of both subsamples we find four indicators which show only nonsignificant differences: justice, economic welfare, understanding, and symmetrical relations. The meanings of the first three are self-evident. The fourth, symmetrical relations, refers to all the responses of diplomats which stressed mutuality and equilibrium as distinct qualities of international peace. Although the means of these four indicators are not significantly different, we notice that they are consistently higher for the developing countries, which would suggest that these indicators are relatively more important for diplomats from this group of countries. The two items on the list for developed countries that do not appear on the other list are military security and dialog. Despite their inclusion in this top-ten list, their means do not differ significantly from the means of the same indicators for developing countries. Therefore we would tend not to consider them as sources of variation among diplomats in their assessment of the peacefulness of the international environment. The two indicators on the list of diplomats from developing countries that do not appear on the previous list are respect

TABLE 6.2

Indicators of Peace for Diplomats from Developed and Developing Countries

	Means*			Means*
Developed countries, N = 102 (≥ 8)		Developing countries, N = 117 ($<$ 8)		
1 Absence of violence	.529	1	Absence of violence	.367
2 International cooperation	.254	2	Absence of structural	
3 Stability and order	.098		violence	.162
4 Justice	.078	3	No domestic interference	.153
7 No domestic interference	.068	4	International cooperation	.136
7 Economic welfare	.068	5	Economic welfare	.128
7 Understanding	.068	6	Symmetrical relations	.119
7 Symmetrical relations	.068	7.5	Understanding	.111
7 Military security	.068	7.5	Respect and dignity	.111
10 Dialog	.058	9.5	Justice	.102
		9.5	Equality	.102

Developed versus developing countries		p-value
	t-value	$<$
1 Absence of structural violence	-2.99	.005
2 Absence of violence	2.07	.02
3 Friendly relations	-2.02	.02
4 Respect and dignity	-1.82	.05
5 No domestic interference	-1.78	.05
6 Stability and order	1.74	.05
7 New economic order	-1.66	.05
8 Freedom	-1.64	.05
9 Equality	-1.58	.10
10 Empathy	-1.56	.10

*Obtained by dividing the total number of responses provided by the diplomats from each type of country by the number of diplomats in the sub-sample.

Note: In the interpretation of all scores arrived at by means of content analysis based on mention versus nonmention (rather than intensity of mention) as measures of saliency of the measured object in the minds of diplomats, I invite the reader to join me in exercising reasonable caution. The difference between the scores of the diplomats from developed and developing countries may have been influenced by the fact that the latter group tended to talk more so that the theme was more likely to emerge. The data are not controlled for this factor.

Source: Compiled by the author from his own research.

and dignity and equality. The saliency of the respect and dignity indicator is significantly higher for diplomats from developing countries than for their colleagues from developed countries (t = -1.82, p < .05). The mean of the equality indicator, though not significantly different, is clearly higher and therefore suggests that diplomats from developing countries also assign a greater importance to this indicator. Not included in either top-ten list but clearly different are the friendly relations, freedom, and empathy indicators. The first two are significantly more salient for diplomats from developing countries.

What do these results tell us? They illustrate without doubt that diplomats have different "sets of indicators" for assessing the degree of peacefulness of international relations, depending on the systemic position of their countries. This means that different appraisals of the degree of peacefulness of a particular international situation are probably based on the use of different sets of indicators; and similar appraisals could be based on the use of different or similar sets of indicators. Our understanding of the perceived peacefulness of the world should become clearer when the existence of different sets of indicators is taken into account.

Inhibitors of Peace

We now turn to some of the conditions in the world today that the diplomats consider to be antagonistic to peace. As mentioned earlier, the data for this analysis are derived from responses to the following question:

> Looking at the world today, what are the three or
> four most important problems which cause dissatis-
> faction and tension, and are directly or indirectly a
> threat to peace?

As in the case of the indicators of peace, we listed all the answers and grouped them into meaningful categories. An overview of these categories for the total sample of diplomats can be found in Table 6.3, and all the data that we will use for contrasting diplomats from developed and developing countries are presented in Table 6.4. For diplomats from both developing and developed countries, the Middle East conflict is perceived as the condition most antagonistic to peace. This could be explained by the fact that the Middle East is seen by most diplomats as the cockpit for multiple competitions between the superpowers, North and South, different races, Eastern and Western cultures, and different religions. The second condition

TABLE 6.3

Sources of Dissatisfaction and Direct or Indirect Threats
to International Peace for the Total Sample
(frequencies)

Middle East conflict	76
North-South polarization	60
Structural violence	40
Energy problem	35
Domestic and regional interference	34
State of the international economic system	33
Big-power relations	33
Unequal distribution of wealth	33
Racism and discrimination	30
Economic conditions	29
Food crisis	27
Ideological approach in foreign politics	26
Population growth	20
Limits of growth	20
Nationalism	20
Economic development	19
Cultural conflicts	18
Detente	18
Cyprus	18
East-West relations	17
Misperception	16
Relations between communism and capitalism	16
Expansionism	15
South Africa	14
Southeast Asia	13
Power politics	11
Communication problems	10
China-Soviet Union	10
Boundary conflicts	10
Internal problems	9
Balance of power	8
Inadequate adaptation to new realities	8

Source: Compiled by the author from his own research.

TABLE 6.4

Sources of Dissatisfaction and Direct or Indirect Threats
to International Peace for Diplomats from Developed
and Developing Countries

		Mean
Developed countries (≥ 8)		
1	Middle East conflict	.323
2	North-South relations	.225
3	Energy problem	.186
4	Big-power relations	.127
6	Unequal distribution of wealth	.107
6	Nationalism	.107
6	East-West relations	.107
9	Economic conditions	.102
9	Food crisis	.102
9	Detente	.102
Developing countries (< 8)		
1	Middle East conflict	.282
2	Structural violence	.239
3	North-South relations	.230
4	State of the international economic system	.213
5	Domestic and regional interference	.170
6	Economic conditions	.145
7.5	Big-power relations	.128
7.5	Unequal distribution of wealth	.128
9.5	Racism and discrimination	.119
9.5	Food crisis	.119

Developed versus developing countries	t-value	p-value $<$
1 State of the international economic system	-4.09	.005
2 Structural violence	-2.79	.005
3 China-Soviet Union	2.49	.01
4 Economic development	-2.43	.01
5 Cultural conflicts	-2.05	.02
6 Domestic and regional interference	-2.00	.02
7 East-West relations	1.80	.05
8 Misperception	1.73	.05

Source: Compiled by the author from his own research.

that is perceived as a source of dissatisfaction and tension is North-South relations. The frequency with which this problem is mentioned is similar for both developing and developed countries. The reasons for the dissatisfaction expressed by the two groups of diplomats are, however, different. From several interviews I could infer that in addition to humanitarian considerations, the basic reason for the dissatisfaction of the Western developed countries was the impact of the North-South conflict on the energy market and the consequent economic and financial problems.

This serious concern with the energy crisis is reflected in the high ranking of this problem in the list of diplomats from developed countries. On the other hand, for diplomats from developing countries, the North-South conflict is perceived as antagonistic because of its association with structural violence, domestic and regional interference, the unbalanced state of the international economic system, and their general dissatisfaction with their economic condition and state of development--problems that are most salient for diplomats from developing countries. Structural violence, the unbalanced state of the international economic system, and domestic and regional interference all appear in the top-ten list for diplomats from developing countries; their means are also significantly different from those of the diplomats from developed countries.

I will clarify the meaning of each of these categories by specifying which responses they include. All statements that explicitly disapprove of economic imperialism, penetration, intervention, colonization, or a system of domination with controllers and controlled were classified as structural violence. Under the "unbalanced state of the international economic system" category, we grouped such problems as inequitable terms of commerce and trade, artificial barriers for free exchange of goods, unfair prices for commodities, cartels formed to control exports, biased market, degradation of the terms of exchange, the impact of economic difficulties experienced by industrialized countries in their economic relations with developing countries, and so on. The category of "domestic and regional interference" includes all statements that explicitly mentioned domestic or regional interference as a threat to international peace. The dissatisfaction of diplomats from developing countries with their state of economic development, although it does not appear in their top-ten list, has a mean of .111, which is significantly higher than for diplomats from developed countries ($t = -2.43$, $p < .01$).

Having highlighted some of the most important conditions that are perceived as antagonistic to international peace, let us now quickly look at the other problems mentioned by one or both groups of diplomats. In the top-ten lists of both subsamples of diplomats, we find three problems that are more or less equally salient for both: big-power relations, unequal distribution of wealth, and food crisis. The meaning of the last two problems is self-evident, but the problem of big-power relations requires some clarification. This problem refers essentially to relations between the Soviet Union and the United States, especially as they affect the security of the world, the evolution of conflicts in their spheres of influence, and also the impact of these relations on the economic life of the Third World countries.

The four problems on the list of diplomats from developed countries that do not appear on the other list are energy, nationalism, East-West relations, and detente. With respect to these problems, the means for diplomats from developed countries are higher than those for their colleagues from developing countries. Only one, however, is significantly different: that for East-West relations ($t = 1.80$, $p < .05$). The only other problem on the list of diplomats from developing countries that does not appear on the list for the developed-country diplomats, and has not already been mentioned, is racism and discrimination. Some of the specific points mentioned by diplomats which were placed in this category are: the joke of ethnic superiority; the white domination in Africa; pockets of racism; the great unsolved problem of China and the Soviet Union, wherein racism is very strong; the education of antisemitism; and institutional racism. The mean for this problem is clearly higher for diplomats from developing countries, although it falls short of statistical significance. The trend suggests greater saliency of this problem for diplomats from those countries. Not included in either top-ten list, but significantly different for the two groups, are the China-Soviet Union, misperception, and cultural conflict problems. The first two problems are much more salient for diplomats from developed countries; the last problem, however, is more salient for developing countries. The meaning of the misperception problem can best be communicated by listing some of the points mentioned by the diplomats that were placed in this category: the misperceptions between the two superpowers and, in consequence, possible miscalculations; the yes-no thinking of the military; the distorted newsreels about the Middle East; the gap in international understanding; the tendency to infer, for example, from the knowledge of a person the character of a whole people; the frictions caused by cultural misconceptions; the existence of indoctrination; the myth of oil money; the tendency to deny real problems; and the misperception by leftists of communist dictatorships. The dissatisfaction of diplomats from developing countries with the state of cultural relations was indicated through their comments about issues such as cultural imperialism, cultural revolution, cultural rigidity, cultural gap, cultural condescension, and inability to communicate cross-culturally.

What do these results tell us about conditions antagonistic to peace? We have noticed a consensus among all diplomats about the antagonistic impact on peace of the Middle East conflict, the North-South polarization, big-power rivalry, unequal distribution of wealth, economic conditions, and the food crisis. In contrast to this consensus, we also find some significant differences, especially with respect to the conditions of the international economic system. For example, for developing countries, the dissatisfaction with their position in what we could call "the global dominance system" is very prominent. This and other differences in the perception of conditions antagonistic to international peace add support to the proposition that diplomatic thinking, here specifically with respect to the issue of peace, is a function of the international position of the diplomat's country.

Conditions for Peace

The third aspect of thinking about peace is the diplomat's peace profile. The questions and the conceptual framework for analysis were adapted from Hveem (1968), who used them in a comparative study of foreign-policy thinking in Norway. The diplomats' peace profiles could be operationalized as their responses to a set of stimuli which represent concrete peace proposals. The set of proposals can be found in Appendix D. It consists of 24 items, 16 of which were taken from Hveem. The list contains a representative sample of important and relevant peace proposals that have been put forward. In Table 6.5, the numbers at the left indicate the order in which the proposals were presented to the respondents; these numbers will later be used to represent the particular proposal. The proposals are ranked according to the degree of favorable responses elicited from the total sample of diplomats, that is, according to their assigned importance. This ranking gives us an idea of the ideal conditions for peace as seen by the diplomats, which will be called their optimal peace profile. To permit examination of differences in peace profiles as a function of the position of the diplomat's country, Table 6.6 presents the profiles of diplomats from developed and developing countries. Significant differences in the judgments of these two groups are listed in Table 6.7. Let us first look at the peace profile of the total sample of diplomats. It is fair to consider the proposals that received a mean of 4 or higher on a 0-5 scale as the main ingredients of an "ideal" world. Thus, an ideal world is one without poverty, with general and complete disarmament, with reduced tension between East and West, and with a stronger United Nations, and, finally, one in which the individual is considered a relevant unit of concern in the building and preservation of peace. In contrast to these ingredients of an optimal international peace, we find at the bottom of the list a cluster of items which are perceived as not important to or even inhibiting the achievement of international peace in the short and long term. Seven items received a mean judgment below 3. Most of these items (17, 11, 14, 7, 10, 21, 24) reflect the perception of the diplomats that diminution of the nation-state's internal and external control would have minimal or even negative consequences for international peace.

Table 6.6 shows to what extent this general profile reflects the preferences of diplomats from developed and developing countries. If we focus on the top five proposals for each group, we find that both groups included items 2, 9, and 12 in this list. However, the importance of each of the three items was stressed more by diplomats from developing than from developed countries. As can be seen in Table 6.7, the means on these three items were significantly higher for diplomats from developing countries. These proposals refer to the alleviation of the poverty problem and the improvement of communication between countries. Two proposals rank among the top five for diplomats from developed countries only, but the means of the two groups are not significantly different. These items refer to the improvement of detente and cooperation. On the other hand, the two proposals that rank among the top five only for the diplomats from developing countries do show significant differences: strengthening the United Nations ($t = -5.22$, $p < .005$), and general and complete disarmament ($t = -4.77$, $p < .005$).

Let us now focus on the five lowest-ranked proposals, which the diplomats consider to have a minimal or negative effect on the realization of international peace. Diplomats of both groups agree in their negative appraisal of four items: 7, 21, 11, and 17. There is no significant difference between the two groups of diplomats with respect to their negative appraisals of the establishment of a world government or the idea of one-nation one-state. The idea that nations should become more similar and that the world should consist of small self-sufficient states received significantly more negative judgments from diplomats from developed countries ($t = -2.08$, $p < .02$, and $t = -3.12$, $p < .005$). One proposal which appears among the five lowest items only for the diplomats from developed countries refers to the increase of socialism in the world. In contrast to diplomats from developed countries, their colleagues from developing countries, although they also rank this item quite low, consider it significantly more positive ($t = -1.92$, $p < .05$). One proposal which appears only in the bottom-five list for diplomats from developing countries refers to the preservation of military alliances. In contrast to their colleagues from developed countries,

TABLE 6.5

The Optimal Peace Profile of the Diplomats
(percentage distribution of responses to 24 peace proposals, N = 200)

Proposal Item Number	Proposal	Especially Important to Peace	Somewhat Important to Peace	Unimportant to Peace.	Against Peace	Other	Mean
2	Abolish hunger and poverty in the world	76.6	19.9	2.5	0.0	1.0	4.4
13	General and complete disarmament must be realized	69.9	16.6	9.3	3.1	1.0	4.1
18	Western and Eastern countries must improve detente	64.6	28.8	4.5	0.5	1.5	4.2
9	More effective communication is necessary	64.3	31.2	1.5	2.0	2.0	4.1
1	The individual person must be educated to peace	64.0	26.0	7.5	1.0	1.5	4.1
19	We must strengthen the United Nations	62.9	28.4	7.6	0.5	0.5	4.0
12	Rich countries must give aid to the poor	60.7	34.7	3.1	0.0	1.5	4.1
23	States that naturally belong together must cooperate	50.6	42.1	5.1	1.1	1.1	3.8
22	Ideological disputes ought to be diminished	45.5	40.1	13.4	0.5	0.5	3.6
3	Relations between individuals must be more peaceful	45.5	33.3	19.2	0.0	2.0	3.5
8	Population growth must be controlled	43.1	37.1	16.2	2.0	1.5	3.4

16	There must be a military balance between states so that nobody dares to attack	40.8	36.7	9.2	12.8	0.5	3.2
6	We must strengthen regional organizations	40.1	45.7	12.2	0.0	2.0	3.5
5	The states must be more democratic	40.1	31.0	26.9	0.0	2.0	3.2
20	National boundaries ought to become more open	38.3	40.8	16.3	2.0	2.5	3.3
15	Free trade must be established between all countries	35.5	48.6	11.2	3.7	0.9	3.3
4	The small countries must have greater influence	33.7	45.1	16.6	3.1	1.5	3.2
24	Restrictions to migration should be gradually lifted	27.3	34.1	31.8	6.8	0.0	2.7
21	Each national group should be given its own country	19.3	27.3	23.0	29.4	1.1	2.0
10	The military alliances must be preserved	18.8	35.4	17.2	28.6	0.0	2.1
7	A world government must be established	18.4	23.8	46.5	10.3	1.0	2.1
14	Countries must become more socialistic	14.4	33.7	46.2	4.8	1.0	2.2
11	The nations must become more similar	12.7	27.5	48.1	11.1	0.5	1.9
17	One should create a world with small self-sufficient states	12.7	20.6	45.1	20.6	1.0	1.7

Source: Compiled by the author from his own research.

137

TABLE 6.6

Conditions for Peace, Ranked by Importance, as Judged by Diplomats
from Developed and Developing Countries
(mean judgments of importance, ranked for each group)

Proposal Item Number	Proposal		Developed Countries		Developing Countries
18	Western and Eastern countries must improve detente	(1)	4.25	(7)	4.09
2	Abolish hunger and poverty in the world	(2)	4.16	(1)	4.80
9	More effective communication is necessary	(3)	3.91	(5)	4.36
12	Rich countries must give aid to the poor	(4)	3.89	(4)	4.36
23	States that naturally belong together must cooperate	(5)	3.87	(8)	3.95
1	The individual person must be educated to peace	(6)	3.86	(6)	4.25
8	Population growth must be controlled	(7)	3.78	(13).	3.41
16	There must be a military balance between states, so that nobody dares to attack	(8)	3.63	(17)	3.06
13	General and complete disarmament must be realized	(9)	3.61	(2)	4.62
19	We must strengthen the United Nations	(10)	3.51	(3)	4.51)
22	Ideological disputes ought to be diminished	(11)	3.43	(10)	3.81
20	National boundaries ought to become more open	(12)	3.36	(16)	3.39
6	We must strengthen regional organizations	(13)	3.29	(11)	3.74
15	Free trade must be established between all countries	(14)	3.22	(15)	3.39
24	Restrictions to migration should be gradually lifted	(15)	3.16	(18)	3.05
5	The states must be more democratic	(16)	3.13	(14)	3.40
3	Relations between individuals must become more peaceful	(17)	2.96	(9)	3.93
10	The military alliances must be preserved	(18)	2.80	(24)	1.67
4	The small countries must have greater influence	(19)	2.75	(12)	3.62
7	A world government must be established	(20)	1.92	(22)	2.34
14	Countries must become more socialistic	(21)	1.90	(19)	2.58
21	Each national group should be given its own country	(22)	1.81	(21)	2.27
11	The nations must become more similar	(23)	1.78	(20)	2.28
17	One should create a world with small self-sufficient states	(24)	1.06	(23)	2.06

Source: Compiled by the author from his own research.

they perceive the existence of military alliances or blocs as con-
tributing significantly less to peace ($t = 4.15$, $p < .005$).

TABLE 6.7

Significant Differences between Diplomats from Developed
and Developing Countries in Their Judgments
of Conditions for Peace
(t-tests between means)

Proposal Item Number	Proposal	t-value	p-value $<$
19	We must strengthen the United Nations	−5.22	.005
13	General and complete disarmament must be realized	−4.77	.005
2	Abolish hunger and poverty in the world	−4.54	.005
3	Relations between individuals must become more peaceful	−4.37	.005
10	The military alliances must be preserved	4.15	.005
4	The small countries must have greater influence	−3.88	.005
17	One should create a world with small self-sufficient states	−3.12	.005
12	Rich countries must give aid to the poor	−2.79	.005
9	More effective communication is necessary	−2.44	.01
19	We must strengthen regional organizations	−2.19	.02
16	There must be a military balance	2.16	.02
11	The nations must become more similar	−2.08	.02
1	The individual person must be educated to peace	−1.93	.05
14	Countries must become more socialistic	−1.92	.05
22	Ideological disputes ought to be diminished	−1.67	.05

Source: Compiled by the author from his own research.

Finally, let us briefly look at some other proposals on which the two groups differ significantly. The diplomats from developing countries assign significantly greater importance to items 3, 4, 6, 1, and 22. An increase in the power of small countries (4) and the strengthening of regional organizations (6) are considered significantly more important by developing than developed countries. Further, items 3, 1, and 22 suggest that diplomats from developing countries are more inclined to approve "soft proposals" than their colleagues from developed countries. This conclusion is supported by the finding that developed countries are significantly higher on two typical hard proposals: 10 and 16. For developed countries the existence of a military balance (16) and the preservation of military alliances (10) are considered as significantly more positive conditions ($t = 2.16$, $p \lessgtr .02$, and $t = 4.15$, $p < .005$).

How can we interpret these findings on diplomats' optimal peace profiles? Although I will consider the optimal peace profile as a reflection of the real preferences of the diplomats, I do so with some reservation. Instead of expressing preferences that are really felt, their judgments may be part of the diplomats' effort at impression-management. As one diplomat strikingly pointed out: "Most people will favor democracy, but for some it barely covers their acceptance of the right to die of hunger, or their preference for the perfect peace as in Greece's slave democracy." Despite the possible intrusion of lip service, we had the feeling that most of the diplomats who made personal comments about the questionnaire or filled it out in my presence expressed their real personal preferences. But even if the optimal peace profiles express real personal preferences, they are not necessarily indicative of real policy preferences. According to Hveem, proposals have to pass through a filtering process before becoming policy. "One such filter is the respondent's perception of how the real world meets the ideal proposals and makes them realistic-applicable or workable--or not" (Hveem 1968: 151). To assess the effect of the real-world filter in the process, we asked the diplomats if they believed that the respective proposals for international peace were likely to be realized, moderately likely to be realized, or unlikely to be realized in the short or long term. The results for the total sample and our subsamples of diplomats from developing and developed countries are presented in Table 6.8. If we focus first on the bottom-five items, we see that the same items appear on the lists for the total sample and the two subsamples. This means that there is general consensus that the following five proposals are most unlikely to be realized: one should try to create a world with small self-sufficient states, general and complete disarmament must be realized, each national group should be given its own country, the nations must become more similar, and a world

TABLE 6.8

Conditions for Peace, Ranked by Realism, as Judged by Diplomats
from Developed and Developing Countries
(mean judgments of realism, ranked for each group on a 1-5 scale)

Proposal Item Number	Proposal	Total		Developed Countries		Developing Countries
10	The military alliances must be preserved	3.5	(1)	3.7	(4)	3.4
18	Western and Eastern countries must improve detente	3.3	(4)	3.4	(5)	3.2
6	We must strengthen regional organizations	3.3		3.1	(3)	3.4
23	States that naturally belong together must cooperate	3.3	(5)	3.3	(2)	3.4
9	More effective communication is necessary	3.2	(3)	3.4	(1)	3.6
24	Restrictions to migration should be gradually lifted	3.1		4.3		2.6
12	Rich countries must give aid to the poor	3.0		3.2		2.9
1	The individual person must be educated to peace	2.9		2.2		2.3
16	There must be a military balance between states so that nobody dares to attack	2.7	(2)	3.5		2.3
19	We must strengthen the United Nations	2.6		2.4		2.7
14	Countries must become more socialistic	2.6		2.9		2.6
8	Population growth must be controlled	2.5		2.4		2.8
3	Relations between individuals must become more peaceful	2.4		2.2		2.7
15	Free trade must be established	2.4		2.8		2.3
4	The small countries must have greater influence	2.4		2.3		2.6
20	National boundaries ought to become more open	2.3		2.5		2.2
2	Abolish hunger and poverty in the world	2.2		2.9		3.0
5	The states must be more democratic	2.0		1.9		2.2
22	Ideological disputes ought to be diminished	1.9		1.9		2.0
17	One should create a world with small self-sufficient states	1.6	(20.5)	1.7	(20.5)	1.6
13	General and complete disarmament must be realized	1.5	(23)	1.3	(22)	1.5
21	Each national group should be given its own country	1.5	(22)	1.5	(20.5)	1.6
11	The nations must become more similar	1.5	(20.5)	1.7	(23)	1.4
7	A world government must be established	1.1	(24)	1.1	(24)	1.2
	Average			2.4		2.4

Source: Compiled by the author from his own research.

government must be established as soon as possible. Supporting the conclusion that there is consensus about the five unrealistic proposals is the fact that no significant differences were found between diplomats from developed and developing countries on these items.

We also find a rather high consensus on the five most realistic proposals among the two groups. Four proposals appear among the top five for both (10, 23, 18, and 6). There are also no significant differences between the means on these four items. These results indicate that there is a high consensus that the following four proposals are realistic: military alliances must be preserved, Western and Eastern countries must improve detente, states who naturally belong together must cooperate, and more effective communication is necessary.

One proposal that ranks second in the list for developed countries and does not appear on the other list refers to the existence of a military balance as a precondition for peace. A strong significant difference is found between the means of the two groups on this proposal ($t = 5.48$, $p < .005$), indicating that diplomats from developed countries attribute greater realism to this proposal. The item that ranks third in the list for the developing countries, and does not appear on the other list, is concerned with strengthening regional organizations as a means toward peace. The mean of this item is somewhat greater for developing than developed countries, suggesting that they consider this proposal more likely to be realized than their colleagues from developed countries.

Let us now look briefly at the other proposals in which the two groups differ significantly (see Table 6.9). We find one additional item to which the diplomats from developed countries assign a greater likelihood of being realized: national boundaries ought to be more open. On the other hand, diplomats from developing countries are significantly higher on items 2, 3, 5, and 8. For them, the abolition of hunger and poverty, the control of population growth, the realization of more peaceful relations between individuals, and the increased democratization of states are proposals whose realization they perceive as more probable than do their colleagues from developed countries.

Comparison of the results of the two groups of diplomats indicates clearly a relatively high degree of consensus among them in their assessments of the realism of the peace proposals. This conclusion is further supported by the greater consensus in the attribution of realism than in the attribution of importance; whereas we found 15 significant differences for the latter, there were only 6 for the former. After examining the two profiles separately, we combined them to construct the operational peace profile of diplomats. We did this by bringing together the two dimensions--importance and

TABLE 6.9

Significant Differences between Diplomats from Developed
and Developing Countries in Their Attribution of
Realism to Conditions for Peace
(t-tests between means)

Proposal Item Number	Proposal	t-value	p-value <
16	The military balances must be preserved	5.48	.005
2	Abolish hunger and poverty in the world	-2.67	.01
3	Relations between individuals must become more peaceful	-2.50	.01
8	Population growth must be controlled	-2.11	.02
20	National boundaries ought to become more open	1.77	.05
5	The states must become more democratic	-1.72	.05

Source: Compiled by the author from his own research.

perception of realism--in one matrix, where the horizontal coordinate represents realism and the vertical coordinate the importance
assigned to the proposals. We entered the means of each single proposal on each of the two coordinates and plotted one point for each
proposal. An overview of the results for the total sample can be
found in Figure 6.1. To separate different clusters, we can distinguish three levels on each coordinate of the matrix: high, medium,
and low. This gives us nine groups of proposals:

High/high	18, 9, 23
Medium/high	6
Medium/medium	20, 4, 3, 8, 15, 16
High/medium	2, 19, 1, 12
Low/high	24, 10
Low/medium	14
Low/low	7, 21, 11, 17
Medium/low	5, 22
High/low	13

The broken lines in the figure indicate the cuts between the three
levels mentioned; the ranges of the levels are somewhat larger on

FIGURE 6.1

Operational Peace Profile for the Total Sample of Diplomats
(means)

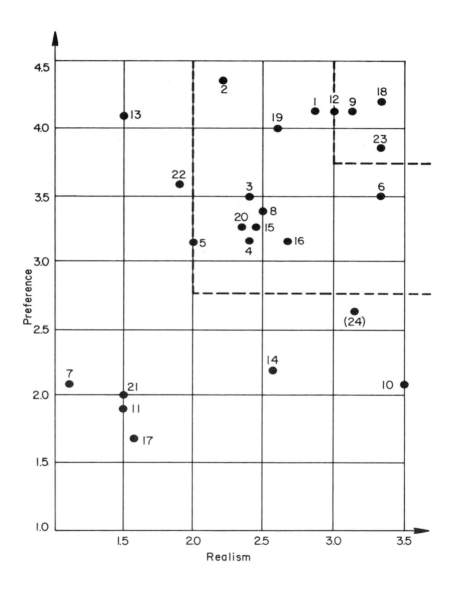

Source: Compiled by the author from his own research.

the "importance" coordinate because of the higher average means on that dimension. The cuts were made visually, to correspond to clustering patterns. For comparative purposes, we also constructed two separate matrixes, one for diplomats from developed countries and one for diplomats from developing countries (see Figures 6.2 and 6.3).

Figures 6.1, 6.2, and 6.3 show that on several items the differences between the degree of importance and the degree of perceived realism are considerable. This finding answers the question about the relation between realism and aspiration in the respondents' thinking.

Another test of this difference is the Pearson correlation coefficient. Scores on the importance and realism dimensions for the total sample yield an average correlation of .27, which supports the conclusion that the aspiration-realism difference is considerable. An overview of the correlation coefficients, item by item, for the total sample and the subsamples of diplomats can be found in Table 6.10. If we compare the correlations of diplomats from developed and developing countries we see that the latter are generally smaller. The average r for developed countries is .32; for the developing countries .22. This indicates that there is a greater convergence between aspirations and realistic expectations in the peace profiles of diplomats from developed countries than among their colleagues from developing countries. Several explanations could be given for this dissonance in the views about peace. One explanation is that the aspirations of these diplomats are in fact higher than the aspirations of their colleagues from developed countries. They see most of the proposals as more congruent with their national interests, as reflected in their optimal peace profiles, than do the diplomats from developed countries. Diplomats from developing countries assigned significantly greater importance than their colleagues from developed countries to 13 of the proposals, while the latter assigned significantly greater importance to only two proposals (see Table 6.7). These data indicate that, given the higher aspirations, the same level of realism would yield larger discrepancies. Another possible explanation is that diplomats from developing countries compensate the power of word politics for their lower real-power position. In other words, they believe more than their colleagues that rhetoric can make a difference in international affairs. This greater belief in word politics, expressed in a tendency to accentuate aspirations more strongly, could account for the greater discrepancy found in developing countries.

Another expression of the discrepancy between aspirations and realistic expectation is the level of trust or distrust in the different proposals. The measure of trust is the mean difference between

FIGURE 6.2

Operational Peace Profile for the Diplomats
from Developed Countries
(means)

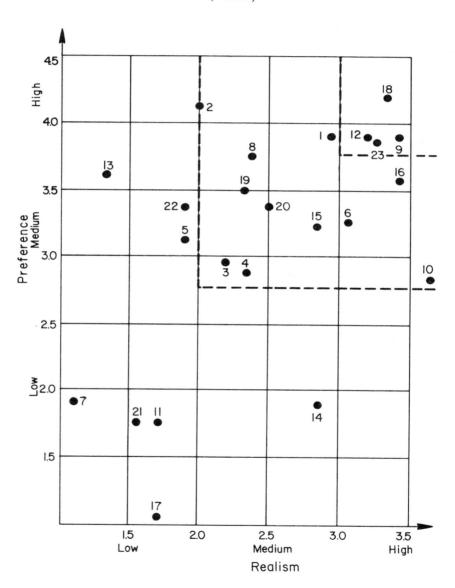

FIGURE 6.3

Operational Peace Profile for the Diplomats
from Developing Countries
(means)

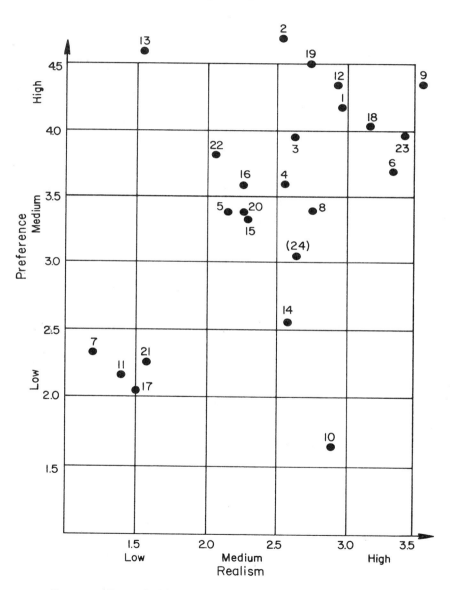

Source: Compiled by the author from his own research.

TABLE 6.10

Pearson Correlations between the Importance and Realism Scores of
Each Condition for Peace for Diplomats from Developed and Developing Countries

Proposal Item Number	Proposal	Total	Developed Countries	Developing Countries
1	The individual person must be educated to peace	.21	.31	.06
19	We must strengthen the United Nations	.40	.58	.12
10	The military alliances must be preserved	.28	.29	.24
2	Abolish hunger and poverty in the world	.21	.24	.07
15	Free trade must be established between all countries	.33	.29	.39
21	Each national group should be given its own country	.47	.45	.50
22	Ideological disputes ought to be diminished	.16	.12	.19
8	Population growth must be controlled	.02	.05	.00
9	More effective communication is necessary	.19	.17	.19
7	A world government must be established	.34	.41	.30
11	The nations must become more similar	.21	.33	.15
12	Rich countries must give aid to the poor	.01	.14	.08
3	Relations between individuals must become more peaceful	.34	.51	.08
4	The small countries must have greater influence	.36	.43	.25
5	The states must be more democratic	.27	.33	.21
6	We must strengthen regional organizations	.40	.40	.40
13	General and complete disarmament must be realized	.17	.22	.10
14	Countries must become more socialistic	.25	.24	.31
16	There must be a military balance between states, so that nobody dares to attack	.32	.44	.13
17	One should create a world with small self-sufficient states	.46	.39	.52
18	Western and Eastern countries must improve detente	.27	.25	.27
20	National boundaries ought to become more open	.26	.29	.23
23	States that naturally belong together must cooperate	.21	.25	.17
24	Restrictions to migration should be gradually lifted	.16	.45	.25
	Average correlation	.27	.32	.22

Source: Compiled by the author from his own research.

perceived realism and importance, as shown in Table 6.11, which presents the trust status of all proposals, ranked from most to least trusted, for the total sample and the two subsamples. A highly preferred proposal that is perceived as highly unrealistic represents an extremely distrusted proposal (reflected in a negative score). A highly realistic proposal which is less preferred might, on the contrary, be called a trusted proposal (reflected in a positive score).

Let us first look at the most- and least-trusted peace proposals for the total sample. The "migration" item calculations are based on a very small number of diplomats (n = 32) and will therefore not be discussed. We will also not comment on items 14 and 17 because of their low levels of importance. The remaining proposals with high-trust status for the total sample of diplomats are: the military alliances must be preserved, and we must strengthen regional organizations. These two trusted proposals are low/high level and medium/high proposals.* A comparison of two arms policy proposals in Table 6.11--preserve alliances and disarmament--indicates that tough proposals like the former are trusted more than soft proposals like the latter. This conclusion is further supported by the greater trust status of military balance and detente. The most distrusted proposals for the total sample are general and complete disarmament must be realized, abolish hunger and poverty in the world, ideological disputes ought to be diminished, and we must strengthen the United Nations. These four items are all located in the high/low and high/medium spaces of our operational peace profile.

Let us now find out if there are differences between diplomats from the two subgroups with respect to the trust status of their proposals. Excluding from both lists high-trust items with a low/low or low/medium operativeness, we are left with the following two lists of most trusted proposals: for the developed countries, the military alliances must be preserved, there must be a military balance, and we must strengthen regional organizations; for developing countries, the military alliances must be preserved, and we must strengthen regional organizations. Regional integration and military alliance have the highest trust status for both groups. The groups differ, however, with respect to the military balance proposal; the trust status of this item is clearly higher for diplomats from developed countries than for their colleagues from developing countries. These three proposals are all located in the medium/high or low/high spaces of the respective operational peace profiles.

---

*In the terms "low/high" and "medium/high" the word before the slash refers to preference, and the second word refers to the realism level of the proposal.

TABLE 6.11

Conditions for Peace Ranked According to the Amount of
Difference between Realism and Importance Attributions

Total Sample		
10	Preservation of military alliances	+1.4
24	Lifting of migration restrictions	+0.4*
14	More socialism	+0.4
17	Self-sufficient states	-0.1
6	Strengthening regional organizations	-0.2
11	More similarity between nations	-0.4
23	Cooperation	-0.5
16	Military balance	-0.5
21	Each national group its country	-0.5
4	Small countries more power	-0.8
18	East-West detente	-0.9
9	More effective communication	-0.9
8	Control population growth	-0.9
15	Free trade between all countries	-0.9
20	More open boundaries	-1.0
7	Establishment of world government	-1.0
3	Peace between individuals	-1.1
12	Rich countries aid poor countries	-1.1
5	More democratic states	-1.2
1	Educate individuals to peace	-1.2
19	Strengthening of the United Nations	-1.4
22	Diminishment of ideological disputes	-1.7
2	Abolish hunger and poverty	-2.2
13	Disarmament	-2.6

Developed Countries		
24	Lifting of migration restrictions	+1.1*
14	More socialism	+0.9
10	Preservation of military alliances	+0.9
17	Self-sufficient states	+0.6
11	More similarity between nations	-0.0
16	Military balance	-0.1
6	Strengthening regional organizations	-0.1
21	Each national group its country	-0.2
4	Small countries more power	-0.4
15	Free trade between nations	-0.4
23	Cooperation	-0.5

9	More effective communication	-0.5
12	Rich countries aid poor	-0.7
3	Peace between individuals	-0.7
7	World government	-0.8
20	More open boundaries	-0.8
18	East-West detente	-0.9
1	Educate individuals to peace	-0.9
19	Strengthening of the United Nations	-1.1
5	More democratic states	-1.2
8	Population control	-1.4
22	Diminishment of ideology	-1.5
2	Abolish hunger and poverty	-2.1
13	Disarmament	-2.2

Developing Countries

10	Preservation of military alliances	+1.7
14	More socialism	-0.0
6	Strengthening regional organizations	-0.3
24	Lifting migration restrictions	-0.4*
17	Self-sufficient states	-0.4
23	Cooperation	-0.5
8	Control population growth	-0.6
21	Each national group its country	-0.7
9	More effective communication	-0.7
16	Military balance	-0.8
10	Preservation of military alliances	-0.8
18	East-West detente	-0.9
15	Free trade between all countries	-1.1
7	Establishment of world government	-1.1
20	More open boundaries	-1.2
5	More democratic states	-1.2
3	Peace between individuals	-1.2
1	Educate individuals to peace	-1.3
12	Rich countries aid poor countries	-1.4
22	Diminishment of ideology	-1.7
19	Strengthening of the United Nations	-1.8
2	Abolish hunger	-2.2
13	Disarmament	-3.0

*N = 32.
Source: Compiled by the author from his own research.

The three most distrusted items that can be found in both lists are general and complete disarmament must be realized, abolish hunger and poverty in the world, and ideological disputes ought to be diminished. The groups differ, however, with respect to the population control, foreign aid, and United Nations proposals. The diplomats from developed countries have a greater distrust of population-control proposals than their colleagues. On the other hand, diplomats from developing countries show greater distrust of the foreign aid and the United Nations proposals. These six proposals are located in the high/medium and high/low spaces of the respective operational peace profiles.

Looking back at the operational profiles, which were intended to categorize the proposals according to their degree of operativeness, the following qualification should be added. We feel it is fair to assume that diplomats would tend to opt for realistic policy proposals if they had to choose between optimal and realistic, or if they found that the highly preferred alternatives were not working over time or turned out to be unrealistic. Thus we would suggest giving greater weight to the perceived realism side of the operational profile, which in turn means that the medium preference/ high realism proposals emerge as relatively more operational. It also means that the regional middle-range proposals, which are highly trusted, are also the most operational (see Table 6.12). Regional peace policies are generally perceived as more operational than global, national, or subnational ones for the total sample and the two subsamples. This global–subnational dimension also raises the question whether and to what extent one or more specific levels in the international system are preferred for peace policies. Comparing the preferences of diplomats from developed and developing countries, we see that the former give the highest preference to the inter- and intraregional level, and the latter put more emphasis on the global and subnational levels. From all this we may conclude that the diplomats from developed countries do not go to extremes in their thinking about peace: they neither prefer nor perceive as very realistic the global approach or approaches that start with the individual or at the microsociological level. On the other hand, diplomats from developing countries emphasize the medium level as operational, while preferring the global and subnational as optimal.

Finally, let us look in somewhat greater detail at the relatively high discrepancy found between the aspirational and realism scores in the peace profiles. We can group the response tendencies of diplomats in four categories (see Table 6.13). A diplomat, most of whose responses are high on preference and low on realism, could be called an idealist or sophisticated realist, who also believes in the impact of verbal strategy and is able to live with this discrepancy.

TABLE 6.12

Preference, Realism, and Trust Status of Conditions
for Peace Grouped According to System Level
for Diplomats from Developed and
Developing Countries
(means)

	(0–5) Optimal Profile Average	(1–5) Realism Perception Average	Optimal– Realistic Difference Average
Total sample			
Global	3.58	1.96	−1.62
Interregional	3.40	3.10	−0.30
Intraregional	3.65	3.30	−0.35
National	2.58	2.06	−0.52
Subnational/individual	3.80	2.65	−1.15
Developed countries			
Global	3.49	1.92	−1.58
Interregional	3.65	3.43	−0.22
Intraregional	3.63	3.22	−0.41
National	2.36	2.16	−0.20
Subnational/individual	3.41	2.53	−0.88
Developing countries			
Global	3.94	2.18	−1.76
Interregional	3.26	2.93	−0.33
Intraregional	3.89	3.40	−0.49
National	2.92	2.08	−0.84
Subnational/individual	4.10	2.81	−1.29

Global items	2, 7, 19, 13, 15
Interregional items	10, 12, 16, 18
Intraregional items	6, 23
National items	4, 5, 11, 20, 14, 17
Subnational/individual items	1, 3

Source: Compiled by the author from his own research.

TABLE 6.13

Aspirational-Realism Discrepancy in the Peace Profile
of Diplomats

Realism	Importance	
	High	Low
Total sample		
High	3.13	2.86
Low	9.51	2.94
Developed countries sample		
High	3.37	2.79
Low	8.46	3.35
Developing countries sample		
High	2.90	2.93
Low	10.57	2.54
Developed versus developing	t-value	p-value
High-high	.88	
High-low	-.46	
Low-high	-3.24	<.005
Low-low	2.49	<.01

Note: The numbers represent the mean number of items that have the particular characteristics of the quadrant.

Source: Compiled by the author from his own research.

Another position may be that of high preference/high realism, which is a more balanced state of thinking about peace. Realists or cynics, I assume, could be found in the high realism/low preference quadrant. Finally, a diplomat with a peace profile low on preference and low on realism may be called a defeatist. Although of interest, it is not within the scope of this study to test the validity of these tentative labels but rather to inquire into the differences between the diplomats of developing and developed countries with respect to these four types. To that end, we classified all proposals scored by each diplomat as belonging to one of the four types. A proposal was classified as balanced if both the importance and realism scores were 5; as defeatist if both scores were 1; as idealist or sophisticated realistic if the realism score was lower than the importance score; and realistic or cynical if the realism score was higher than the importance score. The mean frequencies of each of these types, for the total sample and the subsamples, can be found in Table 6.13. The table clearly indicates that for both subsamples of diplomats, the idealistic or sophisticated-realistic pattern of low realism/high importance prevails. However, this pattern is significantly more frequent among diplomats from developing countries (t = -3.24, p < .005). The only other significant difference relates to the defeatist type of consonance. The data indicate that diplomats from developed countries tend to be higher on this type of consonance (t = 2.49, p < .01). This last finding should, however, be considered with some reservation because of the lower-than-possible validity of our measure of defeatism, which could have been made more valid if, instead of classifying a proposal as defeatist when both scores were 1, we would have classified it as such when it had a preference score of 1 or 0, and a realism score of 1.

The relatively higher dissonance of the diplomats from developing countries seems to be due in large part to a greater percentage of idealists in that sample. This is indicated by Table 6.14, which contrasts the two groups of diplomats on some selected items. The diplomats from developing countries are shown as more soft and more idealistic (believe more in the individual and the world state approach). Interestingly, while the two samples differ markedly on the importance they attach to the different proposals, there is much more agreement between them as to how realistic they deem the proposals to be. This explains much of the relatively higher dissonance of developing-country diplomats.

TABLE 6.14

Diplomats from Developed and Developing Countries
on Some Selected Proposals
(mean scores)

	Important to Peace		Realistic	
	Developed Country	Developing Country	Developed Country	Developing Country
Keep the balance	3.6	3.0	3.4	2.2
Preserve alliances	2.9	1.6	3.7	3.3
Educate individuals	3.8	4.2	2.1	2.2
World state	1.9	2.3	1.1	1.1

Source: Compiled by the author from his own research.

Preferred World Order

We turn, finally, to analysis of the diplomats' view of a preferred world order. Our primary focus is on the extent of agreement between diplomats representing developed and developing countries. We will also examine whether and to what extent the world-
order values of the World Order Model Project (Mendlovitz 1975)
are reflected in the diplomats' thinking about their preferred world
order.

The data on which this analysis is based were gathered during
the interviews in Washington and were evoked by the following question:

> How would the world you'd like to see for your children
> differ from that of today; or how would you describe
> your preferred world order?

We did not develop an a priori system for categorizing the answers
but instead listed all the responses obtained and grouped them into
meaningful categories. The list of the qualities of a preferred world
order for the total sample can be found in Table 6.15, and the data
on which we will base our description of the differences between
diplomats from developed and developing countries are presented in
Table 6.16.

As can be seen in Table 6.16, the two subsamples agree with
respect to six qualities of a preferred world order: international
cooperation, a viable United Nations, reduced polarity between the
North and South, absence of domestic interference, economic welfare, and global approach. The global approach category includes
all qualities that explicitly stressed the need for a global solution to
a particular problem. With respect to these six qualities of a preferred world order, there are no significant differences between the
two samples.

There are five qualities on the list for developed countries,
which do not appear on the list for the developing countries: international democracy, improvement of communication, arms control,
disarmament and arms reduction, and tolerance of differences. Of
these five qualities, only one has a significantly higher mean for
developed-country diplomats: improvement of communication. Although this category included all qualities relating to the improvement of international communications in general, most statements
were specifically related to East-West relations. Regional integration did not emerge in the list of top-ranked qualities for developed-
country diplomats, but it did have a significantly higher mean in this
subsample than among developing-country diplomats ($t = 1.76$, $p < .05$).

TABLE 6.15

Preferred-World-Order Qualities for the Total
Sample of Diplomats
(frequencies)

International cooperation	44
A viable United Nations	33
Reduced polarity between North and South	28
No domestic interference	27
Open borders and migration	24
Absence of violence	22
Economic welfare	22
Mutual understanding	17
Equitable distribution of world resources	17
Arms control	16
Dignity and respect	16
International democracy	16
Global approach	16
Moral and humane international relations	15
New economic system	15
Disarmament	14
Communication improvement	14
Justice	14
Tolerance	14
Equality	11
Economic development	11
Detente	9
Mutuality of exchange	9
More meaningful interdependence	9
Population control	9
Absence of racism	8
Freedom	8
Regional integration	8
International legal order	7
Environmental improvement	6
World government	6

Source: Compiled by the author from his own research.

TABLE 6.16

Preferred–World–Order Qualities as Judged by Diplomats
from Developed and Developing Countries

		Means*
Developed countries		
1	A viable United Nations	.127
2	International cooperation	.107
4.5	Economic welfare	.088
4.5	No domestic interference	.068
4.5	International democracy	.088
4.5	Communication improvement	.088
7	Reduced polarity North–South	.078
8	Arms control	.068
10	Global approach	.058
10	Disarmament and arms reduction	.058
10	Tolerance	.058
Developing countries		
1	International cooperation	.196
2.5	Reduced polarity North–South	.145
2.5	Open borders and migration	.145
5	A viable United Nations	.111
5	Absence of violence	.111
5	No domestic interference	.111
7	Economic welfare	.094
8	Equality	.076
10	Equitable distribution of world resources	.068
10	Global approach	.068
10	Justice	.068

Developed versus developing countries		t-value	p-value <
1	Open borders and migration	−3.05	.005
2	Communication improvement	2.32	.01
3	Justice	−2.31	.05
4	Moral and humane international relations	−2.08	.05
5	Equality	−2.02	.05
6	Absence of violence	−1.94	.05
7	Regional integration	1.76	.05
8.5	Reduced polarity North–South	−1.58	
8.5	Dignity and respect	−1.58	

*Obtained by dividing the total number of responses provided
by diplomats from each type of country by the number of diplomats
in the subsample.

Source: Compiled by the author from his own research.

158

It is not surprising that this category is high for developed countries, for most of the statements included referred specifically to the further integration of the European Common Market.

In the list of top-ranked qualities for the developing-country diplomats, we found five qualities which did not appear on the other list: open borders and migration, absence of violence, equality, equitable distribution of world resources, and justice. All these qualities, with the exception of equitable distribution of world resources, appear significantly more in the preferred world order of the diplomats from developing countries (see Table 6.16). The meaning of these qualities, with the exception of open borders, is self-evident. I will illustrate the meaning of this latter quality by quoting some statements which were placed in this category: a world with more open borders--political, economic, and cultural; traveling should be easier; a world without borders; easier immigration; greater freedom of movement of people around the world; opening of frontiers; no boundaries; and lifting restrictions and stimulating contact between peoples from East and West. This quality is uniquely characteristic of the preferred world order of developing-country diplomats; this is underscored by the fact that it occupies second place in their list, and also accounts for the most highly significant difference between preferred qualities for the two subsamples ($t = -3.05$, $p < .005$). Not included in the top list for developing-country diplomats, but appearing more frequently in the preferred world order of diplomats of developing countries, are moral and humane international relations, and dignity and respect.

Let us now see whether and to what extent the world-order values of the World Order Model Project (Mendlovitz 1975) are reflected in the preferred-world-order thinking of our diplomats. The World Order Model Project recognizes the absence of war, poverty, social injustice, ecological imbalance, and indignity as values having a global scope. In order to relate our data to these world-order values, we added all categories that were related to each of these world-order values together. The results can be seen in Table 6.17. For the diplomats from developed countries, we can divide the world-order values into two groups. Highly important and roughly equal are the absence of poverty and war, and markedly lower in importance are the absence of injustice, ecological instability, and indignity. The picture for diplomats from developing countries is more complex. The most salient value in their preferred world order is the absence of poverty; second in importance and more or less equal to each other are the absence of violence and injustice; third is the absence of indignity; and finally, the absence of ecological instability. The greatest differences are noticed in relation to the justice, dignity, and economic security values. These values are more salient

TABLE 6.17

Qualities of Preferred World Order of the Diplomats Grouped According to Six World-Order Values
(mean frequencies)

Quality	Developed Countries	Developing Countries
Absence of war		
Absence of violence	.039	.111
Arms control	.068	.042
Disarmament and arms reduction	.059	.059
Detente	.049	.034
Total	.215	.246
Absence of poverty		
Reduced polarity between North and South	.078	.145
Economic welfare	.088	.094
Economic distribution	.049	.068
Economic development	.029	.042
Total	.244	.349
Absence of justice		
Moral and humane international relations	.000	.059
Justice	.009	.068
Equality	.019	.076
Mutuality of exchange	.029	.042
Freedom	.029	.017
Total	.086	.262
Absence of ecological instability		
Environmental improvement	.029	.025
Population control	.029	.042
Total	.058	.067
Absence of indignity		
Dignity and respect	.019	.059
Absence of racism	.029	.034
Total	.048	.093

Note: The six world-order values are those that are recognized by the World Order Model Project as being global in scope.
Source: Compiled by the author from his own research.

in the preferred-world-order view of the developing-country diplomats. We also observe that all five values have higher scores
among diplomats of developing countries. This is caused because
our preferred-world-order question yielded a somewhat higher response rate from the diplomats of developing countries (1.8) than
from diplomats of developed countries (1.5). But, even if we take
into account this systematic bias, we see that the earlier presented
interpretation would still be valid. From these results we can infer
three conclusions: that the world-order values are represented in
the diplomats' thinking about their preferred world orders; that
some values are more salient than others; and that diplomats from
developed and developing countries differ with respect to the priority
ordering of these five values.

In summary, we may say that our investigation of the views of
preferred world order has given us useful information about the
future of international relations. Dreams of different future orders
may not bring them about, but they may prevent the consolidation of
the present order or enhance or inhibit the implementation of a particular future order.

CONCLUSION

These results give support to the propositions which we made
explicit at the beginning of this chapter. First we observed the existence of significant differences among diplomats in their operationalization of peace and preferred world order. We also found
that the gap between the present state of international peace and the
ideal state is considerable. The greatest discrepancies between
the aspirational and the realism levels were noticed by diplomats
from developing countries. The larger discrepancy was accounted
for by the stronger accentuation of their aspirations. Proposals at
the inter- and intraregional levels were indicated as more operational than were proposals at the global or national or subnational
levels. The values espoused by the diplomat were also shown to be
a function of the systemic position of the country he represents.
The impact of the systemic position was found to be greater on the
appraisal of peace proposals in terms of their importance or preference than on the diplomat's assessment of the likelihood of peace
proposals to be carried out. In other words, the systemic position
tended to affect more the accentuation of aspirations rather than the
appraisal of reality by diplomats.

More generally, these data indicate that the meanings and
weights associated with peace and preferred-world-order values
generally reflect the particular interests of their respective

proponents. Certain concerns and interests sensitize the diplomat to some indicators of peace and to particular international problems, and at the same time cause him to neglect a number of alternative indicators and problems that other diplomats deem important. This implies, for example, that if we want to create a greater consensus about international values, we have to cope not only with such problems as the improvement of international communication or empathy but also with a structural problem. In other words, universal consensus can be brought about only when we want to deal with the particularity of the systemic vantage points from which these terms are given meaning and are translated into action.

7

Analytic Style

ANALYTIC STYLE AND THE COMPARATIVE
STUDY OF DIPLOMATIC THINKING

The third component of diplomatic thinking explored in this
study is the style of analysis, which refers to the "how" of diplomatic
thinking. Different styles of analysis constitute a variable of some
importance for the comparative study of the diplomatic thinking.
This importance is underscored by the fact that students of foreign
policy have disagreed vehemently about what the proper analysis of
international relations ought to be (Lijphart 1974). Different ways
of looking at things imply seeing somewhat different worlds. As a
consequence, they lead to diverse substantive conclusions or at least
various working hypotheses. An excellent example of the existence
of two styles of analysis can be found in the not totally dormant controversy between the proponents of the traditional and the behavioral
paradigms in the field of international relations. According to Kuhn
(1970: 150), "both are looking at the world, and what they look at is
not changed. But in some areas they see different things, and they
see them in different relations one to the other." The way in which
proponents of the competing paradigms in international relations
judge each other's findings and conclusions illustrates such tendencies. Lijphart (1974: 62-63) feels that

> each school considers the other's results to be not just
> wrong, but absurd. In fact, the result is not necessarily
> wrong at all; it is the problem to which the other school
> addresses itself that is wrong. And the answer to a
> wrong question can only be irrelevant and absurd. Each
> side accuses the other of imposing a model upon reality
> and looking at the model instead of at the real world.

Such mutual charges demonstrate that these two schools look at different worlds, and this underlines the importance of studying various styles of analysis for comprehending the thinking about international relations.

In this chapter we intend to examine whether and to what extent such differences also exist in the thinking about international relations by professional diplomats. The central proposition of this chapter is that diplomats analyze international issues in systematically different ways, and that their modes of analysis diverge along several dimensions. A second proposition is that variation in analytic styles can partly be explained by systemic and perceptual variables. For example, we would expect that diplomats who perceive the international environment as very Hobbesian would also tend to model international transactions as a zero-sum game rather than as a variable-sum game, for such a model best fits the environment they perceive. As for systemic positions, we would expect, for example, that diplomats from periphery countries would be more inclined to use structural analysis than their colleagues from developed countries. The basis for this prediction is that they experience a greater discrepancy between their real and preferred status in the world and should therefore be more acutely aware of the stratified nature of international relations. In support of this prediction, we can mention Lagos, a Latin American student of international relations, who identifies himself with a Third World point of view. He not only models international relations as a highly stratified system, but even proposes the rise in the real status for underdeveloped countries to be the correct interpretation of the international dimensions of their national interests (Lagos 1963: 30).

Let us now operationalize the component of diplomatic thinking that we call analytic style. Some diplomats tend to think of international relations as a great social system composed of diverse countries interacting and occupying various positions, while others do not use such a structural mode of analysis. Some model international transactions in zero-sum terms, while others see them as a variable-sum game. Some place issues in a historical context. Some attribute blame for problems, while others phrase their analysis in neutral terms. Some accept uncritically the foreign policy of their own country, while others tend to have less-partisan attitudes. Some conceive conflict as inherent in the nature of international relations. Some tend to be cynical about the state of international relations and detect discrepancies between words, acts, and intentions. Some conceive relations among nations as more interdependent than others. Some analyze international relations predominantly as a function of national interests. Some focus mainly on technologic or financial aspects of international relations. Some concentrate on broad political, economic, or moral principles, while others emphasize specific situations and details. Some even refer explicitly to particular doctrines, such as capitalism or socialism. I shall use the term "analytic style" to refer to this complex of attributes. The essence of analytic style is not what diplomats think about international politics, but how they do so.

In the next section we will look in greater detail at each of these attributes or stylistic characteristics and describe the way we rank-ordered diplomats with respect to them.

STYLISTIC CHARACTERISTICS

Variable-Sum versus Zero-Sum Analysis

One of the questions highly relevant to understanding the style of analysis is whether diplomats tend to model international relations as a zero-sum or a variable-sum game.

> A zero-sum game is a game in which the payoffs to all players add up to zero . . . whatever one competitor wins in a zero-sum game, he can win only from the losses of the rival, so that any winnings must come out of the losses of others. A zero-sum game is a merciless form of competition. What is good for one player must be bad for some other player (Deutsch 1970: 26).

Another model for viewing international transactions is a variable-sum game: "One in which players compete with one another, but all can win jointly" (Deutsch 1970: 25). We measured that aspect of the style of analysis by using the diplomats' responses (on a five-point scale, ranging from strongly disagree to strongly agree) to the following two statements in our questionnaire:

> When a country or group of countries gains, it usually means that another country or group of countries loses.

> Those countries that get ahead usually get ahead at the expense of others.

Structural Analysis

A second source of variation in the analytic style of diplomats is their propensity to analyze the world as a system of international stratification that determines relationships of superordination and subordination among nations. To characterize diplomats according to this aspect of analytic style, we used four measures applied to data collected during the interviews. The first measure, use of structural framework, ranked the diplomats on a three-point scale. The highest score (3) was assigned to a diplomat who explicitly used such terms as international stratification, position, or class, and who gave a central place to structural relationships between countries or groups of countries in his discussion. A score of 1 was assigned to diplomats who made no use of such an analytic framework. An intermediate score (2) was assigned for the less-explicit and central use of structural analysis. The reliability for this and other measures was assessed by correlating (Pearson r) my scores and the scores of another independent coder on a sample of 20 interviews. The reliability coefficient of this measure was .35, and only 5 percent were rated more than one point apart.

The second indicator of this style of analysis measured the diplomat's positional awareness. A high score (3) for positional awareness was given if the diplomat explicitly referred to his country's structural position (power, economic position, and so on) and discussed the impact of this position on his country's foreign policy, or on the behavior of other countries vis-a-vis his country. The following example illustrates a response that received a rating of 3:

> A vital point in our diplomacy is that foreign policy of a small power is "adaptation" to the international environment, decided by the superpowers; it is intelligent adaptation, in the sense that we try to know beforehand what we can and see the signs, and turn and twist around within the existing framework.

Again, a low score (1) was assigned when no reference to the country's position appeared in the interview and an intermediary score (2) when position was referred to only vaguely or in passing. The reliability of the measure was .62, and only 5 percent of the scores were rated more than one point apart.

The third indicator of this analytic style could be referred to as dependency sensitivity. The highest score (3) was given to a diplomat who explicitly mentioned his country's dependency on a foreign commodity (for example, natural resources, military security, financial aid). The following comment from an Asian diplomat, for example, was scored high on dependency sensitivity:

> [My country] is totally dependent on international relations. Ninety percent of the resources are coming from

other countries. We have to convince [our people] that
to have harmonious relations is vital for [my country's]
standard of living. We would advocate strongly the
necessity of free trade—not because our destiny is dependent on free trade, but also because the entire world
is benefiting from free exchange of goods, investments,
persons, and communications.

The intermediate score was given to an indirect reference to dependency, for example, when the diplomat referred to it as a characteristic of a group of countries to which his own country belonged.
A score of 1 was given if there was no mention of dependency at all.
The reliability coefficient was .75 and no scores were rated more
than one point apart.

The last indicator of a structural style of analysis can be
called penetration sensitivity. Here the highest score was given
when the diplomat explicitly refrred to any form of domestic interference in his own country. A respondent, for example, who began
his plea for less domestic interference in his country by saying that
"big powers should leave small people alone and give bread instead
of serpents and scorpions" was rated 3 on our three-point scale.
The intermediate score (2) was used when penetration was mentioned
indirectly, for example, by referring to it as a characteristic of a
group of countries to which his country belongs. The lowest score
was received when there was no mention of this issue at all. The
reliability coefficient for this measure was .63 and 15 percent of
the scores were rated more than one point apart.

Historical Context

The next analytic style concerns the extent to which the respondent placed his analysis of issues in a historical context. A
respondent for whom the historical context was an important factor
in his explanation of a problem was rated high (3) on this three-
point scale. A score of 2 was given to a simple recounting of the
recent history of the problem, some dates, or attempted solutions.
A 1 was assigned in the absence of any mention of historical factors.
The reliability coefficient for this stylistic characteristic was .67
and the percentage of scores rated more than one point apart was 5.

Discussion Moralized

Another three-point scale rated the extent to which the respondent moralized an issue by assigning blame to someone or using

such terms as justice, rights, duties, and so on. Here, for example, a high rating was assigned to a Latin American diplomat who attributed the ignorance about foreign policy of the people to the media, which are among the greatest delinquents. "Lots of reporters are like cobblers—they fail to ask important questions and use terms without defining them—they are scaremongers." An intermediate score (2) was assigned when the blame or moral terms were used vaguely or in passing. The reliability coefficient obtained was .58, and no scores were placed at the opposite ends of the three-point scale.

Partisanship

Another aspect of analytic style could be characterized as partisan. It refers to the strength of the diplomat's prejudice in favor of his own country. This stylistic characteristic was measured by the diplomat's response on a five-point scale, ranging from strongly disagree to strongly agree, to the following statement:

> In its disputes with other countries, my country is usually right; its ideals and standards are usually fair and wise.

National Interests

The next and related stylistic characteristic concerns the use of national interests as a criterion in judging policies. Here we gave a high score (3) when the diplomat said explicitly that national interests was the predominant criterion of good foreign policy. Statements such as "The role of the diplomat is to bring understanding only in the interests of his country," or "There is no 'just' or 'unjust' in international relations, just national interests" were rated as high on this three-point scale. An intermediate score (2) was given for just mentioning national interests. The reliability score was .46, and 10 percent of the scores were placed at the opposite ends of the three-point scale.

Reference to Ideology

We also coded arguments that pertained to the use of ideology. More specifically, we noted the presence of arguments based explicitly on a named ideology or doctrine, such as a demand for a more socialist world or the protection of liberalism. A code of 1 was given for the absence of any mention of ideology; 2 was given for an explicit mention; and 3 if the respondent defended or promoted a particular ideology. The intercoder reliability was found to be .52, and 15 percent of the scores were rated more than one point apart.

International Relations as a Conflict System

The next stylistic characteristic that we focused upon was the diplomats' conception of international relations as inherently a conflict system. This was measured by the diplomats' responses on a five-point scale, ranging from strongly disagree to strongly agree, to the following statement: "There is always bound to be conflict among various groups in the world." In addition to this measure, we also collected information about the diplomats' perceptions of the degree of conflict present in today's world. Conflict of interests implies, at a minimum, that one policy would be good for one group, another for another group. Using a five-point scale, we ranked how prominent conflicting interests were in the diplomat's discussion of international issues. The highest score (5) was given when the interviewee discussed, explicitly, specific conflicts of interest and when this discussion occupied a central part of his analysis of international relations. A score of 4 was given when conflict among interests was explicit, but not central, or central and implicit in the discussion. A score of 3 indicated an answer that mentioned whose interests were opposed, but included no discussion of these conflicts among interests. A score of 2 was assigned when different opinions or perspectives were mentioned without the implication of conflicting interests; and a score of 1 was assigned when no differences were mentioned at all. The reliability coefficient of this measure was .33, and only 5 percent of the scores were placed more than one score apart.

Cynicism

Diplomats also differed with respect to the degree of cynicism expressed during the conversation. The degree of cynicism is here inferred from references to disparities between words and actions or intentions in international relations. The following two statements, for example, were scored as high on cynicism:

The world tends to become very hypocritical. The evolution of thought and the widening of public opinion creates

a need for shoe brushing. This is also true internationally; propaganda is more and more sophisticated now
that the means of information have grown. As Pascal
said "Repeat . . . and they will believe."

(West European diplomat)

People speak loud, but do very little; they attend meet-
ings at the United Nations and conclude from speeches
that change is coming about.   (African diplomat)

The difference between a score of 3 and 2 is a question of degree;
for a score of 3 the cynical observation had to have a touch of
sarcasm or several cynical remarks had to be made. A score of
1 was given when no cynical remarks were expressed. The reliability coefficient for this stylistic characteristic is .63, with
10 percent of the scores deviating more than one point from each
other.

Particularizer versus Generalizer

Another stylistic characteristic concerns the scope of the
diplomat's discussion. Sometimes a respondent would take an
issue and deal with it in terms of sweeping principles; others would
move immediately to specific details. Here again, a three-point
scale was used. A high score (3) was given when issues were
treated in very general terms or on a high level of abstraction. A
low score (1) was assigned if the approach was more operational
and the respondent focused essentially on concrete conflicts and
cases. An intermediate score (2) was used when there was no
clear predominance of either a generalizing or a particularizing
tendency. The reliability score for this measure was .55, and no
scores were placed at the opposite ends of the three-point scale.

Predominance of Financial or
Technological Issues

Other characteristics rated, on a three-point scale, include
references to financial and technological issues. The highest
score (3) was given when the discussion of financial issues (aid,
capital, monetary system) predominated. A score of 2 was
assigned when such issues were touched upon, but were less central; and 1 when no mention was made of them. The reliability
coefficient for financial aid was .79, and no scores were found

TABLE 7.1

Means and Standard Deviations of All Measures of Stylistic
Characteristics for the Total Sample of Diplomats

	Scale	Mean	Standard Deviation
Variable-sum/zero-sum analysis			
"When a country or group of countries gains, it usually means that another country or group of countries loses."	1-5	2.76	.90
"Those countries that get ahead usually get ahead at the expense of others."	1-5	2.94	.94
Structural analysis			
Use of structural framework	1-3	1.81	.88
Positional awareness	1-3	2.02	.87
Dependency sensitivity	1-3	1.71	.85
Penetration sensitivity	1-3	1.92	.97
Historical context given	1-3	1.76	.80
Discussion moralized	1-3	1.65	.78
Partisanship			
"In its disputes with other countries my country is usually right. Its ideals and standards are usually fair and wise."	1-5	3.43	.91
National interests	1-3	1.70	.53
Reference to ideology	1-3	1.45	.73
International relations as a conflict system			
"There is always bound to be conflict among various groups in the world."	1-5	3.70	.89
Saliency of conflicts in the present world	1-5	3.62	1.27
Cynicism	1-3	1.52	.82
Particularizer versus generalizer	1-3	2.16	.63
Predominance of technological issues	1-3	1.43	.77
Predominance of financial issues	1-3	1.55	.81
Interdependency	1-3	1.79	.87

Source: Compiled by the author from his own research.

at opposite ends. The reliability coefficient for technological issues was .60, and 10 percent of the scores were ranked at the opposite ends of the scale.

Interdependency

Finally, the last stylistic characteristic concerns whether and to what extent the diplomat referred to the world as an interdependent system. A diplomat who used the term "interdependency" explicitly and gave it a central place in his image of the world was scored high (3). A score of 1 was assigned when interdependency was not mentioned; and an intermediate score (2) when it was referred to implicitly. The reliability coefficient was .48, and 5 percent of the scores were located at opposite ends of the scale.

These then are the main aspects of analytic style investigated in this research. Table 7.1 presents the means and standard deviations of these stylistic characteristics for the total sample of diplomats.

DIMENSIONS OF ANALYTIC STYLE

Do these stylistic characteristics cluster into any intelligible pattern, and if so, what are the main dimensions of analytic style? One way of proceeding with an answer to this question is to examine the correlations among the several stylistic variables across different respondents. If diplomats who tend to be high on one stylistic characteristic also tend to be high on another, we can infer that these characteristics form a stylistic cluster. An efficient way to distinguish such clusters is factor analysis. The scores of the 18 variables listed in Table 7.1 were intercorrelated and the resultant matrix of intercorrelations was factor-analyzed, using the varimax rotation procedure. Table 7.2 identifies the 11 factors which were extracted from the data. To make up composite variables representing each factor, we included those variables that had a loading above .35 on that particular factor. Each diplomat was given a score which is the composite of those variable scores, weighted by their factor-score coefficients. For example, on the first factor, a diplomat's positional awareness score was multiplied by .430 (factor-score coefficient). Each diplomat's score for the other two variables that loaded above .35 was likewise multiplied by their factor-score coefficients and the sum of the weighted variable scores was used as the factor score for "structural analysis." For the calculation of all factors, see Appendix I.

TABLE 7.2

Factors of Analytic Style Derived from a Factor Analysis of
Stylistic Characteristics for the Total Sample of Diplomats

Factor 1: Structural analysis	
4 Positional awareness	.692
5 Dependency sensitivity	.680
3 Use of structural framework	.356
Factor 2: Historical analysis	
7 Historical context given	.736
Factor 3: Zero-sum analysis	
1 When a country gains . . .	.671
2 Those countries that get ahead . . .	.425
Factor 4: National interest analysis	
10 Saliency of national interests	.825
Factor 5: Faultfinding	
9 In its disputes with other countries . . .	-.553
14 Cynicism	.404
8 Discussion moralized	.382
Factor 6: Technology and finance	
16 Predominance of technological issues	.394
17 Predominance of financial issues	.354
Factor 7: Interdependency	
18 Interdependency	.891
Factor 8: Particularizer versus generalizer	
15 Particularizer versus generalizer	.728
Factor 9: Reference to ideology	
11 Reference to ideology	.592
Factor 10: Disapproval of external control	
6 Penetration sensitivity	.428
8 Discussion moralized	.398
13 Saliency of conflict in the present world	.372
Factor 11: World is conflict-system analysis	
12 There is always bound to be conflict	.692

Note: Entries are loadings of the stylistic characteristics on
factors; cutoff point was loading $\geq .35$. Varimax rotation was used.
Source: Compiled by the author from his own research.

ANALYTIC STYLE, SYSTEMIC POSITION, AND MORAL-POLITICAL CLIMATE

This section will focus on each of the factors and examine whether and to what extent they are a function of systemic and/or perceptual (international climate) variables. For each of the factors we will proceed as follows: First we will look at the mean for the total sample to get an idea of the central tendency of the factor scores. Then we will compare diplomats from developed and developing countries by means of the t-test. Of the remaining independent variables (seven systemic and six perceptual), we will describe only those that are significantly correlated with the dependent variable. Finally, we will form a block of systemic variables and a block of perceptual variables and examine whether and to what extent these two blocks, separately or in combination, have an impact on the dependent variables. To measure the single and joint impact of systemic and perceptual variables we regressed each dependent variable on six systemic variables (economic development, aid received, economic interdependency, penetratedness, military expenditure, and security force investment) and four perceptual variables (Hobbesian, Marxian, instrumental-exchange, and international law climates). We did not include the center-periphery variable because of its high correlation with degree of development and military expenditure (r = .85 and .83, respectively). For a similar reason, we excluded the we-ness and the shared principled agreement climates. The intercorrelation between these two variables was .75, and both had a high negative correlation with the Hobbesian environment (r = .84 and -.81, respectively). For each dependent variable we did two regression analyses. In the first we entered the block of systemic variables first, and the block of perceptual variables second. In the second analysis, the order of entry was reversed. Such a procedure gives an idea of the predictive power of both types of variables combined. Moreover, it allows us to assess the impact of each block of variables separately. Finally, it gives us an idea of the impact of one block of variables after the effect of the other block is taken out.

Factor 1: Structural Analysis

Factor 1 represents the clustering of three primary characteristics: positional awareness, dependency sensitivity, and use of structural framework. This factor reflects the degree of concern with the status of one's nation in the international stratified structure, especially as that status relates to dependency. From the mean of 1.84 on a 1-3 scale we can infer that diplomats in general do not tend to use structural analysis as their predominant style of analysis. There are, however, marked differences between sub-groups of diplomats. The greatest difference is found between diplomats from developed and developing countries. A comparison of the means of the two groups yields a highly significant t-value of -4.69 (p < .005). This indicates that diplomats from developing countries use this style of analysis more frequently than their colleagues from developed countries. This finding could be explained by their greater experience of atimia (Lagos 1963) or dissonance between their real international status and their formal or preferred status; and by their greater concern with the enhancement of their country's status and hence greater consciousness about the stratification in the world. If we look at the significant correlations of this style with the systemic variables (see Table 7.3), we find that diplomats from economically and militarily weak powers tend to be higher on this style of analysis than their colleagues from economically and militarily strong powers. Of the different styles of analysis that we studied, structural analysis is the one that most sharply distinguishes the thinking of diplomats representing weak states from those from strong states (see Table 7.14).

Let us now look at the impact of the perceived international environment on the propensity to use this particular style. We see that level 1 climates, that is, the Hobbesian and Marxian climates, are positively correlated with this analytic style (r = .15, p < .02; r = .13, p < .07), and the we-ness and shared principled agreement environment are negatively correlated (r = -.18, p < .01; r = .17, p < .02). Thus, this style of analysis seems more congruent with
· a world perceived as Hobbesian or Marxian than with a higher-level international environment.

Comparing the strength of the correlations of our dependent variables with the systemic and perceptual variables, we see that the latter is much weaker. This conclusion is further underscored when we look at the results of the regression analysis. In Table 7.3 we see that the climate block, when introduced first, predicts only 4 percent of the variance; and when introduced second adds only 1 percent. The block of systemic variables is the only significant predictor of this style of analysis (multiple R^2 = .26, p < .001). Jointly, the blocks predict 27 percent of the variance of this variable.

Factor 2: Historical Analysis

The extent to which the diplomat places his analysis of an issue in a historical context does not seem to be a source of variation between diplomats from developed and developing countries; nor is this stylistic characteristic a function of the single and joint impact of the blocks of systemic and climate variables. Together they account for only 8 percent of the variance, and the effect is not significant (see Table 7.4). The only systemic variable that is significantly associated with this style of analysis is the security force investment of a country (r = .15, p. < .02). That is, diplomats from countries high on security force investment have a higher propensity to analyze problems within a historical context.

TABLE 7.3

T-test, Significant Correlations, and Regression
Analysis Data of Structural Analysis
(t-value -.4.69; p-value < .005)

Significant correlations

With systemic variables

Economic development	-.39	< .001
Security force investment	-.37	< .001
Military expenditure	-.36	< .001
Center-periphery	-.34	< .001
Economic interdependency	-.18	< .007
Aid receipt	.19	< .01

With international climates

We-ness	-.18	< .01
Shared principled agreement	-.17	< .02
Hobbesian	.15	< .04
Marxian	.13	< .07

Single and combined impact of a block of six systemic variables
and a block of four international climates (Multiple R^2):

systemic	.26[a]	climate	.04
climate	.01	systemic	.23[b]
	.27[c]		.27[c]

Multiple R = .52.

[a]p < .001.
[b]p < .01.
[c]p < .05.
Source: Compiled by the author from his own research.

TABLE 7.4

T-test, Significant Correlations, and Regression Analysis
Data for Historical Style of Analysis
(t-value .09)

Significant correlations

With systemic variables
    Security force investment   .15   < .02

With international climates
    None

Single and combined impact of a block of six systemic variables
and a block of four international climates (Multiple R^2):

systemic	.07	climate	.00
climate	.01	systemic	.08
	.08		.08

Multiple R = .28

Source: Compiled by the author from his own research.

Factor 3: Zero-Sum Analysis

    From the mean of 2.85 (on a five-point scale, ranging from
strongly disagree to strongly agree), we can infer that diplomats
analyze the world somewhat more as a variable-sum game than as
a zero-sum game (see Table 7.5). Again, however, there are
marked differences between subgroups of diplomats. For diplomats
from developing countries, the variable-sum game seems to be a
less-appropriate model for international transactions (t = -1.88,
$p < .05$). This suggests that they tend to model international relations as a merciless form of competition in which the gains of one
are the losses of the other, rather than as a competition in which
all parties can win or improve their positions jointly. The significant correlations with systemic variables in Table 7.5 suggest that
"weaker" states, economically and militarily, tend to take the
zero-sum game as a truer mirror of international transactions
more often than their colleagues from "stronger" states. There
is, however, one exception, namely, the amount of aid received

($r = -.24$, $p < .01$). This finding suggests that, in the subgroup of countries that receive aid, the ones who receive the most aid tend to see the world in more variable-sum terms than their colleagues at the opposite end of the scale. Thus the giving of foreign aid seems to have some positive effect on the analytic style of the recipient. The international climates that are negatively correlated with the zero-sum style of analysis are the shared principled agreement and the we-ness climates; the Hobbesian climate is positively associated. These correlations are not unexpected, for the zero-sum modeling of the world is congruent with the perceived reality of the latter climate and incongruent with the former.

TABLE 7.5

T-test and Significant Correlations for Zero-Sum
Style of Analysis
(t-value -1.88; p-value $< .05$)

Significant correlations		
With systemic variables		
Military expenditure	-.23	$< .002$
Aid receipt	-.24	$< .01$
Center-periphery	-.17	$< .02$
With international climates		
Shared principled agreement	-.21	$< .009$
We-ness	-.20	$< .01$
Hobbesian	.19	$< .01$

Single and combined impact of six systemic variables and a block of four international climates (Multiple R^2):

R^2 is unreliable because of multicolinearity and a substantial degree of cooperative suppression.

Source: Compiled by the author from his own research.

We did not present the multiple-regression data because the multiple R^2 was unreliable; within the blocks, multicolinearity and a substantial degree of cooperative suppression were going on, so that, for example, the total R^2 for the six systemic variables was much greater than the summation of the R^2 of the variables which make up the block.

Factor 4: National Interests

The mean of 1.7 indicates that most diplomats use national interests as a criterion in judging policies. Further, the data suggest clearly that the perception of national interests as a criterion for evaluating foreign policy is similar across different system positions (see Table 7.6). If we look at the significant correlations with international climates, we find that the shared principled agreement climate is positively correlated ($r = .22$, $p < .006$), and the instrumental exchange climate negatively correlated ($r = -.19$, $p < .01$). The impact of the block of perceptual variables is somewhat higher than the block of systemic variables; however, neither predicts variation on this factor significantly. Jointly, the two blocks of variables predict only 7 percent of the variance. On the basis of these results, it would be fair to say that the salience of national interests in the diplomat's style of analysis can be considered more as a constant than as a variable.

TABLE 7.6

T-test, Significant Correlations, and Regression Analysis
Data for National Interests
(t-value .40)

Significant correlations		
With systemic variables		
None		
With international climate		
Shared principled agreement	.22	< .006
Instrumental exchange	-.19	< .01

Single and combined impact of a block of six systemic variables and a block of four international climates (Multiple R^2):

systemic	.01	climate	.05
climate	.06	systemic	.02
	.07		.07

Multiple R = .27

Source: Compiled by the author from his own research.

Factor 5: Faultfinding

Factor 5 represents a clustering of three variables: partisanship, cynicism, and discussion moralized. High loadings on this factor mean: saying that your country is not fair and wise; considering countries hypocritical, and so on; and tending to blame others. Faultfinding does seem to be the common denominator. Note that partisanship is negatively related to the tendency to moralize. This means that the less partisan a diplomat is, the more he tends to moralize or attribute blame. Between the tendency to moralize and to be cynical, there is a positive link. We consider it fair to assume that to people for whom moral principles are more salient, violations will be more visible and the perception of multiple transgressions will more easily result in widespread cynicism about political motives and standards. If we compare diplomats from developed and developing countries, we see that the latter express significantly more faultfinding ($t = -2.50$, $p < .01$). This is also the case for periphery countries and low military spenders. In both cases the correlations are significant (see Table 7.7). Negatively associated with faultfinding is the perception of the world as a shared principled agreement environment; positively associated is the Hobbesian climate. The two blocks of variables are able to predict 17 percent of the variance. To explore some specific hypotheses in relation to the component variables of this factor, each component will be discussed separately (see Table 7.7).

Partisanship

The means of the partisan scores for the total sample of diplomats is 3.43, which indicates the expression of a moderate positive partisan attitude of the diplomats to their respective countries. If we compare diplomats from developed and developing countries, we see that the latter express slightly more detachment ($t = 1.46$, $p < .10$). This is also the case for periphery countries and low military spenders. In both cases the correlations are significant. If we consider partisanship as an expression of national loyalty, then this finding corroborates Guetzkow's (1955: 21) hypothesis that "members of smaller, and less powerful, and less prestigeful nations in general have less loyalty to their nations than will citizens of larger, world leading nations." Positively associated with national loyalty is the perception of the world as a shared principled agreement environment; negatively associated is the Hobbesian climate. Neither block of variables, singly or in combination, is a significant predictor of this aspect of the analytic style of the diplomat. Together they account for 9 percent of the variance.

TABLE 7.7

T-test, Significant Correlations, and Regression Analysis
Data for Faultfinding
(t-value -2.50; p-value < .01)

Significant correlations

With systemic variables

Military expenditure	-.27	< .001
Center-periphery	-.27	< .001
Economic development	-.26	< .001

With international climate

Shared principled agreement	-.21	< .009
Hobbesian	.18	< .02

Single and combined impact of a block of six systemic variables
and a block of four international climates (Multiple R^2):

systemic	.10		climate	.07
climate	.07		systemic	.10
	.17			.17

Multiple R = .41

Partisanship
(t-value 1.46; p-value < .10)

Significant correlations

With systemic variables

Military expenditure	.14	< .03
Center-periphery	.14	< .03
Economic development	.13	< .04

With international climate

Shared principled agreement	.20	< .006
Hobbesian	-.18	< .01

Single and combined impact of a block of six systemic variables
and a block of four international climates (Multiple R^2):

systemic	.07		climate	.03
climate	.02		systemic	.06
	.09			.09

Multiple R = .41

(continued)

TABLE 7.7 (continued)

Cynicism
(t-value -.69)

Significant correlations

With systemic variables

Military expenditure	-.13	< .03
Center-periphery	-.13	< .04
(Security force investment	-.12	< .08)

With international climates

Shared principled agreement	-.16	< .03
International law	-.12	< .03
(We-ness	-.12	< .08)

Single and combined impact of a block of six systemic variables and a block of four international climates (Multiple R^2):

systemic	.03	climate	.01
climate	.04	systemic	.06
	.07		.07

Multiple R = .27

Discussion Moralized
(t-value -3.31; p-value < .005)

Significant correlations

With systemic variables

Economic development	-.31	< .001
Center-periphery	-.26	< .001
Military expenditure	-.26	< .001
Economic interdependency	-.20	< .003
Security force investment	-.15	< .04

With international climate

International law	.28	< .001

Single and combined impact of a block of six systemic variables and a block of four international climates (Multiple R^2):

systemic	.13	climate	.11*
climate	.10	systemic	.12*
	.13*		.23*

Multiple R = .48

*p < .05.
Source: Compiled by the author from his own research.

Cynicism

Cynicism, or the tendency to consistently perceive discrepancies between words, acts, and motives in international relations, seems to be more associated with diplomats from countries with a low military and economic status. International climates which tend to evoke less cynicism are the shared principled agreement and the international law climates. This finding is expected, for both environments are defined as being governed by legal and moral principles. The two blocks singly and in combination predict only a small portion (7 percent) of the variance.

Discussion Moralized

From the low mean (1.65 on a 1-3 scale) we can infer that diplomats in general do not tend to moralize about international issues. However, although diplomats from developing and developed countries are both low on moralizing, the latter (mean = 1.43) are significantly lower than the former (mean = 1.83). If we look at the significant correlations, we find that the economic development and the periphery-center variables are significantly and negatively correlated with this dependent variable. These findings are consistent with Hveem's (1972: 74-75) prediction that periphery country milieus tend to use a more moralistic approach, and center nation milieus a more pragmatic way of looking at problems. Table 7.7 also indicates that not only economically weak powers but also militarily weak powers are high on this stylistic characteristic. Thus, in general, weak positions tend to enhance the propensity of adding a moral dimension to a discussion of problems. Among the international climates, the type that is significantly correlated with the tendency to moralize is the international law climate (r = .28, p < .001). This means that a diplomat who describes the international environment as basically governed by international law tends to moralize more than his colleague, who considers the impact of international law as less consequential. The two blocks of variables are able to predict 23 percent of the variance. The block of climate variables predicts the dependent variable at a significance level of .05; and the block of systemic variables does not reach, but approximates, the .05 significance level.

Factor 6: Technology and Finance

Factor 6 includes the presence of references to technological and financial issues. On a scale from 1 to 3 the mean score for this factor was 1.6. This indicates that issues specifically related to finance and technology were frequently touched upon but did not tend to occupy a central place in most discussions. These issues were much more salient for developing-country diplomats ($t = -5.36$, $p < .005$). Their concerns relate to such issues as investments, transfer of capital, debts, transfer of technology, and so on. If we look at the significant correlations in Table 7.8 we see that this style of analysis is present in the thinking of diplomats from both economically and militarily weak countries. No significant correlations were found with international climates. Twenty-two percent of the variance of this style of analysis could be predicted by the systemic variables block ($p < .01$). The impact of the block of perceptual variables was nil.

TABLE 7.8

T-test, Significant Correlations, and Regression Analysis Data
for Technology and Finance
(t-value –5.36; p-value $< .005$)

Significant correlations

With systemic variables

Economic development	–.39	$< .001$
Center-periphery	–.35	$< .001$
Military interdependency	–.27	$< .001$
Economic interdependency	–.25	$< .001$
Security force investment	–.25	$< .001$

With international climate
None

Single and combined impact of a block of six systemic variables and a block of four international climates (Multiple R^2):

systemic .21[b]	climate .00
climate .01	systemic .22[a]
.22[b]	.22[b]

Multiple R = .47

---

[a]$p < .01$.

[b]$p < .05$.

Source: Compiled by the author from his own research.

Factor 7: Interdependency

The analysis of the world as interdependent received an over-all mean score of 1.8 (on a scale ranging from 1 to 3). A concern with issues of interdependency appeared most often in the discus-sions of diplomats from less-developed countries and countries with a low security force investment (see Table 7.9). In addition to recognizing interdependency as a central aspect of their world image, the diplomats of these countries stress the need for greater interdependency, as illustrated, for example, in this statement by a Latin American diplomat: "There is a future for regional move-ment—we are not sure that we want a U.S.-Latin America or Europe-Africa bloc—what we seek is real interdependency, the U.S. also dependent on Latin-America; what we need is multiple-interdependency." No significant relations with the perceptual variables were found. The perceptual and systemic variables to-gether account for 10 percent of the variance.

TABLE 7.9

T-test, Significant Correlations, and Regression Analysis
Data for Interdependency
(t-value -1.30; p-value < .10)

Significant correlations

With systemic variables
Security force investment	-.19	< .006
Economic development	-.12	< .05

With international climate
None

Single and combined impact of six systemic variables and a block of four international climates (Multiple R^2):

systemic	.06		climate	.05
climate	.04		systemic	.05
	.10			.10

Multiple R = .33

Source: Compiled by the author from his own research.

Factor 8: Particularizer-Generalizer

From the mean score (2.16) of this factor, we can infer that most discussions fell between the extreme categories and included some reference to both principles and details. In Table 7.10 we observe that diplomats from countries low on security force investment and on military and economic power have a greater tendency to generalize. It is characteristic of a generalizer that he sees important lines rather than technical questions and that he moves easily and quickly from specific cases to general principles. This finding lends support to Hveem's (1972: 14) hypothesis that center country milieus are more means-oriented and periphery country milieus more end-oriented. The international environments that are associated significantly with this analytic style are the Hobbesian climate ($r = -.18$, $p < .02$) and the we-ness environment ($r = .17$, $p < .02$). This means, for example, that a diplomat from a developing country who perceives the world as high on we-ness would tend to have a higher propensity to generalize than a colleague whose country occupies a similar international position, but who pictures the world in more Hobbesian terms. Both blocks of variables together explain 14 percent of the variance.

TABLE 7.10

T-test, Significant Correlations, and Regression Analysis
Data for Particularizer-Generalizer
(t-value -2.62; p-value $< .005$)

Significant correlations		
With systemic variables		
Security force investment	$-.28$	$< .001$
Degree of economic development	$-.17$	$< .01$
Economic interdependency	$-.15$	$< .02$
Center-periphery	$-.13$	$< .04$
Military expenditure	$-.11$	$< .05$
With international climates		
Hobbesian	$-.18$	$< .02$
We-ness	$.17$	$< .02$

Single and combined impact of a block of six systemic variables and a block of four international climates (Multiple R^2):

systemic	.10	climate	.06
climate	.04	systemic	.08
	.14		.14

Multiple R = .37

Source: Compiled by the author from his own research.

Factor 9: Reference to Ideology

From the mean of the total sample (1.4) we can infer that arguments based explicitly on a named ideology or doctrine are rare. The overall assessment of the role of ideology in international relations is negative. Some of the following quotations illustrate this debunking attitude:

> Any ideology is an honest attempt, but also a simple answer to a complex question.

> Ideology is a problem when there is an attempt to impose it on others.

> I don't give attention to ideologies; Morgenthau said that ideology is a veil for power politics.

> Countries are not run by ideologies, but by national interests.

> Ideology is a weapon of those who lack power.

> The world is not so much divided ideologically, but in relation to interests.

> There are no real ideological disputes—it is part of the public game—the free world used to include Portugal.

> Ideology has a role in secondary things.

Somewhat unexpectedly, we notice that diplomats from countries high on security force investment and from "center" countries have a higher propensity to base their argument on a named ideology or doctrine (see Table 7.11). The ideologies most often mentioned by these diplomats are liberalism, free enterprise, capitalism, democracy, Christianity, and neutralism. There is no effect whatsoever of international climate, and the two blocks together explain 8 percent of the variance.

Factor 10: Disapproval of External Control

Factor 10 represents the clustering of three primary characteristics: penetration sensitivity, discussion moralized, and perception of the present world as conflictual. This factor reflects a central concern with domestic interference, combined with a tendency to blame the responsible country or group of countries, and to perceive the present world as conflictual. We elected to call this factor "disapproval of external control." Concern with sovereignty seems to be a much more salient factor in the analysis of diplomats from countries with low economic and military power (see Table 7.12). This finding is congruent with Nye's (1971: 41) observation that sovereignty seems to be more jealously guarded by the poorer states." The mean score for disapproval of external control is 2.92, on a scale ranging from 1 to 5. Also important to notice, and somewhat unexpected, is the significant and negative correlation with the penetration variable ($r = -.18$, $p < .02$). This correlation indicates that within the subgroup of penetrated countries, the least penetrated tend to be the most articulate in their expression of disapproval of domestic interference. No significant correlations with the perceptual variables are found. Both blocks combined predict 30 percent of the variance, and only the system variables block contributes significantly to the prediction.

TABLE 7.11

T-test, Significant Correlations, and Regression Analysis
Data for Reference to Ideology
(t-value 1.10)

Significant correlations

With systemic variables

Security force investment	.19	$< .006$
Center-periphery	.14	$< .02$

With international climate
None

Single and combined impact of a block of six systemic variables and a block of four international climates (Multiple R^2):

systemic	.07	climate	.00
climate	.01	systemic	.08
	.08		.08

Multiple R = .29

Source: Compiled by the author from his own research.

TABLE 7.12

T-test, Significant Correlations, and Regression Analysis
Data for Disapproval of External Control
(t-value -5.43; p-value $< .005$)

Significant correlations

With systemic variables

Center-periphery	-.43	$< .001$
Degree of development	-.45	$< .001$
Military expenditure	-.30	$< .001$
Economic interdependency	-.21	$< .001$
Security force investment	-.16	$< .02$
Penetration	-.18	$< .02$

With international climate
None

Single and combined impact of a block of six systemic variables
and a block of four international climates (Multiple R^2):

systemic	.28[a]	climate	.03
climate	.02	systemic	.27[b]
	.30[b]		.30[b]

Multiple R = .58

[a]$p < .001$.
[b]$p < .01$.
Source: Compiled by the author from his own research.

Factor 11: World is Inherently Conflictual

A mean score of 3.7 clearly indicates that the analysis of the
world as a place where conflicts are intrinsic is widely shared by
all diplomats (see Table 7.13). However, in the analytic style of
diplomats from highly penetrated countries, this characteristic
tends to be most salient ($r = .18$, $p < .02$). The international climate that is significantly associated with this analytic style is the
instrumental-exchange climate ($r = .25$, $p < .001$). This seems to
indicate that diplomats who perceive the world as a level 2 environment have a higher propensity to accept conflict as a given or a
constant in international relations than do diplomats who score low
on "instrumental exchange" climate. Twelve percent of the variance
on this factor can be predicted by the two blocks of variables combined.

TABLE 7.13

T-test, Significant Correlations, and Regression Analysis
Data for World is Inherently Conflictual
(t-value .34)

Significant correlations		
With systemic variables		
Penetration	.18	$< .02$
With international climate		
Instrumental-exchange	.25	$< .001$

Single and combined impact of a block of six systemic variables
and a block of four international climates (Multiple R^2):

systemic	.04	climate	.07
climate	.08	systemic	.05
	.12		.12

Multiple $R = .34$

Source: Compiled by the author from his own research.

CONCLUSION

    The results indicate a strong effect of the systemic position
of a country on the style of analysis of its diplomats. For example,
when we compare the diplomatic styles of analysis from developed
and developing countries, we find significant differences in the
tendency to analyze the world in structural terms, to model international relations as a zero- or nonzero-sum game, to moralize
about an issue, to focus on technology and financial problems, and
to show concern with noninterference or national sovereignty. The
least affected by this structural position are the tendency to include
the historical context in the discussion of an issue, to refer to
national interests as a criterion of good foreign policy, and to model
the world as a conflictual system. An overview of the largest and
smallest differences in analytic style between diplomats from developed and developing countries can be found in Table 7.14.

TABLE 7.14

Overview of the Largest and Smallest Differences
in Analytic Styles between Diplomats from
Developed and Developing Countries

	t-value	p-value <
Sensitivity to external control	−5.43	.005
Technology/finance	−5.36	.005
Structural analysis	−4.69	.005
Discussion moralized	−3.31	.005
Particularizer-generalizer	−2.62	.005
Zero-sum analysis	−1.88	.05
National loyalty	1.46	.10
Interdependency	−1.30	.10
Reference to ideology	1.10	
Cynicism	−.69	
National interests	.40	
World is inherently conflictual	.34	
Historical style of analysis	.09	

Source: Compiled by the author from his own research.

The systemic variables that on average explain most of the
variation of the analytic styles are the periphery-center position
and the degree of economic development of a country; they are followed by military expenditure and the degree of security force
investment, and further, in order of diminishing impact: economic
interdependency, aid received, and penetration (see Table 7.15).
For the analytic styles with respect to which the diplomats differ
most (see Table 7.14), the block of systemic variables can, on the
average, predict 22 percent of the variance. The fact that aid
receipt, for example, has low impact overall does not mean this
systemic variable can be neglected. It happens to be an important
variable in relation to one specific analytic style, the zero-sum
style of analysis. The same is true for the other systemic variables that have a low overall impact. The impact of the perceptual
variables is markedly lower than that of the systemic variables

TABLE 7.15

Overview of the Correlations of Systemic and Climate Variables with Analytic Style Dimensions

	Structural Analysis	Historical Analysis	Zero-sum Analysis	National Interests	Fault-finding	Partisan-ship	Cynicism	Moralized Discussion	Technology and Finance	Interde-pendency	Particularizer-Generalizer	Reference to Ideology	Disapproval of External Control	World is Inherently Conflictual	Number of Correlations ≥10	≥20	≥30	Average Correlation
Center-periphery	-.34	-.00	-.17	.00	-.26	.14	-.13	-.26	-.35	-.09	-.13	.14	-.43	.06	10	5	3	18
Economic development	-.39	-.00	-.12	-.00	-.25	.13	-.03	-.31	-.39	-.12	-.17	.10	-.45	.03	10	5	4	18
Security force	-.37	.15	-.04	.03	-.12	.04	-.10	-.19	-.25	-.19	-.28	.19	-.16	-.10	11	3	1	16
Military expenditure	-.36	.05	-.23	-.00	-.27	.14	-.13	-.26	-.27	-.07	-.11	.08	-.30	-.03	9	6	2	16
Economic interdependency	-.18	-.10	-.05	-.00	-.05	-.04	.07	-.20	-.25	.01	-.15	.11	-.29	-.03	7	3	0	11
Aid receipt	.19	.12	-.24	-.05	.02	-.08	-.10	-.01	.11	.06	.01	.10	.04	-.11	7	1	0	9
Penetration	.09	-.12	.15	.00	-.06	-.04	.04	-.15	.03	.01	-.06	-.04	-.18	.18	5	0	0	8
Hobbesian	.15	.04	.19	-.06	.18	-.18	.12	.04	.07	.08	-.18	-.02	.08	.02	6	0	0	10
Marxian	.13	-.00	-.01	-.06	-.01	-.03	.01	-.07	-.01	.00	.04	.01	.00	.01	1	0	0	3
Instrumental-exchange	.01	-.00	.06	-.19	-.01	.03	.00	-.03	-.00	.12	.13	-.02	.07	.25	4	1	0	7
We-ness	-.18	-.10	-.20	.07	-.13	.09	-.12	-.01	-.08	-.10	.17	-.04	-.09	-.10	8	1	0	10
International law	.07	.01	-.02	-.06	.09	.01	-.05	.28	-.00	.12	.09	.05	.10	.08	3	1	0	7
Shared principled agreement	-.17	-.05	-.21	.22	-.22	.20	-.16	-.05	-.00	-.05	.06	.03	-.09	-.08	6	4	0	12

Source: Compiled by the author from his own research.

(see Table 7.15). Again, this does not mean that they are irrelevant. Although their overall impact is much lower than that of the systemic variables, in relation to some specific variables their impact is greater. Therefore, they have to be considered for a better understanding and prediction of certain analytic styles. For example, the analytic style that is most affected by differences in the perception of the international environment is the tendency to moralize. Eleven percent of the variance of this analytic style is accounted for by the block of perceptual variables ($p < .05$).

8

Strategic Approach

STRATEGIC APPROACH AND THE COMPARATIVE
STUDY OF DIPLOMATIC THINKING

The fourth component of diplomatic thinking is strategic approach. It refers to the ways in which time and means are combined for the purpose of achieving goals. In this chapter we are interested in identifying and structuring different predispositions of diplomats to act toward the foreign policy environment. To distinguish and understand differences in these predispositions contributes to foreign policy prediction (D'Amato 1967) and also helps us to understand changes in the history of international relations (Kissinger 1974). For example, Kissinger (1974: 46–47) describes, as the deepest problem of contemporary international order, the cleavage between two styles of policy, namely the style of the statesman and that of the prophet.

> The statesman manipulates reality; his first goal is sur-
> vival; he feels responsible not only for the best but also
> for the worst conceivable outcome. His view of human
> nature is wary; he is conscious of many great hopes
> which have failed, of selfishness and ambition and vio-
> lence. He is therefore inclined to expect hedges against
> any possibility that even the most brilliant idea might
> prove abortive and that the most eloquent formulation
> might hide ulterior motives. He will try to avoid cer-
> tain experiments, not because he would object to the
> results if he succeeded, but because he would feel him-
> self responsible for the consequences if they failed.
> He is suspicious of those who personalize foreign

policy, for history teaches him the fragility of structures dependent on individuals. To the statesman
gradualism is the essence of stability; he represents
an era of average performance, of gradual change and
slow reconstruction.

By contrast,

the prophet is less concerned with manipulating than
with creating reality. What is possible interests him
less than what is "right." He offers his vision as a
test and his good faith as a guarantee. He believes in
total solutions; he is less absorbed in methodology than
in purpose. He believes in perfectibility of man. His
approach is timeless and not dependent on circum-
stances. He will risk everything because his vision is
the primary significant reality to him. Paradoxically,
his more optimistic view of human nature makes him
more intolerant than the statesman. If truth is both
knowable and attainable, only immorality or stupidity
can keep man from realizing it.

These two descriptions are good examples of different strategic approaches.

Do diplomats tend to be statesmanlike, or are they more like
prophets? Do they resemble doves more than hawks? Is the propensity to compromise one of their dominant characteristics? These
and other questions are addressed in this chapter. In addition to examining differences in the strategic thinking of diplomats, we will
inquire whether and to what extent variations in strategic approach
between diplomats can be explained in terms of the international
positions of their countries and their perceptions of the international
environment. To do so, we will start by listing some relevant characteristics that can be used for describing and classifying different
strategies. These characteristics (variables) will then be factor-
analyzed to determine which factors are most useful in economically
describing the phenomenon under study. Subsequently, on the basis
of factor scores, we will inquire into the relationships between
strategic approach and systemic and perceptual variables.

Let us now look in greater detail at some strategic characteristics and the way we measured the diplomats' positions on them.
The selection and the definition of relevant characteristics grew out
of intuition, reading, and discussions with students of international
relations.

STRATEGIC CHARACTERISTICS

Unwillingness to Compromise

The first source of variation in strategic style that we distinguished related to the diplomat's unwillingness to compromise or his flexibility or inflexibility in decision making. We have two indicators of the degree of presence of this characteristic, namely, the diplomat's response on a five-point scale from strongly disagree to strongly agree to the following statements:

> In a situation of an international controversy where it seems that one side is clearly right and the other side is clearly wrong, I would be inclined to stick to my position.

> To compromise with foreign opponents is dangerous because it usually leads to the betrayal of our side.

Degree of Extremism

Somewhat related to the willingness to compromise is the diplomat's propensity to extremism. This predisposition was operationalized as the diplomat's response on a five-point scale (from strongly disagree to strongly agree) to the following item:

> Generally speaking, in international controversies extreme positions should be avoided, for the proper approach lies somewhere in the middle.

Degree of Gradualism (Timing)

The next characteristic relates to the timing of desired change. In other words, we are focusing on preference for gradual versus instant changes in the existing world. The responses (on a five-point scale) to "Changes in the international relations system have to be made gradually," were used as indicators of differences in the employment of time.

Incremental versus Avulsive

In addition to differences in strategic approach in terms of timing, we can also classify them in terms of the scope of change that the actor envisages. This variable could be labeled "Incremental-Avulsive" (D'Amato 1967) and reflects the degree to which an actor attempts to change existing policy to shape it more in the direction of his own preferred image. The alternatives are no or marginal variation from the status quo to a drastic change. As a measure of the diplomat's stand vis-a-vis these options, we used his response on a five-point scale (from strongly disagree to strongly agree) to the following item:

> To bring about a stable peace in the world, total and radical changes are necessary.

Dove versus Hawk

The next strategic characteristic has been given several names, from dove/hawk (D'Amato 1967) to tender versus tough-minded (Eysenck 1954; Rokeach 1956), and refers to the degree to which a person indicates a militant attitude in his proposals or recommendations for change. The toughminded will tend to advocate the use of force in foreign policy, whereas the tenderminded will be reluctant to use force. To locate the diplomats on this dimension, we used two indicators: The first was response to the following item in our questionnaire: "To bring about greater changes for the benefit of mankind often requires the use of arms." The second indicator was derived from the interview data. A content analysis was done of the diplomats' recommendations to achieve peace and their preferred world order. We gave a score of 1 when the use of physical force was not mentioned. A 2 was assigned when physical force was considered as a last resort or when it was mentioned as an option, but with reservations. Then the scale jumped to a score of 4, used for any comment that referred to force as a necessary ingredient of a peaceful world. The reliability of the score for this variable was .43, and 5 percent of the scores were positioned at the opposite sides of the scale.

Self-Reliance

The next two strategic characteristics are related in the sense that they both reflect strategic thinking dominated by a concern with self-reliance. The first variable was labeled "plea for less domestic interference and more independence." A score of 1 was given when no such plea was expressed at all; 2 for expressing this particular plea vaguely or in passing; and 3 for a plea that occupied a

central place in the set of recommendations and proposals made by
the diplomat. The reliability coefficient of this indicator was .46,
and 20 percent of the scores were rated more than one point apart.
We will refer to the next variable as "plea for self-sufficiency."
The coding procedure was similar to the one described above. Here,
for example, a high rating was assigned to an Asian diplomat who
strongly argued for his country: "We must develop maximally ourselves, because we can't depend on others." The reliability coefficient for this variable was .26, and 15 percent of the scores were
placed at opposite sides of the scale.

Degree of Expedience

Another characteristic concerns the extent to which the respondent approaches issues expediently or, in other words, tends
to adhere to expedient means and methods more than to principles.
Differences in relation to this particular predisposition were measured by means of the diplomat's response on a five-point scale
(from strongly disagree to strongly agree) to this item: "I don't
mind the diplomat's methods if he manages to get the right thing
done."

Idealism versus Realism

Another five-point scale rated the extent to which the diplomat
balanced realism and idealism. His response to the following statement was used as a measure of this strategic characteristic: "Foreign policy is the art of the possible and the government should not
worry about grand plans and distant goals."

Optimism versus Pessimism about the Future

Diplomats also differ in terms of their expectations about the
chances of success in the achievement of their goals. In this connection, we used two indicators of the degree of optimism or pessimism vis-a-vis two different goals: the absence of violence and
the realization of peace and justice in the world. To assess the diplomats' optimism or pessimism about the realization of these goals,
we used their responses on a five-point scale (from strongly disagree to strongly agree) to the following items:

In the next four years we will have an increase of violence in the world.

I am basically optimistic that progress will be made
toward a more peaceful and just world.

Structural Equality

The next two strategic characteristics are related in that they
both focus on structural changes in the international system. The
first strategy aims at structural equality and is measured by the
diplomat's response to this item: "A genuine and lasting peace could
be achieved only after the establishment of a classless world." The
second strategy concerns itself with the problem of the distribution
and enlargement of the world economic pie. The responses on a
five-point scale (from strongly disagree to strongly agree) to the
item, "We should opt for faster economic growth, rather than for a
redistribution of wealth and income to solve the poverty problem"
were used as indicators of this strategic characteristic.

Plea for Global Cooperation

The next characteristic concerns the extent to which the diplomat considers "cooperation on a global basis" as an appropriate
strategy. We coded the diplomat's proposals and recommendations
for peace and his preferred world order on a three-point scale. A 1
was given when there was no mention of cooperation at all; a 2 when
global cooperation was mentioned vaguely or in passing; and a 3 when
the reference to cooperation was central to his argument. A reliability score of .58 was obtained, and 10 percent of the scores were
located at the opposite sides of the scale.

Plea for Integration

Diplomats also differed with respect to their promotion of integration as a means toward the realization of peace and their preferred world order. The procedure for coding responses was similar to the one described above. An East European diplomat, for example, who began his set of recommendations with the following comment was given the highest score: "What is needed is a development
of circular integration, starting with the strengthening of regional
links between countries and then further growth as the ripples of a

pond." The intercoder reliability for this variable amounted to .37, and 10 percent of the scores were more than one point apart.

Use of Nuclear Weapons

Finally, we obtained the diplomats' stand vis-a-vis the use of nuclear weapons in international relations. To ascertain their stand concerning this issue, we asked them if they could imagine any goal, value, or ideal that could justify the use of nuclear weapons. The answers to this question were coded in two ways. The first code distinguished yes (2) and no (1) answers. The second code ranked the answers in terms of the strength of the reservations expressed. A score of 1 was given when there was no mention of reservations. The difference between an intermediate score (2) and the highest score (3) was in the strength with which the reservation(s) were expressed. For example, a score of 2 was assigned to diplomats expressing their reservations as follows:

> If you want to kill people, you can kill them with conventional weapons.

> There are too many disadvantages linked with its use.

> Its use must be commensurable to the cause that makes you apply such a force.

A score of 3 was given, for example, to the following responses:

> Its use is totally unacceptable and beyond all the limits of morality.

> It would be horrendous; even thinking about it causes people to have a sober moment.

> It ceases to be a war on a specific enemy, but a war on mankind.

> It would be the most repugnant crime.

No reliability coding was performed in relation to the last two variables.

These, then, are the main characteristics of the strategic approach investigated in this research project. Table 8.1 presents the means and the standard deviations for the total sample of diplomats.

TABLE 8.1

Means and Standard Deviations of the Strategic Approach
Variables for the Total Sample of Diplomats

	Scale	Means	Standard Deviation
Unwillingness to compromise			
In a situation of an international controversy where it seems that one side is clearly right and the other side clearly wrong, I would be inclined to stick strongly to my position.	1–5	3.58	1.03
To compromise with foreign opponents is dangerous because it usually leads to the betrayal of our side.	1–5	2.38	.96
Degree of extremism			
Generally speaking, in international controversies, extreme positions should be avoided, for the proper approach lies somewhere in the middle.	1–5	3.82	.88
Degree of gradualism (timing)			
Changes in international relations have to be made gradually.	1–5	4.15	.912
Incremental versus avulsive (scope of change)			
To bring about a stable peace in the world, total and radical changes are necessary.	1–5	3.21	1.15
Dove versus Hawk			
To bring about greater changes for the benefit of mankind often requires the use of arms.	1–5	1.92	1.04
Inclination to use of military or other violent force	1–4	1.55	.997
Self-reliance			
Plea for self-determination	1–3	1.94	.968
Plea for self-sufficiency	1–3	1.49	.796

(continued)

Table 8.1 continued

	Scale	Means	Standard Deviation
Degree of expediency			
I don't mind a diplomat's methods if he manages to get the right thing done.	1-5	2.70	1.24
Idealism versus realism			
Foreign policy is the act of the possible and governments should not worry about grand plans and distant goals.	1-5	2.88	1.07
Optimism versus pessimism about the future			
In the next four years we will have an increase in armed violence in the world.	1-5	2.92	.778
I am basically optimistic that progress will be made toward a more peaceful and just world.	1-5	3.59	.752
Structural equality			
A genuine and lasting peace could be achieved only after the establishment of a classless world.	1-5	2.34	1.18
Enlargement versus redistribution of the economic pie			
We should opt for faster economic growth, rather than for a redistribution of wealth and income to solve the poverty problem.	1-5	2.76	1.11
Global cooperation			
Plea for global cooperation	1-3	2.09	.923
Integration			
Plea for integration	1-3	1.89	.964
Use of nuclear weapons			
There are conditions that justify the use of nuclear weapons.	1-3	1.34	.475
Expression of reservations.	1-3	2.64	.719

Source: Compiled by the author from his own research.

DIMENSIONS OF STRATEGIC APPROACH

Do these strategic characteristics cluster into any intelligible pattern, and if so, what are the main dimensions of the strategic approach? To answer this question we follow the same procedure that was used for the analytic style of the diplomats (see Chapter 7). We will examine the correlations among the several strategic characteristics across different respondents. If diplomats who tend to be high, for example, on the first characteristic also tend to be high on the fourth characteristic, we can infer that these characteristics form a strategic-group cluster. An efficient way for identifying such strategic groups is factor analysis. We performed a factor analysis on all the variables listed in Table 8.1, with the exception of items 12, 13, 14, and 15. The decision to include these four variables in the analysis of strategic approach was made quite late, after the factor analysis had already been performed. The scores of the 15 remaining variables listed in Table 8.1 were intercorrelated and the resultant matrix of intercorrelations was factor analyzed, using the varimax rotation procedure. Table 8.2 identifies the eight factors which were extracted from the data. Having obtained these eight factors, we calculated factor scores for each diplomat. We chose to include in the calculation only those variables that had a loading higher than .35. Each diplomat was then given a score on each factor which is the composite of the variable scores that load on the factor, weighted by their factor score coefficients. For example, for the self-reliance strategy, each diplomat's "plea for self-sufficiency" score was multiplied by .322 (factor-score coefficient). A diplomat's score for the other variable that loaded above .35 on Factor 1 was likewise multiplied by its factor-score coefficient and the sum of the two was used to obtain the factor score for self-reliance strategy. (For the calculation of all factor scores see Appendix J.)

STRATEGIC APPROACH, SYSTEMIC POSITION, AND MORAL-POLITICAL CLIMATE

In this section we will focus on each of these factors consecutively and examine whether and to what extent they are a function of systemic and perceptual variables (international climates). For each factor we will proceed as follows: First, we will look at the mean of the total sample, to get an idea of the central tendency of the factor scores. Then we will compare diplomats from developed and developing countries by means of t-tests. Of the remaining independent variables (seven systemic and six perceptual) we will

TABLE 8.2

A Factor Analysis of the Strategic Characteristics
for the Total Sample of Diplomats

Factor 1: Self-reliance strategy	
8 Plea for self-determination	.675
9 Plea for self-sufficiency	.569
Factor 2: Prudence	
3 Generally speaking, in international controversies . . .	.635
4 Changes in international relations . . .	.491
11 Art of possible	.426
Factor 3: Global cooperation	
16 Plea for global cooperation	.613
Factor 4: Degree of expediency	
10 Goal justifies means	.483
6 To bring about greater changes . . .	.474
Factor 5: Radical nonviolent change	
7 Use of military or other violent force	-.373
5 To bring about a stable peace . . .	.305
Factor 6: Flexibility-unflexibility	
1 In a situation of international controversy . . .	.666
2 To compromise is dangerous	.547
Factor 7: Nonuse of nuclear weapons	
19 Expression of reservations	.771
18 There are conditions that justify the use of nuclear weapons	-.481
Factor 8: Integration	
17 Plea for integration	.656

Note: Entries are loadings of the strategic characteristics on factors--cut-off point was loading $\geq$ .30.

Source: Compiled by the author from his own research.

describe only those that are significantly correlated with the dependent variable. Finally, we will form a group of systemic variables and a group of perceptual variables, and study whether and to what extent these two blocks, separately or in combination, have an impact on each dependent variable. To measure the single and combined impact of these two blocks, we regressed our dependent variables on six systemic variables (economic development, penetratedness, economic interdependency, military expenditure, security force investment, and aid received), and four perceptual variables

(Hobbesian, Marxian, instrumental-exchange, and international law climates). We did not include the center-periphery variable because of its high correlation with the degree of development and military expenditure ($r = .85$ and $.83$, respectively). For similar reasons excluded the we-ness and the shared principles agreement climates. The intercorrelations between these two variables was $.75$, and both had a high negative correlation with the Hobbesian climate ($r = -.84$ and $-.81$, respectively). For each dependent variable we did two multiple regressions. In the first we entered the block of systemic variables first, then the block of perceptual variables. In the second analysis, the order of entry was reversed. Such a procedure gives us an idea about the predictive power of both blocks of variables combined, it allows us to assess the impact of the blocks of variables separately, and it gives us an idea of the impact of one block of variables after the effect of the other block is removed.

Factor 1: Self-Reliance Strategy

Factor 1 represents the clustering of two primary characteristics: plea for less domestic interference and plea for self-sufficiency. This factor reflects the strength of the tendency to consider the achievement of more self-reliance as a necessary condition for the realization of peace or of preferred world order. From a rather low mean of 1.71, on a scale from 1 to 3, we can infer that this strategy is not predominant for most diplomats. However, there are significant differences between subgroups of diplomats. In the strategic approach of diplomats from developing or periphery countries, this factor occupies a much more central place (see Table 8.3). Significant negative correlations are also found between this strategy and military expenditure and security force investment. This means that diplomats from countries that are both economically and militarily weak have a predominant concern with independence. For weaker powers political independence is perceived as a means to an end. Its value lies in its use to establish new economic, social, and cultural conditions, which their current position restrains. A last systemic variable that was found to be significantly and negatively correlated with the self-reliance strategy is economic interdependency. This indicates that diplomats from countries whose standard of living is very dependent on foreign trade and import tend to be less in favor of the self-reliance strategy than their colleagues from countries that are economically less interdependent. The degree of saliency of this strategy in the strategic approach of the diplomat is mainly influenced by systemic variables. If we look at Table 8.3, we notice that the contribution of the block of perceptual variables to the prediction of this strategy is nearly nil; on the other hand, the block of systemic variables is able to account for approximately 25 percent of the variance ($p < .05$).

TABLE 8.3

T-test, Significant Correlations, and Regression Analysis
Data for Self-Reliance Strategy
(t-value -4.74; p-value $< .005$)

Significant correlations
  With systemic variables

Center-periphery	-.42	$< .001$
Economic development	-.39	$< .001$
Military expenditure	-.31	$< .001$
Security force investment	-.17	$< .01$
Economic interdependency	-.16	$< .01$

  With international climate
    None

Single and combined impact of a block of six systemic variables and a block of four international climates (Multiple R^2):

systemic	.24		climate	.01
climate	.02		systemic	.25
	.26			.26

Multiple R = .51

Source: Compiled by the author from his own research.

Factor 2: Strategy of Prudence

Factor 2 includes three variables: the degree of nonextremism, gradualism, and realism of the diplomat. This factor should probably be termed "strategy of prudence." This strategy reflects circumspection as to the danger or risks involved in the management of practical affairs. With respect to this strategy, no significant differences were found between diplomats from developed and developing countries. The mean for the developing countries was somewhat higher but not significant. The most prudent diplomats seem to come from countries who are high on aid received and low on security force investment (see Table 8.4). On the other hand, developing countries that receive the least aid and countries that have highly invested in security forces tend to produce the least prudent diplomats. None of the international climates produced a significant correlation with this strategy. We did not present the multiple regression data because the multiple R^2 was unreliable; within the blocks, multicolinearity and a substantial degree of cooperative suppression were going on, so that, for example, the total R^2 for the six systemic variables was much greater than the summation of the R^2 of the variables which make up this block.

TABLE 8.4

T-test and Significant Correlations for Prudence
(t-value -.47)

Significant correlations		
With systemic variables		
Aid receipt	.25	<.004
Security force investment	-.15	<.03
Penetration	-.13	
With international climates		
None		

Source: Compiled by the author from his own research.

Factor 3: Global Cooperation

The extent to which diplomats are proponents of global cooperation is another source of variation in their strategic approach. As we see in Table 8.5, there is no significant difference between the diplomats from developed and developing countries, and the only systemic position which has an effect on this strategy is the amount of aid received ($r = .14$, $p < .05$). This means that, among the subgroups of aid-receiving countries, those that receive the most aid are also most favorable toward increasing cooperation at a global level. There is one perceptual variable that is highly correlated with this strategy: the instrumental exchange environment ($r = -.19$, $p < .01$). This indicates that a diplomat who characterizes the international environment in instrumental exchange terms tends to downplay global cooperation as an appropriate strategy to realize his goals. The combined and single impact of our blocks of variables is nonsignificant; together they explain 13 percent of the variance.

TABLE 8.5

T-test, Significant Correlations, and Regression Analysis
Data for Global Cooperation
(t-value -.17)

Significant correlations
  With systemic variables
  Aid receipt   .14   <.05

  With international climate
  Instrumental exchange   -.19   <.01

Single and combined impact of a block of six systemic variables
and a block of four international climates (Multiple R^2):

systemic	.04		climate	.06
climate	.09		systemic	.07
	.13			.13
Multiple R = .36				

Source: Compiled by the author from his own research.

Factor 4: End Justifies Means Strategy

   Factor 4 represents the clustering of two primary characteristics: the degree of expediency (item 10) and the assertion that
greater changes for mankind often require the use of arms (item 6).
It would be fair to label this factor "end justifies means strategy."
As indicated by the means of both component variables, this strategy
is highly disapproved of by the diplomats, especially when it concerns the use of arms. The degree of disapproval, however, differs
for diplomats from developing and developed countries. Diplomats
from developing countries tend to express a less-negative attitude
vis-a-vis this strategy (t = -2.10, p< .02). A similar disposition
is found among diplomats from countries low in military power.
Thus the economically and militarily weaker powers tend to express
a higher degree of expediency. The environments that are associated
significantly with this strategy are instrumental exchange and the
Marxian environments. On the basis of these findings, we could
predict that the diplomats who describe themselves as most expedient tend to come from weaker countries and perceive the world as
exploitative, as a stratified system, or as an instrumental exchange
environment. Both blocks of variables together explain approximately 20 percent of the variance (see Table 8.6).

TABLE 8.6

T-test, Significant Correlations, and Regression
Analysis Data for Degree of Expediency

I don't mind a diplomat's methods
      t-value -1.88; p-value <.05
Use of arms
      t-value -1.51; p-value <.10
Together: factor 4
      t-value -2.10; p-value <.02

Significant correlations
  With systemic variables

Center-periphery	-.24	<.001
Military expenditure	-.23	<.001
Economic development	-.18	<.008
Economic interdependency	-.17	<.01
Security force investment	-.16	<.02

  With international climates

Instrumental exchange	.23	<.002
Marxian	.17	<.01

Single and combined impact of a block of six systemic variables
and a block of four international climates (Multiple R^2):

systemic	.12	climate	.08
climate	.08	systemic	.12
	.20		.20

Multiple R = .45

Source: Compiled by the author from his own research.

Factor 5: Radical Change/Nonviolent

On this factor two primary characteristics loaded higher than
.30: incremental versus avulsive change and the tendency to mention use of military power for establishing or preserving peace or a
preferred world order. The last variable has a negative loading.
This factor differentiates diplomats who promote radical changes in
a nonviolent manner from those who consistently talk in more incremental terms and consider military power as a necessary ingredient
of the preservation or establishment of peace. As can be seen in
Table 8.7, diplomats from developing countries are significantly

more in favor of this strategy (t = -3.54, p < .005). This conclusion is further supported by the significant negative correlations between this strategy and the periphery-center and economic interdependency variables. The other systemic variables which are significantly and negatively correlated are military expenditure, penetratedness, and the degree of security force investment. With the exception of the highly penetrated countries, this strategy seems to be more typical for the "weaker" countries. None of the perceptual variables is significantly correlated with this strategy. The systemic variables block accounts for approximately 16 percent of the variance (p < .05).

TABLE 8.7

T-test, Significant Correlations, and Regression Analysis
Data for Radical Nonviolent Change
(t-value -3.54; p-value < .005)

Significant correlations		
With systemic variables		
Economic development	-.36	<.001
Center-periphery	-.28	<.001
Economic interdependency	-.23	<.004
Military expenditure	-.22	<.005
Penetration	-.19	<.03
Security force investment	-.16	<.03
With international climate		
None		

Single and combined effect of a block of six systemic variables and a block of four international climates (Multiple R^2):

systemic	.16*		climate	.01
climate	.04		systemic	.19*
	.20*			.20*
Multiple R = .45				

*p < .05.
Source: Compiled by the author from his own research.

Factor 6: Flexible-Rigid

Factor 6 includes two variables that indicate a disapproval of compromise as a strategy, and it corresponds to the dimension of flexibility versus rigidity in negotiations. Looking at Table 8.8, we notice that none of the systemic variables, except for amount of aid received, are significantly correlated with this strategy. This would indicate that the disposition to favor this strategy is similar for diplomats from different systemic positions. The mean of the total sample of diplomats is 2.98 on a 1-5 scale, an indication of a 50-50 attitude toward this strategy. Some of the meanings associated with such a 50-50 response are illustrated by the following comments of diplomats:

> Compromise--yes, assuming the compromise is not dictated.

> You have to compromise in behavior, not in mind.

As can be seen, responses to the compromise statements tend to be phrased in conditional terms, starting with "It depends. . . ."

TABLE 8.8

T-test, Significant Correlations, and Regression Analysis
Data for Flexibility-Unflexibility
(t-value -.29)

Significant correlations		
With systemic variables		
Aid receipt	-.15	<.05
With international climate		
International law	.14	<.05

Single and combined effect of a block of six systemic variables and a block of four international climates (Multiple R^2):

systemic	.06		climate	.03
climate	.03		systemic	.06
	.09			.09
Multiple R = .30				

Source: Compiled by the author from his own research.

The diplomats who expressed the greatest inflexibility tended to come from developing countries ranking low in the amount of aid received and perceiving international relations as governed by international law (see Table 8.8). The amount of variance explained by both blocks of variables amounted to 9 percent.

Factor 7: Disapproval of the Use of Nuclear Weapons

This factor includes our two measures of the diplomats' attitudes toward the use of nuclear weapons. Differences in attitude with respect to this strategy are here strongly related to the country's economic and military power position. Diplomats from economically and militarily weak powers tend to express stronger reservations about the proposition to use nuclear weapons in international relations than their colleagues from developed and more powerful countries (see Table 8.9). Differences with respect to this strategy are not significantly associated with different perceptions of the international environment. The block of systemic variables is the only one that significantly predicts approximately 22 percent of the variance ($p < .01$).

TABLE 8.9

T-test, Significant Correlations, and Regression Analysis
Data for Use of Nuclear Weapons
(t-value −4.21; p-value $< .005$)

Significant correlations		
With systemic variables		
Center-periphery	−.39	$<.001$
Economic development	−.39	$<.001$
Security force investment	−.33	$<.001$
Military expenditure	−.33	$<.001$

Single and combined impact of block of six systemic variables and a block of four international climates (Multiple R^2):

systemic	.22[a]	climate	.05
climate	.02	systemic	.19[b]
	.24[b]		.24[b]

Multiple R = .49

[a]$p < .01$.   [b]$p < .05$.
Source: Compiled by the author from his own research.

Factor 8: Integration Strategy

This factor reflects the degree of importance the diplomats assigned to integration as a means to furthering international peace and their preferred world order (see Table 8.10). The only significantly related systemic variable is the degree of economic interdependency (t = .18, p < .008). This means that diplomats from countries whose standard of living is very dependent on foreign trade and the import of energy tend to be more in favor of integration than their colleagues from countries that are economically less interdependent. The perceived international environments that are significantly associated with this strategy are the we-ness and the Hobbesian environments (r = .19, p < .01 and r = -.16, p < .03, respectively). From these correlations we could infer that diplomats from countries high on interdependency and on we-ness or low on Hobbesian climate would tend to score highest on this strategy. We did not present the multiple regression data because the multiple R^2 was unreliable; within the blocks, multicolinearity and a substantial degree of cooperative suppression were going on, so that, for example, the total R^2 for the six systemic variables was much higher than the summation of the variables which make up the block.

TABLE 8.10

T-test and Significant Correlations for Integration
(t-value .55)

Significant correlations		
With systemic variables		
Economic interdependency	.18	<.008
Penetration	-.10	<.10
With international climates		
We-ness	.19	<.01
Hobbesian	-.16	<.03

Source: Compiled by the author from his own research.

Let us now look at the other variables which we did not include in the factor analysis, but which can also be considered as relevant strategic characteristics.

Structural Equality

The statement, "A genuine and lasting peace could be achieved only after the establishment of a classless world," received mostly a negative response, as indicated by the low mean (2.34 on a 1-5 scale). Although the difference is not significant, diplomats from developing countries have a higher mean, suggesting a slightly more positive attitude toward this strategy. The significant and negative correlation between this strategy and degree of economic development underscores this conclusion (see Table 8.11). Unexpected is the significant and negative correlation with the degree of penetration, indicating that diplomats from highly penetrated countries consider this strategy less favorably than their colleagues from less-penetrated countries. One possible explanation could be that diplomats from the most-penetrated countries score lower than their colleagues from less-penetrated countries because of their greater exposure to the "reality" of structural penetratedness or inequality; as a consequence they entertain fewer illusions about the feasibility of this strategy. One international climate is positively associated with this strategy, namely, the we-ness climate. The positive correlation between this climate and this strategy makes sense because such an environment is much more amenable to the success of this strategy than lower-level climates, which are negatively correlated. We did not present the multiple regression data because of the unreliability of the multiple R^2; within the blocks, multicolinearity and a substantial degree of cooperative suppression were going on, so that, for example, the total R^2 for the six variables was much more than the summation of the R^2 of the variables which are components of this block.

TABLE 8.11

T-test and Significant Correlations for Structural Equality
(t-value -.68)

Significant correlations		
With systemic variables		
Penetration	-.27	<.002
Economic development	-.12	<.05
With international climate		
We-ness	.16	<.02

Source: Compiled by the author from his own research.

Enlargement versus Redistribution
of the Economic Pie

The mean of this strategic characteristic is 2.76 and indicates
a slight disapproval of the proposal that "we should opt for faster
economic growth, rather than for redistribution of wealth and income
to solve the poverty problem" (see Table 8.12). Most diplomats
conceive both alternatives as complementary. There is a slight indication, however, that diplomats from developed countries favor
this proposal more than their colleagues from developing countries,
but the difference is not significant. There is a strong recognition
by diplomats from developed countries that some form of redistribution is necessary. The general attitude of diplomats from developed
countries is best captured in a quote of a West European diplomat:
"We want to avoid extreme situations. We admit that some form of
redistribution is necessary because we cannot live in the long run in
an hostile environment." Of all our independent variables, the only
variable that is significantly correlated with this strategy is the diplomats' perception of the world as governed by international law
($r = .18$, $p < .01$). This means that diplomats who consider international law to be consequential in international relations tend to favor
economic growth rather than distribution of wealth and income. We
did not present the multiple regression data because the multiple R^2
was unreliable; within the blocks, multicolinearity and a substantial
amount of cooperative suppression were going on, so we obtained a
highly inflated R^2.

TABLE 8.12

T-test and Significant Correlations for Enlargement
versus Redistribution of the Economic Pie
(t-value .45)

Significant correlations
   With systemic variables
      None
   With international climate
      International law   .18   <.01

Source: Compiled by the author from his own research.

Prediction of Increased Violence

With respect to the prediction that we will have an increase in violence in the world in the next four years, we find a slight disagreement (2.92 on a 1-5 scale). There is, however, a significant difference between diplomats from developed and developing countries. Diplomats from developing countries tend to predict more violence than their colleagues from developed countries (see Table 8.13). The international climates that are significantly associated with this prediction are the Hobbesian ($r = .14$, $p < .03$) and the shared principled agreement ($r = -.13$, $p < .04$) climates. The directions of these correlations are meaningful because the prediction of greater violence is more plausible if extrapolated from an environment that is perceived as Hobbesian than from an environment that is free from physical and structural violence. This strategic characteristic is predicted significantly by the block of systemic variables (16 percent, $p < .05$).

TABLE 8.13

T-test, Significant Correlations, and Regression Analysis
Data for Prediction of Increased Violence
(t-value -1.58; p-value $< .10$)

Significant correlations
  With systemic variables
    Economic development   -.12   <.05
  With international climates
    Hobbesian   .14   <.03
    Shared principled agreement   -.13   <.04

Single and combined impact of a block of six systemic variables and a block of four international climates (Multiple R^2):

systemic	.14	climate	.02
climate	.04	systemic	.16*
	.18		.18

Multiple R = .42

*$p < .05$.
Source: Compiled by the author from his own research.

Pessimism–Optimism vis–a–vis
the Realization of Peace

There is moderate optimism about the fact that progress will
be made toward a more peaceful and just world (3.59 on a 1–5 scale).
There are, however, marked differences between subgroups of diplomats. A significant difference is found between diplomats from developed and developing countries; the latter tend to be more optimistic than the former (see Table 8.14).

TABLE 8.14

T-test, Significant Correlations, and Regression Analysis
Data for Pessimism–Optimism vis–a–vis
the Realization of Peace
(t–value –1.51; p–value $<$ .10)

Significant correlations
  With systemic variables

Security force investment	–.30	$<$.02
Economic interdependency	–.17	$<$.01
Military expenditure	–.15	$<$.02
Economic development	–.13	$<$.03

  With international climates

Hobbesian	–.38	$<$.001
We-ness	.37	$<$.001
International law	.28	
Shared principled agreement	.26	$<$.001
Marxian environment	–.14	$<$.03
Instrumental exchange	–.10	

Single and combined impact of a block of six systemic variables and
a block of four international climates (Multiple R^2):

systemic	.12	climate	.18*
climate	.16*	systemic	.12
	.28*		.28*

Multiple R = .53

*p $<$ .01.

Source: Compiled by the author from his own research.

The contradiction between the expectation of more violence and optimism about the realization of peace among diplomats from developing countries can be explained only in terms of their definition of peace, which requires the presence of conditions beyond the mere absence of physical violence. If we look at the list of the significant correlations with systemic variables, we see that the strongest correlation is produced by the security force investment variable $(r = -.30, p < .02)$. We also find a negative correlation between the degree of military force and optimism about the realization of peace. The fact that a diplomat whose country invests heavily in security would tend to be pessimistic about the realization of peace seems quite consonant; in other words, optimism about the realization of peace could not justify such a high investment.

Another systemic variable which is significantly correlated with this strategic characteristic is the degree of economic interdependency of a country $(r = -.17, p < .01)$. From the significant correlations with perceptual variables we can infer that optimism or pessimism about the realization of peace and justice in the world is strongly influenced by the diplomat's perception of the world. The directions of these correlations are as expected: lower-level climates such as the Hobbesian, Marxian, and instrumental exchange can be expected to be associated with pessimism because they contain most of the ingredients that inhibit the realization of peace or justice; the reverse is true for the higher-level environments. Both blocks of variables together are able to predict 28 percent of the variance; however, only the contribution of the block of perceptual variables is significant $(p < .01)$.

CONCLUSION

The results indicate significant effects of systemic variables on the strategic approach of the diplomat. For example, if we contrast the strategic approaches of diplomats from developed countries with diplomats from developing countries, we find significant differences with respect to the self-reliance strategy, the predisposition to consider the use of nuclear weapons, the preference for radical and nonviolent change, expediency, the prediction of violence, and the degree of optimism or pessimism about the realization of a peaceful and just world.

The strategies least affected by the block of systemic variables are global cooperation, flexibility-inflexibility, redistribution versus growth, prudence, integration, and structural equality. An overview of the most and the least different strategic approaches for diplomats of developed and developing countries can be found in Table 8.15.

TABLE 8.15

Overview of the Largest and Smallest Differences in
Strategic Approach Variables between Diplomats
from Developed and Developing Countries

Self-reliance strategy	-4.74	.005
Nonuse of nuclear weapons	-4.21	.005
Radical change/nonviolent	-3.54	.005
Expediency	-2.10	.02
Prediction about violence	-1.58	.10
Optimism about peace	-1.51	.10
Structural equality	-0.68	
Integration	.55	
Prudence	-.47	
Enlargement versus redistribution of the economic pie	.45	
Flexibility-inflexibility	-.29	
Global cooperation	-.17	

Note: A negative sign before the t-value indicates that the
mean of the diplomats from developing countries is larger.
Source: Compiled by the author from his own research.

The systemic variables that explain, on the average, most of the
variation of strategic approach are the degree of economic development and the periphery-center position of a country; they are followed by the security force investment and the amount of military
expenditure; and further, in order of diminishing effect, economic
interdependency, aid received, and penetration (see Table 8.16).
For the strategic approaches with respect to which diplomats differ
most (see Table 8.15), an average of 18 percent of the variance can
be predicted by our block of systemic variables. The fact that, for
example, the degree of penetration variable produces a low overall
effect does not mean that this system variable should be discarded.
On the contrary, it is an important predictor, but only in relation
to some specific strategies—in the present case the radical and
nonviolent and the structural equality strategies. In both cases the
degree of penetratedness is a significant predictor. The overall
impact of perceptual variables is lower than that of the systemic
variables (see Table 8.16). Again, this does not mean that these

TABLE 8.16

Overview of the Correlations of Systemic and Climate Variables with Strategic Approach Dimensions

	Self-Reliance	Prudence	Global Cooperation	Degree of Expediency	Radical Nonviolent Change	Flexibility-Unflexibility	Nonuse of Nuclear Weapons	Integration	Structural Equality	Enlargement versus Distribution of Economic Pie	Increased Violence Prediction	Pessimism-Optimism Peace	Number of Correlations ≥10	≥20	≥30	Average Correlation	Number of Significant Correlations
Periphery-center	-.42	.05	-.00	-.24	-.28	-.00	-.39	.01	-.12	-.03	-.09	-.06	5	4	2	.14	5
Economic development	-.39	-.02	-.00	-.18	-.36	.01	-.39	.03	-.12	-.00	-.12	-.13	7	3	3	.15	7
Security force	-.17	-.15	.02	-.16	-.16	-.03	-.33	-.04	-.11	.09	-.09	-.30	7	2	2	.14	6
Military expenditure	-.31	-.07	.01	-.23	-.22	-.00	-.33	-.06	-.03	.02	-.11	-.15	6	4	2	.13	5
Economic Interdependency	-.16	.03	.02	-.17	-.23	-.02	-.10	.18	-.09	-.07	-.02	-.17	6	1	0	.10	4
Aid receipt	.07	.25	.14	-.14	.07	-.15	.12	.05	.13	-.02	-.13	-.02	7	1	0	.11	3
Penetration	.00	-.13	-.00	-.05	-.19	-.08	.00	-.11	-.27	.00	.09	.03	4	1	0	.08	2
Hobbesian	.00	-.06	-.10	-.02	-.02	-.03	.14	-.16	-.10	-.07	.14	-.38	6	1	1	.10	3
Marxian	.07	-.06	-.02	.17	.02	-.10	.07	-.07	-.06	.05	.08	-.14	3	0	0	.08	2
Instrumental-exchange	.03	.11	-.19	.23	.03	.02	.08	-.08	-.03	.03	.02	-.10	4	1	0	.08	2
We-ness	-.09	.01	.11	.02	.01	-.00	-.12	.19	.16	.04	-.06	.37	5	1	1	.10	3
International law	.06	.06	.16	.07	-.08	.14	.09	.10	.05	.18	-.08	.28	5	1	0	.11	1
Shared principled agreement	-.03	.05	.06	.02	-.07	-.11	-.10	.01	-.06	.07	-.13	.26	4	1	0	.08	2

Source: Compiled by the author from his own research.

variables are less relevant. Although their overall impact is marked-ly lower than that of the systemic variables, their impact on some specific variables is found to be greater than that of systemic vari-ables. Therefore, they have to be included for a better understand-ing and prediction of certain strategic approaches. For example, perceptual differences among the diplomats have a major effect on their degree of optimism or pessimism about the realization of a more peaceful and just world. The block of perceptual variables predicts 18 percent of the variance ($p < .01$).

9

Conclusion

Diplomatic thinking has been the subject of this volume. It is an important intervening variable between the "objective" condition of the world and international behavior. International facts do not speak for themselves, but are given meaning by each international actor from his own point of view. To get an insight into the dynamics of the professional diplomat's conceptual approach of international relations, we studied the impact on diplomatic thinking of two variables: the international climate and the position of the diplomat's country in the international structure. With respect to the international structure, I wanted to test if the proposition, "You stand where you sit," was also valid for diplomats. I am aware that more variation in diplomatic thinking could have been accounted for if we had included in the study other independent variables, such as the diplomat's social and educational background (Hoefnagels 1974), where he received his diplomatic experiences (Alger 1965), and generational effects (Jervis 1976). The impact of these variables could be explored in future studies.

Our purpose required that we decompose several elements in the diplomatic thinking and pull apart the individual strands of a diplomat's political ideas and ideals. I have suggested that diplomatic thinking can best be understood in terms of four analytically distinguishable components: perceptual, analytical, evaluative, and action. The first component that we studied was the international climate, or the diplomat's perception of the international environment. To examine differences in the diplomats' views of the world, we used two classificatory schemes: a theoretically derived ideal-type classification of moral-political climates, and an empirically derived multidimensional scheme of the diplomat's perception of the international environment. The results demonstrate that the perceptual world of the diplomat is multidimensional and that a comprehensive report of the diplomat's environment must provide information about all these dimensions. Our results also suggest that the typology of moral-political climates taps several dimensions of the diplomats' perceived world and ranks them in order of preference. That is, the order of preference in the minds of the total sample of diplomats corresponds, more or less, to the theoretically based ordering of the five levels of moral-political climates. We also found that in terms of present applicability to the reality of international relations, the different climates form a rank-order of diminishing relevance. Despite the universal preference for a higher level of moral-political climates, the moral approach of the diplomat tends to reflect the dominating moral-political climate of the world in which he has to operate. This suggests that a change in this climate is a prerequisite for realizing a higher level of morality in international relations. Higher moral-political climates than those that are attributed to the global international system exist in some international subsystems, such as the European Community. The climates which predominate in the global international system are at level 1: the Marxian and Hobbesian climates. Following in terms of importance is the instrumental-exchange climate. Then there is the international law climate, which could be qualified as an important but not central feature in the diplomat's world. Finally, are the we-ness and the shared principled agreement climates, which both occupy a relatively low profile in the diplomat's perception of the international environment. A comparison between the diplomat's perception of the global and a regional international environment (European Common Market) indicates that the above-described findings are valid only for the perception of the global international environment and cannot be transferred to another international-system level. For this and the other components of diplomatic thinking, we have also studied whether and to what extent the structural position of the country the diplomat represents influences diplomatic thinking. Examining the effects of certain systemic attributes on the diplomat's perception, we found the results positive; the amount of variance that could be predicted by systemic factors is not insignificant. The most consistent predictor of the diplomat's perception of the international environment is the aid receipt and, to a lesser extent, the economic development variables. The other systemic variables which have an impact, but only on a few climates or dimensions, are, in order of importance, center-periphery, security force investment, and military expenditure.

The goals a diplomat seeks in his activity and the rules he follows are informed by his operative values. We have examined the way in which the operative values of peace and preferred world order are interpreted, evaluated, and used by the diplomats. We observed the existence of significant differences between diplomats in their operationalizations of these values. We also found that the gap between the present state of international peace and the ideal state is considerable. The greatest discrepancies between the aspirational and realism levels were noticed in diplomats from developing countries. The larger discrepancy was accounted for by the stronger accentuation of their aspirations. Proposals at the inter- and intraregional levels of international relations were indicated as more operational than were proposals at the global or national or subnational levels. The values espoused by the diplomats were also shown to be a function of the position of the country represented. The impact of this position was found to be greater on the appraisal of the peace proposals in terms of their importance or preference than on the diplomat's assessment of the likelihood of peace proposals to be carried out. In other words, the systemic position tended to affect the accentuation of aspirations rather than the appraisal of reality by diplomats. More generally, these data indicate that the meanings and weights associated with peace and preferred-world-order values generally reflect the particular interests of their respective proponents. Certain concerns and interests sensitize the diplomat to some indicators of peace and particular international problems and at the same time cause him to neglect a number of alternative indicators and problems that other diplomats deem important. There is also the great similarity between the meanings attached to the concepts of peace and preferred world order. These findings imply that if one wants to understand the dynamics of international peace, one should think of the achievement of peace as a competition between different preferred-world-order models. And that, to resolve that competition, or to create a consensus about these international values, we have to cope not only with such problems as the improvement of international communication or empathy but also with a structural problem. In other words, a universal consensus about these values can be brought about only when we deal with the particularity of the systemic vantage points from which these values are given meaning and are translated into action. Without international structural changes, it seems impossible that the diversity of conceptualizations (be it perception of the international environment, style of analysis, strategic style, or value preferences concerning the ultimate direction and purposes of a new world order) and consequently the fragility of the present world order will be reduced.

The empirical judgments a person hazards about a complex and ambiguous world are structured by his style of analysis. We compared the diplomats with respect to 11 analytic style dimensions and found significant differences between groups of diplomats. The results indicated a strong effect of the systemic position of a country on the diplomats' styles of analysis. For example, when we compared the styles of analysis of diplomats from developed and developing countries, we found significant differences in the tendency to analyze the world in structural terms, to model international relations as a zero-sum or nonzero-sum game, to moralize about issues, to focus on technological and financial issues, and to show concern with noninterference or national sovereignty. Least affected by the structural position are the tendency to include the historical context in the discussion of issues, to refer to national interests as a criterion of good foreign policy, and to model the world as a conflictual system. The systemic variables that explain, on the average, most of the variation of the different analytic styles, are the center-periphery position and the degree of economic development of a country; they are followed by military expenditure and the degree of security force investment, and further, in order of diminishing impact, economic interdependency, aid receipt, and penetration. For the analytic style on which the diplomats differed most, the block of systemic variables on the average predicts 22 percent of the variance. The impact of the perceptual variables is markedly lower than that of the systemic variables. This does not mean that they are irrelevant. Although their overall impact is much lower than that of the systemic variables, in relation to some specific analytic styles, their impact is greater than that of systemic variables. Therefore, they have to be considered for a better understanding and prediction of certain analytic styles. For example, the analytic style that is most affected by differences in the perception of the international environment is the tendency to moralize. Eleven percent of the variance of the analytic style is accounted for by the block of perceptual variables.

The way in which a person combines his normative commitments and empirical judgments is regulated by his strategic approach. The results indicate significant differences in the strategic approach among diplomats. Strong effects of systemic variables on the strategic approach are noticed. Contrasting the strategic approaches of the diplomats from developed and developing countries, we found significant differences with respect to self-reliance strategy, the predisposition to consider the use of nuclear weapons, the preference for radical and nonviolent change, expediency, the prediction of violence, and the degree of optimism or pessimism about the realization of a peaceful and just world. The strategies least affected by the block of systemic variables were global cooperation, flexibility-inflexibility, redistribution versus growth, prudence, integration, and structural equality. The systemic variables that explain, on the average, most of the variation of the strategic approaches are the degree of economic development and the center-periphery position of a country. They are followed by the security force investment and the amount of military expenditure, and further, in order of diminishing effect, economic interdependency, aid receipt, and penetration. For the strategic approaches with respect to which diplomats differed most, an average of 18 percent of the variance can be predicted by the block of systemic variables. The overall impact of the perceptual variables is lower than that of the systemic variables. Again, that does not mean that these variables are less relevant. Although their overall impact is markedly lower than that of the systemic variables, their impact on some specific variables is found to be greater than that of systemic variables. Therefore, they have to be included for a better understanding and prediction of certain strategic approaches. For example, perceptual differences have a major impact on the diplomat's degree of pessimism or optimism about the realization of a more peaceful and just world. The block of perceptual variables predicted 18 percent of this aspect of the strategic approach of the diplomat.

The aim of this study was to explore a rather virgin area in the study of international relations, namely, diplomatic thinking. Our contribution consisted of building a framework for systematically studying this aspect of international relations and empirically testing some propositions. In general, I consider the findings of this exploratory inquiry positive and encouraging of further analysis and utilization of this approach in the comparative study of diplomatic thinking. By sharper focusing on the diplomat's conceptualization of the world, we indicated its importance as an intervening variable in the international relations system, the variations of diplomatic thinking, and the links between conceptual and structural variables. To the extent we care about improving the predictive value of the international system models, those conceptual variables should be included.

BIBLIOGRAPHY

Achterhuis, Hans. 1975. Filosofen van de derde wereld.
Bilthoven: Basisbocken.

Alger, Chadwick F. 1965. "Personal Contact in Intergovernmental
Organizations." In International Behavior, ed. H. Kelman.
New York: Holt, Rinehart and Winston.

American Academy of Political and Social Science. 1972. Instruc-
tion in Diplomacy: The Liberal Arts Approach.

Anatoliev, K. 1972. Modern Diplomacy: Principles, Documents,
People. Moscow: Novosti Press Agency Publishing House.

Angell, James B. 1893. "The Inadequate Recognition of Diplomats
by Historians." In Report of Proceedings of Ninth Annual
Meeting of the American Historical Association, Chicago.

Aron, Raymond. 1966 and 1973. Peace and War: A Theory of
International Relations. (Richard Howard and Annette Baker
Fox, eds. and trans.) New York: Doubleday.

_____. 1967. "What Is the Theory of International Relations?" In
Theory and Reality in International Relations, ed. J. C. Farrell
and A. P. Smith. New York: Columbia University Press.

Bennett, George, ed. 1953. The Concept of Empire: Burke to
Attlee, 1774-1947. London: Black.

Bentham, Jeremy. 1952. Handbook of Political Fallacies, ed.
Harold A. Larrabee. New York: Crowell.

Berger, Peter L., and Luckmann, Thomas. 1966. The Social
Construction of Reality. New York: Doubleday.

Bernstein, Robert A., and Weldon, Peter D. 1968. "A Structural
Approach to the Analysis of International Relations." Journal
of Conflict Resolution 2: 159-76.

Bobrow, Davis B. 1972. International Relations: New Approaches.
New York: The Free Press.

Bottomore, T. B. 1965. Elites and Society. New York: Basic Books.

_____, and Rubel, M., eds. 1956. Marx: Selected Writings in Sociology and Social Philosophy. London: Watts.

Boulding, K. 1961. "National Images and International Systems." In International Politics and Foreign Policy, ed. J. M. Rosenau. New York: The Free Press.

_____. 1969. The Image. Ann Arbor, Mich.: The Free Press.

Brecher, M., Steinberg, B., and Stein, J. 1969. "A Framework of Research on Foreign Policy Behavior." Journal of Conflict Resolution 1: 75-101.

Brodin, Katarina. 1972. "Belief Systems, Doctrines and Foreign Policy." Cooperation and Conflict 7: 97-112.

Burgess, Philip M. 1968. Elite Images and Foreign Policy Outcomes: A Study of Norway. Columbus: The Ohio State University Press.

Burton, John. 1969. Conflict and Communication. New York: Macmillan.

Busk, Sir Douglas. 1967. The Craft of Diplomacy: How to Run a Diplomatic Service. New York: Praeger.

Carter, John. 1926. Man Is War. Indianapolis: Bobbs-Merrill.

Cartwright, D. P. 1953. "Analysis of Qualitative Material." In Research Methods in the Behavioral Sciences, ed. Leon Festinger and Daniel Katz. New York: Dryden Press.

Chomsky, Noam. 1974. Peace in the Middle East: Reflections on Justice and Nationhood. New York: Random House.

Choucri, N. 1969. "The Nonalignment of Afro-Asian States: Policy Perception and Behavior." Canadian Journal of Political Science 2: 1-17.

Claude, Inis. 1959. Swords into Plowshares, 2d ed. New York: Random House.

Clausewitz, Carl von. 1968. On War, ed. A. Rapoport. Baltimore: Penguin Books. (Originally published translation 1908.)

Cohen, J., and Cohen, P. 1975. Applied Multiple Regression: Correlation Analysis for the Behavioral Sciences. New York: John Wiley.

Cook, S. W., and Selltiz, C. 1964. "A Multiple Indicator Approach to Attitude Measurement." Psychological Bulletin 62: 36-55.

Cowley, George A. 1976. "Culture et politique étrangère." Perspectives internationales: Revue d'opinion sur les Affaires Étrangères. September-October: 29-34.

D'Amato, Anthony A. 1967. "Psychological Constructs in Foreign Policy Prediction." Journal of Conflict Resolution 11: 295-311.

de Groot, A. D. 1961. Methodologie. s'Gravenhage: Mouton.

Deutsch, Karl. 1970. Politics and Government: How Do People Decide Their Fate? Boston: Houghton Mifflin.

_____. 1972. Peace Research: The Need, the Problems and the Prospects. Middlebury, Vt.: Middlebury College Publications Department.

_____ et al. 1957. Political Community and North Atlantic Area: International Organization in the Light of Historical Experience. Princeton, N.J.: Princeton University Press.

_____, Edinger, Lewis, Macridis, R., and Merritt, R. 1967. France, Germany and the Western Alliance. New York: Scribner.

_____, and Merritt, Richard. 1965. "Effects of Events on National and International Images." In International Behavior, ed. H. C. Kelman. New York: Holt, Rinehart & Winston.

Dexter, Lewis A. 1970. Elite and Specialized Interviewing. Evanston: Northwestern University Press.

Dougherty, James, and Pfaltzgraff, Robert. 1974. Contending Theories of International Relations. Philadelphia: Lippincott.

Dulles address on Peace in Washington on April 11, 1953. 1955.
New York Times, April 12, p. 6.

Eccles, Henry. 1965. Military Concepts and Philosophy. New
Brunswick, N.J.: Rutgers University Press.

Edelman, Murray. 1972. The Symbolic Uses of Politics. Urbana:
University of Illinois.

Eysenck, H. J. 1954. The Psychology of Politics. London:
Routledge and Kegan Paul.

Ezekiel, M., and Fox, K. A. 1959. Methods of Correlation and
Regression Analysis. New York: John Wiley.

Fanon, Frantz. 1968. The Wretched of the Earth. Trans. C.
Farrington. New York: Grove Press. (Originally published
in 1961.)

Fetscher, Irving. 1968. Modelle der Friedenssicherung.
Munchen: R. Piper.

Fisher, Glen H. 1972. Public Diplomacy and the Behavioral
Sciences. Bloomington: Indiana University Press.

Franck, Thomas M., and Weisband, E. 1972. World Politics:
Verbal Strategy among the Superpowers. New York: Oxford
University Press.

Frankel, Joseph. 1973. Contemporary International Theory and
the Behavior of States. London: Oxford University Press.

Friedheim, Robert L. 1968. "The Satisfied and Dissatisfied States
Negotiate International Law." In Dynamics of World Politics,
ed. L. B. Miller. Englewood Cliffs, N.J. Prentice-Hall.

Gadamar, Hans-Georg. 1968. "Notes on Planning for the Future."
In Conditions of World Order, ed. Stanley Hoffmann. Boston:
Houghton Mifflin.

Galtung, Johan. 1964. "A Structural Theory of Aggression."
Journal of Peace Research 2: 96-119.

_____. 1967. Peace Research: Science or Politics in Disguise.
Oslo PRIO publication 23-6 (Mimeograph.)

_____. 1968a. "Peace." In International Encyclopedia of the Social Sciences, ed. D. L. Sills. New York: Macmillan and The Free Press.

_____. 1968b. "A Structural Theory of Integration." Journal of Peace Research 4: 375-95.

_____. 1969a. "Foreign Policy Opinion as a Function of Social Position." In International Politics and Foreign Policy, ed. James Rosenau. New York: The Free Press.

_____. 1969b. "Violence, Peace and Peace Research." Journal of Peace Research 3: 167-91.

_____. 1971. "A Structural Theory of Imperialism." Journal of Peace Research 2: 81-117.

_____. and Ruge, Mari Holmboe. 1965. "Patterns of Diplomacy: A Study of Recruitment and Career Patterns in Norwegian Diplomacy." Journal of Peace Research 2: 101-35.

Gamson, W., and Modigliani, A. 1971. Untangling the Cold War: A Strategy for Testing Rival Theories. Boston: Little, Brown.

_____. 1974. Conceptions of Social Life. Boston: Little, Brown.

Gerber, Louis. 1973. The Diplomacy of Private Enterprise. Cape Town: Purnell.

Gergen, Kenneth J., and Gergen, M. M. 1974. "Foreign Aid That Works." Psychology Today, June, pp. 53-58.

Gleditsch, Nils P. 1970. "Rank and Interaction: A General Theory with Some Applications to the International System." Proceedings of the IPRA Third General Conference II. Assen: Van Gorcum, pp. 1-21.

Glenn, Edmund S.; Johnson, Robert H.; Kimmel, Paul R.; and Wedge, Bryant. 1970. "A Cognitive Interaction Model to Analyze Culture Conflict in International Relations." Journal of Conflict Resolution 14, no. 1: 35-48.

Graber, Doris A. 1976. Verbal Behavior and Politics. Urbana: University of Illinois Press.

Graubard, Stephen R. 1973. Kissinger: Portrait of a Mind. New York: W. W. Norton.

Green, Bert F. 1976. "On the Factor Score Controversy." Psychometrica 41, no. 2 (June): 263-66.

Guetzkow, H. 1955. Multiple Loyalties. Princeton, N.J.: Princeton University Press.

Gurr, Tedd Robert. 1974. "The Neo-Alexandrians: A Review Essay on Data Handbooks in Political Science." American Political Science Review 68, no. 1.

Halle, Nils H. 1966. "Social Position and Foreign Policy Attitudes. Journal of Peace Research 1: 46-74.

Hamlin, D. L. S., ed. 1961. Diplomacy in Evolution. Toronto: University of Toronto Press.

Hayter, Sir William. 1961. The Diplomacy of the Great Powers. New York: Macmillan.

Heradstveit, Daniel. 1974. Arab and Israeli Perceptions. Oslo: Universitetsforlaget.

Hermann, Charles F. 1969. "International Crisis as a Situational Variable." In International Politics and Foreign Policy, ed. James Rosenau. New York: The Free Press.

Hoefnagels, Marjo. 1974. Secundaire Analyse van de Belgische Diplomatieke Dienst. Brussels: Centrum voor Polemologie, Vrije Universiteit.

Hoffmann, Stanley. 1961. "International Systems and International Law." In The International System: Theoretical Essays, ed. K. Knorr and S. Verba. Princeton, N.J.: Princeton University Press.

_____, ed. 1968. Conditions of World Order. Boston: Houghton Mifflin.

Hoivik, Tord. 1972. "Three Approaches to Exploitation: Markets, Products, and Communities." Journal of Peace Research 3: 262-69.

Hollist, W. L. 1975. "Model Specification of Rival Global Interdependence and Dependency: Theories of International Cooperation." Paper prepared for the Thirteenth North American
Conference of the Peace Science Society (International) in
Cambridge, Mass., November 10-12.

Horn, Klaus. 1973. "Approaches to Social Psychology Relevant to
Peace Research." Journal of Peace Research 3: 305-14.

Howard, Michael. 1971. Studies in War and Peace. New York:
Viking.

Hveem, Helge. 1968. "Foreign Policy Thinking in the Elite and the
General Population." Journal of Peace Research 2: 146-70.

_____. 1970. "Blame as International Behavior." Journal of
Peace Research 1: 49-67.

_____. 1972. "Foreign Policy Opinion as a Function of Interna-
tional Position." Cooperation and Conflict: Nordic Journal
of International Politics 2: 65-86.

_____. 1973a. "The Global Dominance System." Journal of
Peace Research 4: 319-40.

_____. 1973b. "Peace Research: Historical Development and
Future Perspective." Mimeographed. (Now published in IPRA
Studies in Peace Research 5.)

Iklé, Fred Charles. 1967. How Nations Negotiate. New York:
Praeger.

Inkeles, Alex. 1973. "The Emerging Social Structure of the World."
Paper prepared for presentation at the International Political
Science Association meeting in Montreal, Canada, August.

Isaacs, Harold. 1958. Images of Asia. New York: Capricorn
Books.

Jacobson, Harold K. 1967. "Deriving Data from Delegates to International Assemblies: A Research Note." International Organization 21, no. 3.

Janik, Allan, and Toulmin, Stephen. 1973. Wittgenstein's Vienna.
New York: Simon and Schuster.

Jaspers, Karl. 1971. Man in the Modern Age. New York: Doubleday.

Jensen, De Lamar. 1964. Diplomacy and Dogmatism:. Bernardino de Mendoza and the French Catholic League. Cambridge, Mass.: Harvard University Press.

Jervis, Robert. 1970. The Logic of Images in International Relations. Princeton, N.J.: Princeton University Press.

_____. 1976. Perception and Misperception in International Politics. Princeton, N.J.: Princeton University Press.

Kara, Karel. 1968. "On the Marxist Theory of War and Peace." Journal of Peace Research 1: 1-27.

Keefe, Eugene K. et al. 1974. Area Handbook for Belgium. Washington, D.C.: U.S. Government Printing Office.

Kegley, Charles W.; Raymond, Gregory A.; Rood, Robert M.; and Skinner, Richard A., eds. 1975. International Events and the Comparative Analysis of Foreign Policy. Columbia: University of South Carolina Press.

Kelman, Herbert C. 1962. "Changing Attitudes through International Activities." Journal of Social Issues 18, no. 1: 68-87.

_____, ed. 1965. International Behavior: A Social-Psychological Analysis. New York: Holt, Rinehart and Winston.

_____. 1968. A Time to Speak: On Human Values and Social Research. San Francisco: Jossey-Bass.

_____. 1973. "The Challenge of Change." In Man and the Future of Man: A Reader for the First Course by Newspaper, ed. Jane L. Scheiber. San Diego: University of California.

Keohane, Robert O., and Nye, Joseph S. 1977. Power and Interdependence: World Politics in Transition. Boston: Little, Brown.

Kissinger, H. 1957. Nuclear Weapons and Foreign Policy. New York: Harper.

_____. 1965. The Troubled Partnership: A Reappraisal of the Atlantic Alliance. New York: McGraw-Hill.

_____. 1974. American Foreign Policy, expanded ed. New York: W. W. Norton.

Kohlberg, Lawrence. 1971. "From Is to Ought: How to Commit the Naturalistic Fallacy and Get Away with It in the Study of Moral Development." In Cognitive Development and Epistemology, ed. T. Mischel. New York: Academic Press.

Kohn, Hans. 1942. World Order in Historical Perspective. Cambridge, Mass.: Harvard University Press.

Kuhn, T. S. 1970. The Structure of Scientific Revolutions. Chicago: University of Chicago Press.

Lagos, Gustavo. 1963. International Stratification and Underdeveloped Countries. Chapel Hill: The University of North Carolina Press.

Landheer, Bart. 1964. "The Image of the World Society and the Function of Armaments." Journal of Peace Research 3-4: 233-40.

Langholm, Sivert. 1971. "On the Concepts of Center and Periphery." Journal of Peace Research 3-4: 274-78.

Lasswell, Harold D. 1965. "The Climate of International Action." In International Behavior, ed. Herbert Kelman. New York: Holt, Rinehart and Winston.

Lederer, William J., and Burdick, Eugene. 1958. The Ugly American. Greenwich, Conn.: Fawcett.

Levi, Werner. 1964. "On the Causes of Peace." Journal of Conflict Resolution 8, no. 1: 23-35.

Lewis, Clarence Irving. 1956. Mind and the World Order: Outline of a Theory of Knowledge. New York: Dover Publications.

Lumsden, Malvern. 1966. "Perception and Information in Strategic Thinking." Journal of Peace Research 3: 257-77.

_____. 1967. "Social Position and Cognitive Style in Strategic Thinking." Journal of Peace Research 3.

Lijphart, Arend. 1974. "The Structure of the Theoretical Revolution in International Relations." International Studies Quarterly 18, no. 1.

Machiavelli, Niccolo. 1974. The Discourses, ed. Bernard Crick. Middlesex, England: Penguin Books.

Macomber, William B. 1970. Diplomacy for the 70's: A Program of the Management for the Department of State. Washington, D.C.: U.S. Government Printing Office.

_____. 1975. The Angels Game: A Handbook of Modern Diplomacy. New York: Stein and Day.

Mannheim, Karl. 1936. Ideology and Utopia. New York: Harcourt, Brace and World.

Manning, C. A. W. 1962. The Nature of the International Society. New York: John Wiley.

Mazrui, Ali A. 1967. Towards a Pax Africana: A Study of Ideology and Ambition. Chicago: The University of Chicago Press.

McGowan, Patrick J., and Shapiro, H. B. 1973. The Comparative Study of Foreign Policy. Beverly Hills: Sage Publications.

McLellan, David S. 1974. "Diplomacy." In The Theory and Practice of International Relations, ed. David S. McLellan et al. Englewood Cliffs, N.J.: Prentice-Hall.

Mendlovitz, Saul. 1975. On the Creation of a Just World Order: Preferred Worlds for the 1990's. New York: The Free Press.

Merrit, R., and Rokkan, S., eds. 1966. Comparing Nations: The Use of Quantitative Data in Cross-National Research. New Haven, Conn.: Yale University Press.

Minogue, K. R. 1972. "Theatricality and Politicians: Machiavelli's Concept of Fantasia." In The Morality of Politics, ed. Parekh Bhikhu and R. N. Berki. London: George Allen and Unwin.

Modelski, George. 1970. "The World's Foreign Ministers: A Political Elite." Journal of Conflict Resolution 14, no. 2.

Mookerjee, Girija K. 1973. Diplomacy: Theory and History. New Delhi: Trimurti Publications.

Mushakoji, Kinhide. 1970. "Structures for Peace in the North-South Perspectives." Peace Research in Japan 71-85.

Nicolson, Harold George. 1963. Diplomacy. London: Oxford University Press.

Nie, Norman et al. 1975. SPSS: Statistical Package for the Social Sciences, 2d ed. New York: McGraw-Hill.

Niezing, J. 1973. Sociology, War and Disarmament. Rotterdam: University Press.

North, R. C. et al. 1963. Content Analysis: A Handbook with Applications for the Study of International Crisis. Evanston, Ill.: Northwestern University Press.

Northrop, F. S. C. 1946. The Meeting of East and West. New York: Collier Books.

Nye, J. S. 1971. Peace in Parts: Integration and Conflict in Regional Organization. Boston: Little, Brown.

O'Connell, D. P. 1968. Richelieu. Cleveland: World.

Oppenheim, A. N. 1970. Questionnaire Design and Attitude Measurement. London: Heinemann.

Osgood, Charles et al. 1957. The Measurement of Meaning. Urbana: University of Illinois Press.

Plowden, Lord. 1964. Report of the Committee on Representational Services Overseas Appointed by the Prime Minister under Chairmanship Lord Plowden 1962-1963. London: Her Majesty's Stationery Office.

Pope, L. 1958. Millhands and Preachers: A Study of Gastonia. New Haven, Conn.: Yale University Press.

Poullada, Leon B. 1974. "Diplomacy: The Missing Link in the Study of International Politics." In The Theory and Practice of International Relations, ed. David S. McLellan et al. Englewood Cliffs, N.J.: Prentice-Hall.

Puchala, Donald James. 1971. International Politics Today. New York: Dodd, Mead.

Putnam, Robert D. 1973. The Beliefs of Politicians: Ideology, Conflict, and Democracy in Britain and Italy. New Haven, Conn.: Yale University Press.

Rapoport, Anatol. 1971. Various Conceptions of Peace Research. Peace Research Society Papers 19, Ann Arbor Conference.

Rawls, John. 1971. A Theory of Justice. Cambridge, Mass.: The Belknap Press of Harvard University Press.

Reychler, Luc. 1973. "The Relevance of Moral Argument in International Relations." Unpublished paper. Cambridge, Mass.: Harvard University.

Richelieu, Duc de. 1961. The Political Testament of Cardinal Richelieu. Madison: University of Wisconsin Press.

Riesman, David. 1964. Abundance for What? and Other Essays. Garden City, N.Y.: Doubleday.

Roetter, Charles. 1963. The Diplomatic Art: An Informal History of World Diplomacy. Philadelphia: Macrae Smith.

Rokeach, Milton, and Hanley, Charles. 1956. "Eysenck's Tender-mindedness Dimension: A Critique." Psychological Bulletin 53: 169-76.

Rosen, Steven J., and Jones, Walter S. 1977. The Logic of International Relations. Cambridge, Mass.: Winthrop Publishers.

Rosenau, James N. 1966. "Pre-theories and Theories of Foreign Policy." In Approaches to International and Comparative Politics, ed. R. Berry Farrell. Evanston, Ill.: Northwestern University Press.

Rossow, Robert. 1962. "The Professionalization of the New Diplomacy." World Politics 14, no. 4: 561-75.

Rubin, Zick. 1973. Liking and Loving. New York: Holt, Rinehart and Winston.

Rummel, Rudolph. 1966. "The Dimensionality of Nations Project." In Comparing Nations: The Use of Quantitative Data in Cross-National Research, ed. R. Merritt and S. Rokkan. New Haven, Conn.: Yale University Press.

_____. 1969. "Some Empirical Findings on Nations and Their Behavior." World Politics 21: 226–41.

Russell, Robert W.; Doerr, Judith E.; Stauffer, Thomas A.; Lopez, George; and West, James W. 1956. Dependence and Interdependence in the International System: An Introduction to International Political Economy. New York: International Studies Association.

Russett, Bruce, and Lamb, W. 1969. "Global Patterns of Diplomatic Exchange 1963–64." Journal of Peace Research 1: 37–55.

Sampson, E. E. 1971. Social Psychology and Contemporary Society. New York: John Wiley.

Satow, Ernest Mason. 1922. A Guide to Diplomatic Practice, rev. 2d ed. London: Longmans Green.

Scharf, Peter. 1971. "The Moral Atmosphere of the Prison." Cambridge, Mass.: Harvard University, unpublished paper.

Schmid, Herman. 1968. "Peace Research and Politics." Journal of Peace Research 3: 219–32.

Schwartzmann, Simon, and Arauja, Manual Mora y. 1966. "The Images of International Gratification in Latin America." Journal of Peace Research: 236–82.

Scott, William A. 1965. "Effects of Cross-National Contact on National and International Images." In International Behavior, ed. H. Kelman. New York: Holt, Rinehart and Winston.

Senghaas, Dieter. 1974. "Peace Research and the Third World." Journal of Peace Research 2: 158–72.

Sharp, Gene. 1973. The Politics of Non-violent Action. Boston: Porter Sargent.

Singer, J. David. "The Global System and Its Subsystems: A Developmental View." In Linkage Politics: Essays on the Convergence of National and International Systems, ed. J. N. Rosenau. New York: The Free Press.

    _____, and Small Melvin. 1966. "The Composition and the Status Ordering of the International System, 1815-1940." World Politics: 236-82.

Singer, Marshall R. 1972. Weak States in a World of Powers: The Dynamics of International Relationship. New York: The Free Press.

Sivard, Ruth Leger. 1974. World Military and Social Expenditures 1974. Leesburg, Va.: WMSE Publications.

Smelser, Neil J. 1976. Comparative Methods in the Social Sciences. Englewood Cliffs, N.J.: Prentice-Hall.

Snyder, Richard C.; Bruck, H. W.; and Sapin, Burton. 1963. "Decision-making as Approach to the Study of International Politics." In Foreign Policy Decision Making, ed. R. C. Snyder, H. W. Bruck, and B. Sapin. New York: The Free Press.

Solomon, Leonard. 1966. "The Influence of Some Types of Power Relationships and Game Strategies upon the Development of Interpersonal Trust." In Human Behavior and International Politics: Contributions from the Social-Psychological Sciences, ed. J. D. Singer. Chicago: Rand McNally.

Sprout, Harold and Margaret. 1965. The Ecological Perspective on Human Affairs. Princeton, N.J.: Princeton University Press.

Statt, David. 1974. "The Influence of National Power on the Child's View of the World." Journal of Peace Research 3: 245-46.

Steinbruner, John. 1973. "Decisions under Complexity." (Manuscript of book.)

Tagiuri, Renato, and Litwin, George H., eds. 1968. Organizational Climate. Boston: Harvard University Press.

Taylor, Charles Lewis, and Hudson, Michael C. 1972. World Handbook of Political and Social Indicators, 2d ed. New Haven, Conn.: Yale University Press.

t'Hart, W. A. 1955. Het psychologisch aspect van een wereld federatie. In Europa's geestelijke bydrage tot wereld-integratie.

Tiger, Lionel. 1969. Men in Groups. New York: Random House.

Toffler, Alvin. 1971. Future Shock. New York: Bantam Books.

Toulmin, Stephen. 1972. Human Understanding. Vol. I. Princeton, N.J.: Princeton University Press.

Trevalyan, Humphrey. 1973. Diplomatic Channels. Boston: Gambit.

United Nations. 1945. Charter of the United Nations and Statute of the International Court of Justice. New York: United Nations.

_____. 1975. United Nations Statistical Yearbook 1974. New York: United Nations.

Vincent, Jack. 1968. "National Attributes as Predictors of Delegate Attitudes of the U.N." American Political Science Review 62-63: 916-31.

Walbek, Norman V. 1973. "Global Public Political Culture." Peace Research Reviews 5, no. 2.

Waltz, Kenneth N. 1959. Man, the State and War: A Theoretical Analysis. New York: Columbia University Press.

Weinstein, F. B. 1973. "The Uses of Foreign Policy in Indonesia: An Approach to the Analysis of Foreign Policy in the Less Developed Countries." World Politics 24: 356-81.

Weisband, Edward, and Damir, Roguly. 1976. "Palestinian Terrorism: Violence, Verbal Strategy, and Legitimacy." In International Terrorism: National, Regional and Global Perspectives, ed. Yonah Alexander. New York: Praeger.

Wiberg, Hakan. 1968. "Social Position and Peace Philosophy." Journal of Peace Research: 277-92.

Williams, Robin. 1968. "The Concept of Values." In International Encyclopedia of the Social Sciences, ed. D. L. Sills. New York: Macmillan and The Free Press.

APPENDIX A
Codebook

Deck 01

Column Number	SPSS Variable Name	Code
01–03		Number assigned to the interviewee
04		Deck number (01)
05–10	DATE	Date of interview O/B. Missing information (MI)
11	LOCATION	Place of interview 1. Washington 2. New York 3. Ottawa 4. Cambridge O/B MI
12–14	TIME	Duration of interview in minutes O/B. MI
15	AGE	Age of diplomat 1. less than or equal to 30 2. 31–40 3. 41–50 4. 51–60 5. greater than or equal to 61 O/B MI
16	SEX	Sex of the diplomat 1. Female 2. Male O/B MI

Column Number	SPSS Variable Name	Code
17	INTELL	Intellectual background of the diplomat 1. Law 2. Economics and business 3. Political and governmental sciences 4. Social sciences/education 5. Humanities/history 6. Natural sciences 7. Engineering 8. Agriculture 9. Other O/B MI
18-19	EXPERIEN	Years of diplomatic experience O/B MI
20-21	ABROAD	Years of diplomatic experience abroad O/B. MI
22-23	CENTER	Years of diplomatic experience in center countries O/B. MI
24-25	PERIPHER	Years of diplomatic experience in periphery countries O/B. MI
26	RANK	Diplomatic rank 1. Attache 2. Third Secretary 3. Second Secretary 4. First Secretary 5. Counselor 6. Minister Counselor 7. Minister O/B MI

Column Number	SPSS Variable Name	Code
27	DESK	Diplomatic function 1. Chancery 2. Commerce 3. Information 4. Culture and education 5. Scientific 6. Agriculture 7. Finance 8. Press 9. Other O/B MI
28-33	COUNTRY	Name of the country that the diplomat represents
34-36	FRANK3	Comment of interviewee on frankness among diplomats (3)
37-39	FRANK4	Comment of interviewee on frankness among diplomats (4)
40	OPTIME	Diplomat expresses optimism concerning the realization of international peace and his preferred world order 1. In the short term 2. In the long term O/B MI
41	PESTIME	Diplomat expresses pessimism concerning the realization of international peace or his preferred world order: 1. In the short term 2. In the long term O/B MI
42	INVITATI	Interviewee invited me for another interview, if more information was needed 1. No invitation made 2. Invitation made explicit O/B MI

Column Number	SPSS Variable Name	Code
43	INTERES	Degree of interest in the study expressed by the diplomat 1. No explicit expression of interest 2. Expression of interest made explicit 3. Asked me to send an abstract of the results O/B MI
44	QUESTION	Did the diplomat criticize the questionnaire? 1. No 2. Yes O/B MI
45	EXPLICRIT	Content of the critique made by diplomat about the questionnaire.
46	FILLOUT	Did he fill out the questionnaire? 1. No 2. Yes 3. Preferred to comment verbally O/B MI Perception of the international environment: Using the semantic differential method, we scored on a scale ranging from 1 to 7, the diplomats' responses to the following question: "How would you describe the present international relations environment in relation to the following attributes?"
47	DEMOCRA	Democratic-Undemocratic 1. Democratic 2. 3. 4. 5. 6. 7. Undemocratic O/B MI

Column Number	SPSS Variable Name	Code
48	HIERAR	Hierarchical-Egalitarian
49	STATIC	Static-dynamic
50	SATISFACTORY	Satisfactory-unsatisfactory
51	EXPLOIT	Exploitative-unexploitative
52	TENSE	Tense-relaxed
53	CONSCIO	Conscious-unconscious
54	PREDICT	Predictable-unpredictable
55	SHOTERM	Short-term oriented-long-term oriented
56	VIOLENT	Violent-nonviolent
57	GLOOMY	Has a gloomy future-has a bright future
58	OPPORTU	Opportunistic-principled
59	SUPPORT	Supportative-indifferent
60	RATIO	Rational-irrational
61	EGOISM	Enlightened egoistic-blind egoistic
62	INTERDE	Low interdependency-high interdependency
63	TOLERAN	Tolerant for diversity-intolerant for diversity
64	POLAR	Polarized-integrated
65	STABLE	Stable-unstable
66	REACTIO	Reactionary-progressive
67	ANARCH	Anarchic-organized/orderly
68	TRUST	Trustful-distrustful
69	JUST	Just-unjust
70	COMPET	Competitive-cooperative
71	NATIONA	Nationalistic-globalistic
72	ALTRUIS	Altruistic-egoistic
73	HYPOCR	Hypocritical-honest

Column Number	SPSS Variable Name	Code
74	POWER	Power-oriented-moralistic
		Perception of the international environment (2). Diplomats who consistently used only the values 1, 4, and 7 of the scale were coded separately.
75	DEMOCRA2	
76	HIERAR2	
77	STATIC2	
78	SATISFA2	
79	EXPLOIT2	
80	TENSE2	

Deck 02

01–03		Number assigned to the interviewee
04		Deck number (02)
05	CONSCIO2	
06	PREDICT2	
07	SHOTERM2	
08	VIOLENT2	
09	GLOOMY2	
10	OPPORTU2	
11	SUPPORT2	
12	RATIO2	
13	EGOISM2	
14	INTERDE2	
15	TOLERAN2	
16	POLAR2	
17	STABLE2	
18	REACTIO2	

Column Number	SPSS Variable Name	Code
19	ANARCH2	
20	TRUST2	
21	JUST2	
22	COMPET2	
23	NATIONA2	
24	ALTRUIS2	
25	HYPOCR2	
26	POWER2	
		Conditions for international peace: "Evaluate this sample of peace proposals according to their importance for international peace."
27	EDUC	The individual must be educated to peace 1. Against peace 2. Unimportant to peace 3. Somewhat important to peace 4. Especially important to peace O/B MI
28	HUNGER	"Abolish hunger and poverty in the world"
29	INDIVID	"Relations between individuals must become more peaceful"
30	SMALL	"The small countries must have greater influence"
31	DEMOC	"The states must be more democratic"
32	REGION	"We must strengthen regional organizations"
33	WORLD	"A world government must be established as soon as possible"
34	POPUL	"Population growth must be controlled"
35	COMMUN	"More effective communication is necessary"

Column Number	SPSS Variable Name	Code
36	ALLIAN	"The military alliances must be preserved"
37	SIMILAR	"The nations must become more similar"
38	RICH	"Rich countries must give help to the poor"
39	DISARM	"General and complete disarmament must be realized"
40	SOCIAL	"Countries must become more socialistic"
41	FREETRA	"Free trade must be established between all countries"
42	MILBAL	"There must be a military balance between the states so that nobody dares to attack"
43	SSELFSU	"One should try to create a world with small self-sufficient states"
44	DETENTE	"Western and Eastern countries must improve detente"
45	UN	"We must strengthen the United Nations"
46	BOUNDAR	"National boundaries ought to become more open"
47	NATCOUN	"Each national group should be given its own country"
48	IDEOL	"Ideological disputes ought to be diminished"
49	NATCOOP	"States that naturally belong together must cooperate"
50	MIGRAT	"Restrictions to migration should be gradually lifted"

Conditions for international peace:
"Evaluate the same proposals according to whether or not they might be carried out in the short or the long term."

Column Number	SPSS Variable Name	Code
51	EDUC2	
52	HUNGER2	
53	INDIVID2	
54	SMALL2	
55	DEMOC2	
56	REGION2	
57	WORLD2	
58	POPUL2	
59	COMMUN2	
60	ALLIAN2	
61	SIMILAR2	
62	RICH2	
63	DISARM2	
64	SOCIAL2	
65	FREETRA2	
66	MILBAL2	
67	SSELFSU2	
68	DETENTE2	
69	UN2	
70	BOUNDAR2	
71	NATCOUN2	
72	IDEOL2	
73	NATCOOP2	
74	MIGRAT2	

Diplomacy: "How much do you agree with the following statements?"

Column Number	SPSS Variable Name	Code
75	GRADUAL	"Changes in international relations have to be made gradually" 1. Strongly disagree 2. Disagree 3. 50-50 4. Agree 5. Strongly agree O/B MI
76	GUNS	"In a situation of an international controversy where it seems that one side is clearly right and the other is clearly wrong, I would be inclined to stick strongly to my position"
77	COMPROM	"To compromise with foreign opponents is dangerous because it usually leads to the betrayal of our side"
78	ARMS	"To bring about greater changes for the benefit of mankind often requires the use of arms"
79	OKMETHOD	"I don't mind a diplomat's methods if he manages to get the right thing done"
80	RADICAL	"To bring about a stable peace in the world, total and radical changes are necessary"

Deck 03

01-03		Number assigned to the interviewee
04		Deck number (03)
05	CONFLICT	"There is always bound to be conflict among various groups in the world"
06	SIMINTER	"Most nations have a great deal in common and share basically the same interests"
07	ZEROSUM	"When a country or group of countries gain, it usually means that another country or group of countries loses"

Column Number	SPSS Variable Name	Code
08	MIDDLE	"Generally speaking, in international controversies, extreme positions should be avoided, for the proper approach lies somewhere in the middle"
09	ART	"Foreign policy is the art of the possible and the government should not worry about grand plans and distant goals"
10	MYCOUNTR	"In its disputes with other countries my country is usually right. Its ideals and standards are usually fair and wise"
11	ENLIGHT	"Good diplomacy is basically based on enlightened egoism"
12	EXPENSE	"Those countries who get ahead, usually get ahead at the expense of others"
13	PRDEVIOL	"In the next four years we will have an increase in armed violence in the world"
14	PEACE	"I am basically optimistic that progress will be made toward a more peaceful and just world"
15	GROWTH	"We should opt for faster economic growth, rather than for a redistribution of wealth and income to solve the poverty problem"
16	WENESS	"There is a growing feeling of we-ness among nations and a growing consensus about global problems and how to cope with them"
17	SECURDEP	"My country depends highly on foreign support for the protection of its own security"
18	CLASSLES	"A genuine and lasting peace could be achieved only after the establishment of a classless world"

Column Number	SPSS Variable Name	Code
19	RESOUDEP	"The development of my country's economic system depends very much on the import of natural resources"
20	INTLAW	"The relations between nations are basically governed by international law"
21	CONSENT	"Decisions in international relations are usually made by mutual consent, without sacrifice to one or the other party"
22	INVESTOR	"My country's economy is significantly (to a great extent) influenced by foreign investors"
23	DEFCONTR	"Our defense system is to a great extent controlled by another country(ies)"
24	UNINFLUE	"The United Nations ought to get much more influence than it has today"
25	KNOWHOW	"Foreign knowhow is very vital for the development of my country's economy"
26	CAPITDEP	"For its economic development, my country needs a great amount of foreign capital"
27	IDEODECL	"Ideology is a declining factor in international relations"
28	CAPITALI	"The socialist system will eventually replace the capitalist system"
29-31	JOBSAT1	Job satisfaction: "What is the most appealing about being a diplomat?" (Code up to six mentions.)
32-34	JOBSAT2	
35-37	JOBSAT3	
38-40	JOBSAT4	
		(also deck 08 40-42/43-45/46-48)
43	ATTRACT	Degree of satisfaction expressed by diplomat 1. He dislikes it very much—no important satisfactions 2. On the balance he dislikes it. Some attractions, but dissatisfactions are more important

Column Number	SPSS Variable Name	Code
		3. 50-50
		4. On the balance he likes it. Some dissatisfactions, but satisfactions are more important
		5. Likes it very much. No important dissatisfactions--"I really enjoy it"
		O/B MI
44-46	DIPROLE1	Role of the diplomat: (Code up to five
47-49	DIPROLE2	mentions)
50-52	DIPROLE3	
		(also deck 08 49-51/52-54)
54	DIPINFLU	Influence of the diplomat: "Do you make a difference in the making of foreign policy?"
		1. None
		2. Unimportant
		3. Yes and no--some importance
		4. Quite important--explicit
		5. Very important--superlatives used
		O/B MI
55-56	AREI1	Area of influence of the diplomat
57-58	AREA2	
59-60	AREA 3	
61-62	FUNCT1	Influence of the diplomat is a function of:
63-64	FUNCT2	
65-66	FUNCT3	
67-68	NATURE1	Comments on human nature
69-70	NATURE2	
71-72	NATURE3	
73-74	INTMOR1	Comments on international morality
75-76	INTMOR2	
77-78	MORCAUS1	Comments on the causes of the state of
79-80	MORCAUS2	international morality

Deck 04

01-03		Number assigned to the interviewee
04		Deck number (04)

Column Number	SPSS Variable Name	Code
05–06	SYSCHAN1	Causes of change in the international
07–08	SYSCHAN2	system
09–10	SYSCHAN3	
11–12	ACTREACT	"Would you describe your country's foreign policy as active or reactive."
13–15	INDPEAC1	Indicators of peace: "The word peace is
16–18	INDPEAC2	one of the most loosely used words in
19–21	INDPEAC3	international politics: What to you per-
22–24	INDPEAC4	sonally are the essentials of peace?" (Code up to six mentions)
		(also deck 08 55-57/58-59)
25–27	CONDIT1	Inhibitors of peace: "What are the three
28–30	CONDIT2	or four most important problems in the
31–33	CONDIT3	world today which cause dissatisfaction
34–36	CONDIT4	and tension, and are directly or indirect-
37–39	CONDIT5	ly a threat to peace?" (Code up to 10
40–42	CONDIT6	mentions)
		(also deck 08 61-63/64-66/67-69/70-72)
45–47	PWO1	Preferred world order: "How would the
48–50	PWO2	world you'd like to see for your children
51–53	PWO3	differ from that of today (or how would
54–56	PWO4	you describe your preferred world order") (Code up to six mentions)
		(also deck 08 73-75/76-78)
57–59	RECOM1	Recommendations for the improvement
60–62	RECOM2	of international relations: "What can be
63–65	RECOM3	done about it? (inhibiting conditions for
66–68	RECOM4	peace) What practical changes would be be necessary to realize that kind of world? (preferred world order)" (Code up to seven mentions)
		(also deck 09 5-7/8-10/11-13)
71	ATTPEACE	Attitude toward the present state of peace 1. Expressed dissatisfaction 2. Expresses satisfaction O/B MI

Column Number	SPSS Variable Name	Code
73	INDIVIS	Peace is indivisible 1. No such comment made 2. Peace is indivisible--implicit. For example: "There is peace if peace is universally accepted"; Peace is a function of the degree to which the benefits can infiltrate all the levels of the world order" 3. Peace is indivisible--explicit. For example: "In our growing interdependent world peace is indivisible"
74	MORALIZE	Discussion moralized: Here we rate the extent to which the respondent "moralized" an issue by assigning blame to someone or using such terms as justice, rights, duties, and so on. 1. No moralizing 2. Uses moral terms such as justice, rights, duties, and/or blames 3. Uses moral terms and/or blames-- does it strongly. The difference between 2 and 3 is a question of degree. O/B MI
75	HISTORY	Historical context given: Does he place the discussion in a historical context by referring to historical trends or describing the historical development of the problem. 1. No 2. Yes, but only vaguely or in passing; a simple recounting of the recent history; some dates--or attempted solutions justifies a code of 2 3. · Yes--is an important dimension in his analysis of the problem O/B MI
76	FUTURE	Future context: When the diplomat assesses the feasibility of his recommendations, or the probability of realizing international peace or his

Column Number	SPSS Variable Name	Code
		preferred world order, does he qualify his assessment by specifying the timing, and to what extent does he refer to the future as an active agent or catalyzer. 1. No timing specified 2. Specifies the timing 3. Refers to the future as an active agent. For example: "The future is with us." O/B MI
77	YEARS	In referring to the future, what time span does he consider? 1. 1-5 years 2. 6-10 years 3. 11-20 years 4. Over 20 years O/B MI
78	REFIDEOL	Reference to ideology: In his discussion does he refer to a specific named ideology or doctrine for the evaluation of alternative policies? (Do not code answers given to question on capitalism and communism) 1. No 2. Yes 3. Yes--explicit promotion or defense of particular ideology O/B MI
79-80	REFIDEO1	What ideology does he/she refer to? (also deck 04 43-44/69/70)

Deck 05

01-03		Number assigned to the interviewee
04		Deck number (05)
05	TRADI	Tradition: In his/her discussion does he/she refer explicitly to tradition or custom as a relevant criterion for opposing or proposing policies?

Column Number	SPSS Variable Name	Code

1. No
2. Yes, but vaguely or in passing
3. Yes, central element in discussion
O/B MI

06   GENERAL   Particularizer-generalizer: Level of
abstraction in the analysis of a problem.
Does the diplomat deal with issues in
terms of sweeping principles or move
immediately to specific details or cases.
1. Approach is operational, focusing on
concrete cases and conflicts
2. No clear dominance of either generalizing or particularizing
3. Issues treated in very general terms,
or on a high level of abstraction
O/B MI

07   THEORET   Inductive versus deductive approach
1. The diplomat approaches the issues
most exclusively in phenomenological
terms and reasons inductively from
personal experience
2. No clear dominance of either inductive or deductive approach--approach
is basically eclectic
3. Diplomat uses for his analysis one
dominant frame of analysis
O/B MI

08   TECHNOL   Predominance of technological issues:
Does he discuss technology as an im-
portant variable in international relations?
1. No
2. Yes, implicitly
3. Yes, explicitly. This is a central
element in his discussion
O/B MI

Column Number	SPSS Variable Name	Code
09	POLAN	Discussion of international relations in terms of opposite poles: In discussing international relations, does he use such categories as blocs, poles, camps, opposite groups? 1. No 2. Yes, he mentions poles, but with no further analysis 3. Yes, poles occupy a central place in his image of the world and he discusses the conflicts between the respective poles explicitly O/B MI
10-11	POLE1	Specification of the poles (also deck 09 14-15/16-17)
12	PASTUTOP	Past utopia: Does he/she refer to some ideal past society or system of international relations as a goal or standard in discussing the issue? 1. No 2. Yes, but only vaguely or in passing 3. Yes, explicitly and in some detail O/B MI
13	FUTUTOP	Future utopia: Does he/she refer to some ideal future society or system of international relations as a goal or standard in discussing the issue? 1. No 2. Yes, but only vaguely or in passing 3. Yes, explicitly and in some detail O/B MI
14	FINANCE	Predominance of financial issues: Does he/she focus on financial issues during the discussion? 1. No 2. Yes, but only vaguely or in passing 3. Yes, it is a very important aspect of his discussion O/B MI

Column Number	SPSS Variable Name	Code
15	NATINTER	**National interests**: Does diplomat refer to national interests as a criterion for proposing or opposing policies? 1. No 2. Yes, he/she mentions national interests 3. Yes, explicit. It is a central element in the discussion O/B MI
16	MACROINT	**Supranational considerations**: In his interview does he express concern about the interests of other countries besides his own? 1. No 2. Yes, but he refers to a group of countries to whom his country belongs 3. Yes, he refers to a group to whom his country does not belong O/B MI
17–18 19–20 21–22 23–24	MACRO1 MACRO2 MACRO3 MACRO4	What groups of countries are mentioned?
25	SALIENCY	**Saliency of conflicts in the present world**: How prominent are conflicting interests in his discussion of international relations? 1. No differences of interest were mentioned 2. Different opinions and perspectives were mentioned, without the implication of conflicting interests 3. Conflicts of interest were mentioned, but no discussion of the conflicts followed 4. Conflicts of interests were discussed, but did not occupy a central place in the discussion 5. Conflicts of interests were discussed explicitly and occupied a central

Column Number	SPSS Variable Name	Code
		part in his analysis of international relations O/B MI
26	CYNICISM	Cynicism: The degree of cynicism is inferred from references to disparities between words and actions or intentions in international relations. 1. No cynical remarks were expressed 2. Yes, a cynical remark was expressed 3. Yes, cynical remarks were expressed, or if there was only one, it needed to have a touch of sarcasm O/B MI
27	POSITION	Positional awareness: Does he during the discussion refer to the position of his own country in the international relations system? 1. No such reference was made 2. Yes, but only vaguely or in passing 3. Explicitly refers to his country's structural position, and discusses the impact of this position on his country's foreign policy O/B MI
28-29 30-31 32-33	POSIT1 POSIT2 POSIT3	Specification of the positions
34	OWNRESPO	Attribution of responsibility for causing or solving a problem to his own country. 1. No mention 2. Explicit mention of his own country's responsibility O/B MI
35	OTHERRES	Attribution of responsibility to other countries 1. No 2. Yes to a group of countries to whom he belongs

Column Number	SPSS Variable Name	Code

3. Yes to a group of countries to whom his country belongs and to a group of countries to whom his country does not belong
4. Yes, but only countries or groups of countries of which his country is not a member

36-37	RESPONS1	Specification of the responsibilities
38-39	RESPONS2	
40-41Q	RESPONS3	

| 42 | DEPSENS | Dependency sensitivity |

1. No mention of dependency of his country
2. Indirect reference to dependency-- the diplomat refers to it as a characteristic of a group of countries to which his own country belongs
3. He explicitly mentions his country's dependency on a foreign commodity

O/B MI

| 43-44 | DEPSPEC1 | Specification of the dependency |

(also deck 09 18-19)

| 45 | PENSENS | Penetration sensitivity |

1. No reference made
2. Indirect reference to penetration-- the diplomat refers to it as a characteristic of a group of countries to which his own country belongs
3. The diplomat explicitly refers to any form of domestic interference in his own country

O/B MI

| 46-47 | PENSPEC1 | Specification of penetration |

| 48 | DOVE | Dove versus Hawk: Here we code the degree to which a person indicates a militant attitude in his proposals for recommendations for change. |

1. No mention of the use of physical force

Column Number	SPSS Variable Name	Code

<table>
<tr><td></td><td></td><td>2. Physical force was considered as a last resort or was mentioned as an option, but with expressed reservations
4. Any comment that referred to force as a necessary ingredient of a peaceful world
O/B MI</td></tr>
<tr><td>50</td><td>INTEGRAT</td><td>Plea for integration: Does the diplomat promote integration as a means toward the realization of peace or his preferred world order?
1. No mention
2. Integration as a means was mentioned vaguely or in passing
3. The reference to integration was central to his argument
O/B MI</td></tr>
<tr><td>51</td><td>BLOCK</td><td>Block formation: Does the diplomat consider the building of defensive groups of countries as a means to cope with a problem?
1. No
2. Yes
3. Promotes the idea strongly
O/B MI</td></tr>
<tr><td>52</td><td>SELFDET</td><td>Plea for less domestic interference and independence
1. No plea was expressed at all
2. This plea was mentioned but only vaguely or in passing
3. This plea occupies a central place in the set of recommendations and proposals
O/B MI</td></tr>
<tr><td>54</td><td>COOPERAT</td><td>Plea for global cooperation: Here we code the extent to which the diplomat considers "cooperation on a global basis" as an appropriate strategy.
1. No mention at all</td></tr>
</table>

Column Number	SPSS Variable Name	Code
		2. Global cooperation was mentioned vaguely or in passing
		3. The reference to cooperation was central to his argument
		O/B MI
55	FEASIBIL	Assessment of feasibility: To what extent is the diplomat optimistic or pessimistic about the realization of his/her preferred world order or peace?
		1. He says that it is unfeasible
		2. He is pessimistic and considers the chances for realization as very small
		3. 50-50--doesn't know, or expresses reserved optimism
		4. Is optimistic--a good chance; there are still some reservations
		5. Without doubt--absolutely; it is a necessity
		O/B MI
56-57 59-61 62-64	SUPPORT1 SUPPO SUPPORT3	Factors which the diplomat sees as enhancing the realization of peace and preferred world order
		(also deck 09 22-24/25-27)
66-68 69-71	INHIBIT1 INHIBIT2	Factors which the diplomat sees as inhibiting the realization of peace and preferred world order
		(also deck 09 28-30)
72	TURNING	Turning point: Does the diplomat perceive the present state of international relations as a critical turning point in the history of international relations?
		1. No
		2. Does not know--50-50
		3. Yes
		O/B MI
73-75 76-78	TURSPEC1 TURSPEC2	Specification of the turning point characteristics
		(also deck 09 31-33)

	SPSS	
Column	Variable	
Number	Name	Code

Deck 06

01-03		Number assigned to the interviewee
04		Deck number (06)

06   ROLEIDEO   <u>Role of ideology in international relations</u>
1. Ideology does not play a role
2. The impact of ideology is marginal
3. 50-50
4. Ideology has a considerable role
5. Ideology plays a very important role
O/B MI

08-09	IDEOL1	Comments about ideology
10-11	IDEO2	
12-13	IDEOL3	

14   DETENAT   <u>Attitude vis-a-vis detente</u>
1. Against detente
2. Sceptical
3. Pro-con
4. Ok
5. Very good
O/B MI

15-16	DETMEAN1	Comments on detente
17-18	DETMEAN2	

19   CONWEAP   <u>Use of conventional weapons</u>: "Could you imagine any value, goal, or ideal that could justify the use of conventional weapons?"
1. No condition
2. Yes
O/B MI

20   CONRESER   To what extent does the diplomat express reservations about the use of conventional weapons?
1. No reservations expressed
2. Yes, but only vaguely or in passing
3. Yes, very strong reservations
O/B MI

21-22	RES1	Reservations specified
23-24	RES2	

Column Number	SPSS Variable Name	Code
25–26	JUST1	Justifications specified
27–28	JUS2	
29–30	JUST3	
31	NUCES	On the use of nuclear weapons: "Would you imagine any value, goal, or ideal that could justify the use of nuclear weapons?" 1. No condition 2. Yes O/B MI
32	NUCRESER	To what extent does the diplomat express reservations about the use of nuclear weapons? 1. No reservations expressed 2. Yes, but only vaguely or in passing 3. Yes, very strong reservations O/B MI
33–35	NUCRES1	Reservations specified (also deck 09 34–36/37–39)
37–38	NUCJUS1	Justifications specified
39–40	NUCJUS2	
41–42	NUCJUS3	
43–45	MENTOR1	Mentor: What contemporary or historical figures have influenced his thinking about international relations? (also deck 09 40–42/43–45/46–47)
47–48	DIPCAUS1	Causes of variation in diplomat's think-ing: What factors have an influence on diplomatic thinking?
49–50	DIPCAUS2	
51–52	DIPCAUS3	
53	FRANK	Interviewer's ratings of frankness 1. Very closed and reserved 2. Basically reserved 3. Basically frank 4. Very frank and open (4 + 5)
54	PERFRANK	Are diplomats frank? 1. No

Column Number	SPSS Variable Name	Code

<table>
<tr><td>57-59</td><td>FRANK1</td><td></td></tr>
</table>

2. Pro-con
3. Yes
O/B MI

| 57-59 | FRANK1 | Comments on frankness |
| 60-62 | FRANK2 | |

(also deck 01 34-36/37-39)

| 65 | STRUCTUR | Use of a structural framework: Does the diplomat analyze the world as a system of international stratification that determines relationships of superordination and subordination among nations? |

1. No use of structural framework
2. More explicit and central use of structural analysis
3. Diplomat explicitly uses such terms as international stratification, position, or class and gives a central place to structural relationships between countries or groups of countries

O/B MI

| 66-67 | GENPEACE | Comments about peace in general |

| 68 | STRANGUL | Economic strangulation: "When economically strangulated would you consider the use of violence?" |

1. No
2. Yes and no
3. Yes

O/B MI

| 69-70 | SPECSTRA | Comments about economic strangulations and the use of violence |

| 71 | INTERDEP | Interdependency: Here we code whether and to what extent the diplomat refers to the world as an interdependent system. |

1. No
2. Yes, refers to this characteristic implicitly
3. Yes, uses the term explicitly

O/B MI

Column Number	SPSS Variable Name	Code
72-73	SPECINTE	Comments on interdependency
74-76	COMCAP1	Communism versus capitalism: Com-
77-79	COMCAP2	ments on the relations between the capitalist and communist systems.
80	LANGUAGE	Language used during the interview 1. English 2. French 3. Dutch O/B MI

Deck 07

01-03		Number assigned to the interviewee
04		Deck number (07)
		Cross-national indicators
05-09	MILEXPEN	Military expenditure
10-13	MILMANP	Military manpower
14-16	EXPENCAP	Military expenditure per capita
17-20	POPSOLD	Population per soldier
21-23	SECOOO	International security forces per 1,000 working age population (one decimal)
24-27	COUNAGE	Age of the country
28-33	TOTPOP	Population
34-36	DIPREP	Diplomatic representation
37-39	IOS	Memberships in international organizations
40-41	LITERACY	Literacy level
42-48	GNP	Gross national product
49-52	GNPCAP	Gross national product per capita
53-54	INDUSEDP	Industry's output as percent of the GNP
55-58	AIDGIVEN	Amount of foreign aid given
59-60	PENETRAT	Penetration index

Column Number	SPSS Variable Name	Code
61-65	EXPORT	Export
66-70	IMPORT	Import
71-76	PRODENER	Energy production (two decimals)

Deck 08

01-03		Number assigned to the interviewee
04		Deck number (08)
05-10	CONSENER	Consumption of energy (two decimals)
11-14	CENTRAID	Aid received from center countries
15-18	MARKAID	Aid received from developed market economies and disbursements from multilateral institutions (one decimal)
19-25	CAPENER	Per capita energy consumption (two decimals)
26	OPENCLO	Open versus closed status of a country
27-29	PARTY	Party fractionalization (Taylor)
30-33	PRESS	Press freedom (Taylor) (two decimals)
34	ECOSYS	Economical system
35	IDEOSYS	Ideological system
36-39	CAPAID	Per capita aid received (two decimals)
40-42	JOBDIS1	Job dissatisfaction expressed by diplomat
43-45	JOBDIS2	
46-48	JOBDIS3	
49-51	DIPROLE4	Role of the diplomat
52-54	DIPROLE5	
55-57	INDPEAC	Indicators of peace
58-60	INDPEAC6	
61-63	CONDIT7	Inhibitors of peace
64-66	CONDIT9	
67-69	CONDIT9	
70-72	CONDIT10	
73-75	PWO5	Preferred world order
76-78	PWO6	

Column Number	SPSS Variable Name	Code
		Deck 09
01–03		Number assigned to the interviewee
04		Deck number (09)
05–07	RECOM5	Recommendations for the improvement
08–10	RECOM6	of international relations
11–13	RECOM7	
14–15	POLE2	Specification of the poles
16–17	POLE3	
18–19	DEPSPEC2	Specification of dependency
20–21	PENSPEC2	Specification of penetration
22–24	SUPPORT4	Factors which the diplomat sees as en-
25–27	SUPPORT5	hancing the realization of peace and
		preferred world order
28–30	INHIBIT3	Factors which the diplomat sees as in-
		hibiting the realization of peace and
		preferred world order
31–33	TURSPEC3	Specification of the turning point charac-
		teristics
34–36	NUCRES2	Reservations about the use of nuclear
37–39	NUCRES3	weapons specified
40–42	MENTOR2	Mentors
43–45	MENTOR3	
46–48	MENTOR4	

APPENDIX B
Letter of Introduction

HARVARD UNIVERSITY
CENTER FOR INTERNATIONAL AFFAIRS
6 Divinity Avenue
Cambridge, Massachusetts 02138

His Excellency Joao Hall Themido
Ambassador of Portugal
2125 Kalorama Rd N.W.
Washington, D.C. 20008

Excellency:

As a member of the Belgian Royal Institute of International Relations and as a doctoral student at Harvard University, I am doing a study on contemporary diplomatic thinking. Some of the questions which are focused upon are: How does the diplomat define his role in international relations? What is his perception of international environment? What does he consider to be necessary components of a better international peace structure?

In order to achieve a representative sample of the Diplomatic Corps in Washington, I hope to arrange interviews with two diplomats from each Embassy. At the moment I have completed interviews in 59 Embassies. An interview takes approximately one hour and the answers are treated on a confidential basis. This implies that in the book that I hope to write, no names of diplomats, nor of their country, will be associated with any statement, without the permission of the interviewee.

I would very much like to have the opportunity to meet you or other members of your staff to obtain your or their perspective on general issues that are considered in the study.

I would be very grateful if you would let me know whether you or some other members of your staff would be able to talk to me during the month of May. I shall call on your office on May 5 to establish contact.

Thank you for your consideration.

Sincerely

Luc Reychler

APPENDIX C
Interview Questions

1. What is the role of the diplomat in international relations?
2. a. What is most appealing about being a diplomat?
   b. What is least appealing about being a diplomat?
3. The word peace is one of the most loosely used words in international politics. What to you personally are the essentials of peace?
4. a. What are the three or four most important problems in the world today which cause dissatisfaction and tension and are directly or indirectly a threat to peace?
   b. How did this become a problem? (focus on one)
   c. What can be done about it?
   d. Why do what you propose?
   e. How distant is the solution from the problem?
5. a. Could you imagine any value, goal, or ideal that could justify the use of nuclear weapons?
   b. Could you imagine any value, goals, or ideal that could justify the use of conventional weapons?
6. a. How would the world you'd like to see for your children differ from that of today (or how would you describe your preferred world order)?
   b. What practical changes would be necessary to reach this kind of world?
   c. How much progress toward such a world is realistically likely?
7. Would you consider the present period in international politics as a critical turning point in the history of international relations?
8. Are diplomats basically frank?
9. What factors have an influence on diplomatic thinking?
10. Questions pertaining to the biography of the diplomat: age, experience, previous posts, education, and so on.
11. How would you describe the relations today between communist and capitalistic systems?
12. Name some of the figures which have influenced your thinking about international relations as a diplomat.

APPENDIX D
Questionnaire

PERCEPTION OF THE INTERNATIONAL ENVIRONMENT

How would you describe the present international relations environment in relation to the following attributes? (This is a very synthetic and subjective question. Indicate by means of a check on the continuum, for example, __ ✓ __ __ __ __ between each of the two polar attributes, how you would describe "on the average" relations between nations in the world.)

Static	__ __ __ __ __ __	Dynamic
Satisfactory	__ __ __ __ __ __	Unsatisfactory
Nationalistic	__ __ __ __ __ __	Globalistic
Tense	__ __ __ __ __ __	Relaxed
Hierarchical	__ __ __ __ __ __	Egalitarian
Opportunistic	__ __ __ __ __ __	Principled
Low interdependency	__ __ __ __ __ __	High interdependency
Democratic	__ __ __ __ __ __	Undemocratic
Exploitative	__ __ __ __ __ __	Unexploitative
Conscious	__ __ __ __ __ __	Unconscious
Violent	__ __ __ __ __ __	Nonviolent
Polarized	__ __ __ __ __ __	Integrated
Has a gloomy future	__ __ __ __ __ __	Has a bright future
Anarchic	__ __ __ __ __ __	Organized/Orderly
Competitive	__ __ __ __ __ __	Cooperative
Just	__ __ __ __ __ __	Unjust
Trustful	__ __ __ __ __ __	Distrustful
Predictable	__ __ __ __ __ __	Unpredictable
Short-term oriented	__ __ __ __ __ __	Long-term oriented
Supportive	__ __ __ __ __ __	Indifferent
Rational	__ __ __ __ __ __	Irrational
Power-oriented	__ __ __ __ __ __	Moralistic
Enlightened egoistic	__ __ __ __ __ __	Blind egoistic
Stable	__ __ __ __ __ __	Unstable
Reactionary	__ __ __ __ __ __	Progressive
Altruistic	__ __ __ __ __ __	Egoistic
Hypocritical	__ __ __ __ __ __	Honest
Tolerant of diversity	__ __ __ __ __ __	Intolerant of diversity

CONDITIONS OF INTERNATIONAL PEACE

1. Evaluate this sample of proposals to their "importance" for
   international peace (use first column).

5 = especially important to peace	1 = unimportant to peace
3 = somewhat important to peace	0 = against peace

2. Evaluate the same proposals according to whether or not they
   might be carried out in the short or long term (use second column).

   5 = likely to be realized
   3 = moderately likely to be realized
   1 = unlikely to be realized

	Importance	Likelihood of Being Carried Out
The individual person must be educated to peace		
We must strengthen the United Nations		
The military alliances must be preserved		
Abolish hunger and poverty in the world		
Free trade must be established between all countries		
Each national group should be given its own country		
Ideological disputes ought to be diminished		
Population growth must be controlled		
More effective communication is necessary		
A world government must be established as soon as possible		
The nations must become more similar		
Rich countries must give aid to the poor		
Relations between individuals must become more peaceful		
The small countries must have greater influence		
The states must be more democratic		
We must strengthen regional organizations		
General and complete disarmament must be realized		
Countries must become more socialistic		

	Importance	Likelihood of Being Carried Out
There must be a military balance between states so that nobody dares to attack		
One should create a world with small self-sufficient states		
Western and Eastern countries must improve detente		
National boundaries·ought to become more open		
States that naturally belong together must cooperate		
Restrictions to migration should be gradually lifted		

DIPLOMATICS

How much do you agree with the following statements?

    5 = strongly agree
    4 = agree
    3 = 50-50
    2 = disagree
    1 = strongly disagree

Changes in international relations have to be made gradually	
In a situation of an international controversey where it seems to me that my side is clearly right and the other side clearly wrong, I would be inclined to stick strongly to my position	
To compromise with foreign opponents is dangerous because it usually leads to the betrayal of our side	
To bring about greater changes for the benefit of mankind often requires the use of arms	
The relations between nations are basically governed by international law	
I don't mind a diplomat's methods if he manages to get the right thing done	
There is a growing "we-ness" among nations and a growing consensus about global problems and how to cope with them	
Good diplomacy is basically based on enlightened egoism	
A genuine and lasting peace could be achieved only after the establishment of a classless world	

There is always bound to be conflict among various groups in the world

To bring about a stable peace in the world, total and radical changes are necessary

Most nations have a great deal in common and share basically the same interests

I am basically optimistic that progress will be made toward a more peaceful and just world

Those countries who get ahead usually get ahead at the expense of others

Generally speaking, in international controversies, extreme positions should be avoided, for the proper approach lies somewhere in the middle

We should opt for a faster economic growth, rather than for a redistribution of wealth and income to solve the poverty problem

In the next four years we will have an increase in armed violence in the world

Decisions in international relations are usually made by mutual consent, without sacrifice to one or the other party

Foreign policy is the art of the possible and the government should not worry about grand plans and distant goals

In its disputes with other countries my country is usually right. Its ideals and standards are usually fair and wise

My country depends highly on foreign support for the protection of its own security

The development of my country's economic system depends very much on the import of natural resources

My country's economy is significantly (to a great extent) influenced by foreign investors

Our defense system is to a great extent controlled by another country(ies)

Foreign know-how is very vital for the development of my country's economy

For its economic development, my country needs a great amount of foreign capital

Ideology is a declining factor in international relations

The socialist system will eventually replace the capitalist system

BIOGRAPHICAL DATA

At what age did you enter in the diplomatic service? _____

How many years' experience do you have in diplomacy? _____

What is your present diplomatic rank? _____

In what areas of the world were you based? _____

_____

_____

_____

_____

_____

COMMENTS

APPENDIX E
Procedure for Calculating
International Climate Indexes

Hobbesian climate

To calculate this index we add and divide by 8 the scores given on the following scales of our semantic differential:

nonviolent/violent   1 7
globalistic/nationalistic
organized-orderly/anarchic
altruistic/egoistic
moralistic/power-oriented
trustful/distrustful
enlightened egoistic/blind egoistic
supportive/indifferent

Marxian climate

To calculate this index we add and divide by 3 the scores given on the following scales of our semantic differential:

egalitarian/hierarchical   1 7
unexploitative/exploitative
integrated/polarized

Instrumental exchange climate

To calculate this index we add and divide by 6 the scores given on the following scales of our semantic differential:

violent/nonviolent   1 7
cooperative/competitive
irrational/rational
principled/opportunistic
blind egoistic/enlightened egoistic
supportive/indifferent

We-ness environment

To calculate this index we add and divide by 5 the scores given on the following scales of our semantic differential:

competitive/cooperative   1 7
indifferent/supportive
polarized/integrated
egoistic/altruistic
distrustful/trustful

International law climate*

The index of this climate is based on the degree of agreement or disagreement of the diplomat with the following statement:

> The relations between nations are basically governed by international law.   1 . . . 5

Shared principled agreement climate

To calculate this index we add and divide by 7 the scores given on the following scales of our semantic differential:

undemocratic/democratic   1 7
intolerant for diversity/tolerant for diversity
opportunistic/principled
power oriented/moralistic
competitive/cooperative
unjust/just
nationalistic/globalistic

---

*To compare the mean of the international law climate with the means that are based on a 1-7 scale, we converted the mean of international law climate as follows:

$$[(2.9 - 1) \times 1.5] + 1 = 3.85$$

Overview of the T-Test Results
between International Climates

International Climate	Mean	Difference	t-value	p-value
Hobbesian	4.67			
		-.33	-4.88	< .005
Marxian	5.01			
Hobbesian	4.67			
		.35	5.23	< .005
Instrumental exchange	4.32			
Marxian	4.99			
		.66	10.12	< .005
Instrumental exchange				
Instrumental exchange	4.32			
		1.14	15.41	< .005
We-ness	3.16			

APPENDIX G
Mean Scores of the
Semantic Differential Items
for the European Common Market
and Global International Environments

European Common Market Environment	
Organized/orderly	5.80
Nonviolent	5.55
Has a bright future	5.50
High interdependency	5.50
Progressive	5.20
Relaxed	5.10
Integrated	5.10
Long-term oriented	5.10
Honest	5.00
Dynamic	5.00
Egalitarian	4.90
Unexploitative	4.80
Principled	4.70
Cooperative	4.70
Globalistic	4.10
Moralistic	4.10
Egoism	3.60
Indifferent	3.22
Unconscious	3.10
Unsatisfactory	3.00
Unpredictable	3.00
Undemocratic	2.80
Unjust	2.80
Unstable	2.55
Blind egoistic	2.44
Distrustful	2.40
Irrational	2.40
Intolerant of diversity	2.20

N = 10

Global International Environment	
Dynamic	5.19
High interdependency	5.16
Egoistic	5.13
Unjust	5.00
Distrustful	4.87
Unsatisfactory	4.77
Undemocratic	4.76
Unstable	4.52
Unpredictable	4.43
Irrational	4.32
Organized/orderly	4.27
Progressive	4.19
Indifferent	4.15
Intolerant of diversity	4.02
Has a bright future	3.93
Blind egoistic	3.76
Nonviolent	3.58
Unconscious	3.35
Integrated	3.16
Long-term oriented	3.16
Relaxed	3.16
Honest	3.07
Unexploitative	2.95
Egalitarian	2.93
Cooperative	2.90
Principled	2.88
Globalistic	2.60
Moralistic	2.28

$N = \pm 180$

APPENDIX H
Calculation of the Diplomats' Scores on the Eight Perceptual Dimensions

Dimen1 = .17495I(DEMOCRA–4.7679)/1.3841
+.25506*(CONSCIO–3.3537)/1.3510
+.08661*(SUPPORT–4.1585)/1.2820
+.20958*(RATIO–4.32731)/1.3027
+.35935*(EGOISM–3.7692)/1.2910
+.09219*(TOLERAN–4.0240)/1.4435
+.16395*(JUST–5-0059)/1.2125

Dimen2 = .20015*(TENSE–3.1647)/1.1902
+.19314*(EXPLOIT–2.9532)/1.2214
–.15002*(RATIO–4.3273)/1.3027
–.14606*(TOLERAN–4.0240)/1.4435
+.07484*(COMPET–2.9000)/1.1234
–.09641*(ALTRUIS–5.1317)/1.1593
+.40567*(POWER–2.2814)/1.0464

Dimen3 = –.24452(SATISFA–4.7733)/1.3895
+.21717*(TENSE–3.1647)/1.1902
+.16131*(VIOLENT–3.5848)/1.2823
+.19838*(GLOOMY–3.9349)/1.2303
–.35492*(STABLE–4.5294)/1.3854
+.06693*(ANARCH–4.2733)/1.2287

Dimen4 = .05109*(POLAR–3.1667)/1.3071
–.02018*(COMPET–2.9000)/1.1234
+1.0064*(NATIONA–2.6012)/1.2627

Dimen5 = .34793*(STATIC–5.1941)/1.4029
+.23207(*INTERDE–5.1615)/1.4912
–.16393*(TOLERAN–4.0240)/1.4435
+.26072*(REACTIO–4.1905)/1.2523

Dimen6 = –.10706*(SHOTERM–3.1667)/1.4213
–.31927*(OPPORTU–2.8876)/1.2698
+.07505*(SUPPORT–4.1585)/1.2820
+.16279*(STABLE–4.5294)/1.3854
–.15711*(ANARCH–4.2733)/1.2287
+.27613*(TRUST–4.8706)/1.2142
+.18447*(JUST–5.0059)/1.2125
–.08381*(HYPOCR–3.0727)/1.1974
–.06745*(POWER–2.2814)/1.0464

Dimen7 = –.30159*(DEMOCRA–4.7679)/1.3841
+.32510*(HIERAR–2.9394)/1.2430

Dimen8 = .47849*(PREDICT–4.4360)/1.4913

APPENDIX I
Calculation of the Diplomats' Scores
on the Eleven Analytic Style Dimensions

$$\text{Analyt1} = .43088*(\text{POSITION}-2.024)/.871$$
$$+.41800*(\text{DEPSENS}-1.713)/.857$$
$$+.07789*(\text{STRUCTUR}-1.812)/.880$$

$$\text{Analyt2} = .60648*(\text{HISTORY}-1.762)/.807$$

$$\text{Analyt3} = .51891*(\text{ZEROSUM})-2.764)/.905$$
$$+.20365*(\text{EXPENSE}-2.946)/.946$$

$$\text{Analyt4} = .80906*(\text{NATINTER}-1.700)/.536$$

$$\text{Analyt5} = .26124*(\text{MORALIZE}-1.656)/.788$$
$$+.21536*(\text{CYNICISM}-1.521)/.824$$
$$-.37805*(\text{MYCOUNTR}-3.432)/.913$$

$$\text{Analyt6} = .21070*(\text{TECHNOL}-1.431)/.776$$
$$+.19087*(\text{FINANCE}-1.440)/.814$$

$$\text{Analyt7} = .95608*(\text{INTERDEP}-1.791)/.870$$

$$\text{Analyt8} = .62292*(\text{GENERAL}-2.162)/.621$$

$$\text{Analyt9} = .45997*(\text{REFIDEOL}-1.452)/.739$$

$$\text{Anal 10} = .16729*(\text{MORALIZE}-1.656)/.788$$
$$+.17619*(\text{PENSENS}-1.928)/.975$$
$$+.13217*(\text{SALIENCY}-3.632)/1.273$$

$$\text{Analyt11} = .51816*(\text{CONFLICT}-3.707)/.892$$

APPENDIX J
Calculation of the Diplomats' Scores
on the Eight Strategic Approach Dimensions

$$Strateg1 = .50849*(SELFDET-1.947)/.969$$
$$+.32221*(SELFSUF-1.498)/.796$$

$$Strateg2 = .27860*(GRADUAL-4.154)/.912$$
$$+.20260*(ART-2.886)/1.078$$
$$+.44446*(MIDDLE-3.824)/.881$$

$$Strateg3 = .42770*(COOPERAT-2.091)/.923$$

$$Strateg4 = .25182*(ARMS-1.927)/1.040$$
$$+.28906*(OKMETHOD-2.706)/1.248$$

$$Strateg5 = .22446*(DOVE-1.554)/.997$$
$$+.16454*(RADICAL-3.214)/1.157$$

$$Strateg6 = .53370*(GUNS-3.587)/1.032$$
$$+.35207*(COMPROM-2.383)/.968$$

$$Strateg7 = -.13457*(NUCES-1.340)/.475$$
$$+.62705*(NUCRESER-2.642)/.719$$

$$Strateg8 = .54575*(INTEGRAT-1.889)/.964$$

NAME INDEX

SUBJECT INDEX

ABOUT THE AUTHOR

LUC REYCHLER is a professor of international relations at the University of Leuven (K. U. L.). A licentiate from the University of Gent (R. U. G.) and a Ph. D. from Harvard University, he has been a researcher at the London School of Economics and Political Science, and at the University of Oslo, an associate of the Harvard University Center for International Affairs, and a visiting scholar at the Bureau of Social Science Research (B. S. S. R.) in Washington, D. C.

RELATED TITLES ON
PROFESSIONALS AT WORK
Published by
Praeger Special Studies

*IMPROVING PRODUCTIVITY AND THE QUALITY
OF WORK LIFE
Thomas G. Cummings
Edmond S. Molloy

BLACK ADMINISTRATORS IN HIGHER EDUCATION
Robert L. Hoskins

OCCUPATIONAL CHOICES AND TRAINING NEEDS:
Prospects for the 1980s
Leonard A. Lecht

IMMIGRANT PROFESSIONALS IN THE UNITED STATES:
Discrimination in the Scientific Labor Market
Bradley W. Parlin

SOCIAL SCIENTISTS AND POLICY MAKING IN THE USSR
Edited by
Richard B. Remnek

*Also available in paperback.